THE NATURAL

Richard 'Dick' Thornett

THE NATURAL
Richard 'Dick' Thornett

Brendan Morris and Stephan Wellink

FAIRPLAY
PUBLISHING

First published in 2025 by Fair Play Publishing
PO Box 4101, Balgowlah Heights, NSW 2093, Australia

www.fairplaypublishing.com.au

ISBN: 978-1-923236-22-6
ISBN: 978-1-923236-23-3 (ePub)

© Brendan Morris and Stephan Wellink 2025
The moral rights of the authors have been asserted.

All rights reserved. Except as permitted under the *Australian Copyright Act 1968* (for example, a fair dealing for the purposes of study, research, criticism or review), no part of this book may be reproduced, stored in a retrieval system, communicated or transmitted in any form or by any means without prior written permission from the Publisher.

Design and typesetting by Leslie Priestley.

Front cover photograph:
Richard Thornett in his first Test for the Wallabies vs Fiji in Brisbane, 1961
All photographs: Supplied by the authors.

Printed in Australia. Print management by Paradigm Print, Brisbane.

All inquiries should be made to the Publisher via hello@fairplaypublishing.com.au

A catalogue record of this book is available from the National Library of Australia.

Contents

Foreword By Dawn Fraser AC MBE OLY	ix
Foreword By John Eales AM	ix
Foreword By Michael Cronin OAM	ix
Introduction	1
Chapter One: A Time Of Change	3
Chapter Two: Sunrise 1940-1957	7
Chapter Three: Randwick 1958-1959	17
Chapter Four: Rome 1960	27
Chapter Five: 1961 - Fiji In Australia	44
Chapter Six: 1961 - South Africa	53
Chapter Seven: 1962 - The All Blacks	68
Chapter Eight: Rugby League	80
Chapter Nine: Parramatta	88
Chapter Ten: 1963 - Representative Games	96
Chapter Eleven: Perspectives	105
Chapter Twelve: The Kangaroos	109
Chapter Thirteen: England	118
Chapter Fourteen: The Ashes	131

Chapter Fifteen: France	145
Chapter Sixteen: 1964 – The Eels Come of Age	152
Chapter Seventeen: 1965 – The Brothers Thornett Shine	159
Chapter Eighteen: 1966 – The Ashes in Australia	162
Chapter Nineteen: 1967 – A Difficult Season	167
Chapter Twenty: 1968 – The World Cup Australia/NZ	173
Chapter Twenty-One: 1969 – Injury-Plagued	190
Chapter Twenty-Two: 1970 – Annus Horribilis	197
Chapter Twenty-Three: 1971 – Farewell Eels	202
Chapter Twenty-Four: 1972 – The Roosters	210
Chapter Twenty-Five: Post-Career, 1970s	223
Chapter Twenty-Six: Post-Career, 1980s	228
Chapter Twenty-Seven: Post-Career, 1990s	230
Chapter Twenty-Eight: Family	234
Chapter Twenty-Nine: Sunset	243
Career Statistics	247
Honours	248
Acknowledgements	249
Bibliography	252
Endnotes	256

I was pleased to have had a nostalgic journey through my early days in journalism, when I dealt with the Thornett brothers on a regular basis. Congratulations on the book. Whatever happens, the certain thing is that you have added significantly to the record of Australian sport.

Norman Tasker: Journalist

I'm really flattered to get this opportunity to talk about Dick Thornett. He was certainly a guy who is highly regarded, one of the greats of the club, still revered by the fans and the former players. When you walked into a Parramatta reunion, there was that table. That special table – the Dick Thornetts, the Ken Thornetts, the Bob O'Reillys. They had such an aura about them. I saw Dick Thornett play way back in that 1971 semi-final between Parramatta and St George. I was very fortunate to be named in that Parramatta Legends team in the second row alongside him, which to me was such a huge honour, to be named alongside a huge player like him.

Peter Wynn: Parramatta (1979–1990), New South Wales and Australia

What an amazing story brilliantly told and researched. I found it compelling reading from start to finish. 'Moby' was one of a kind and that is portrayed superbly.

Peter Peters: Parramatta (1968) and Manly-Warringah (1969–1974)

Richard 'Dick' Thornett
by Peter Fenton (October 26, 2023)

The brilliant Dick Thornett is a man we well recall
The youngest of a trio who would challenge one and all,
Growing up in Bronte swimming laps in Bronte Baths
Mixing there with household names now treading famous paths.

Playing Water Polo showing strength in roughest water
With older brothers John and Ken who gave no slightest quarter,
Spending countless hours riding waves in open surf
Then watching stars in myrtle green on Coogee's hallowed turf.

This fine young set of brothers may indeed have had no equal
In sixty years that followed have we ever seen a sequel?
Both John and Ken wore green and gold; in different codes they starred,
Yet Dick was not to be outdone; he played a different card.

In those famous Rome Olympics at the age of almost twenty
He joined the Water Polo team to savage foes a-plenty.
Now when he made the Wallabies though still so young in years,
He showed no trepidation for the challenge held no fears.

The All Blacks felt his power in the thickest of the battle
He revelled in those moments when you hear the sabres rattle.
When Rugby League came calling and he joined his brother Ken
He held aloft the Ashes with a host of famous men.

Few men have won the honour that Dick can hold so proudly
For many years his praises rang so widely and so loudly,
To wear your nations colours; three times on different stages
Must make this modest warrior "a sportsman for the ages".

Foreword By Dawn Fraser

Representing Australia is a privilege, an honour. To do so in three sports is extraordinary. Richard stands for all that is good about being an Australian and that is something worth remembering.

Dawn Fraser AC MBE OLY
Olympic Swimming Champion, World Record Holder

Foreword By John Eales

I'm not sure there will ever be another Dick Thornett. In an era of specialisation, it is increasingly inconceivable for an athlete to compete at the top level in three sports. Brendan and Stephan's book allows us to reflect on how unique Dick's career was and celebrate that it included an influential stint in the Wallabies. Representing the Wallabies is an honour and a responsibility, one that doesn't pass as you hand on your jersey to the next man. Your career will pass, but you will always be a Wallaby. Not a former Wallaby, but a Wallaby. Dick's legacy in his time in the gold jersey, and with what he achieved both before and since, will stand the test of time among his peers.

John Eales AM
Wallaby #694 and captain (Australian national rugby team)

Foreword By Michael Cronin

The game wasn't invented yesterday or today, so it's very important that we remember all those players who are part of its history. I was a kid, probably 15 when I first watched Dick play in that Test when he replaced Arthur Beetson at halftime (on July 23, 1966). It has a lasting impression on you, watching those players. Dick Thornett played Water Polo, Rugby Union and Rugby League for Australia. If he was going around today, he'd be a legend. And that shouldn't be lost on people. He played in an era, with his brother, where Parramatta was starting to do things.

Michael 'Mick' Cronin OAM
Parramatta Eels and Kangaroo #469 (Australian national rugby league team)

Introduction

There is something eternally special about the relationship that a father has with his daughter. It was written of my father during the week that there was surprise in his passing, because most who knew him saw him as indestructible. So, while you saw a man who tore sporting teams apart single-handedly, I saw a man whose only ferocity was in the love he gave to me and my sisters.

I will never forget the feeling of safety as my father carried me to bed in his arms after long days out with family and friends. I'd wish that he'd never put me down.
Sophie Morris, October 18, 2011

The passing of Richard Thornett was a shock to many, as his larger-than-life presence on the sporting field seemed to suggest a man who was unbreakable. But, as his daughter so eloquently put it at his funeral, there was more to Richard than met the eye.

I am married to Richard's youngest daughter, Sophie. Before he passed, I had the privilege of enjoying 14 years of not just his company and heartfelt friendship, but his telling of tales, of a life well-travelled, of experiences so remarkable yet so enchanting that they deserve re-telling. They reflect the deep devotion to his family and his friends; tales that extend well beyond the physical wonderment that he was able to conjure as an athlete. Richard Thornett, it turned out, was not just a sportsman of exceptional skill, but also a sensitive, humble and loyal man, and just a little bit cheeky, a man whose gentle nature belied his prowess on the field. There were times of weakness, sure, and moments when mountains stood before him that must have seemed insurmountable. But, as is so often the case, it is the manner in which these challenges are met that is the true measure of any person.

As humans, we have always been drawn to stories about people like Richard, who achieve success in their fields beyond most mortals, yet who lead their lives with quiet dignity and grace. Nonetheless, beyond it all, they are just that, mortal…human. And so, in collaboration with Stephan Wellink who sowed the seeds for this project, I set out to tell his story, to capture the essence of this remarkable man who left an indelible mark on Australian sport, but whose greatest legacy was much, much more.

Brendan Morris

About 17 years ago, I approached John Thornett MBE with the suggestion that a book should be written about the brothers Thornett. Thankfully, John liked the idea and took it to his brothers who also agreed to collaborate with me, and, from that point, I had open access to John, Ken, Richard, their families, friends and former teammates. It was a biographer's dream.

So, what happened? Well, life does, and for various reasons the research, many hours of recorded interviews, piles of reference materials and copious handwritten and typed notes were placed in storage. That is, until early 2023, which is when Brendan Morris asked me if I would like to collaborate on a book about his father-in-law, Richard Thornett. My response was an unequivocal 'yes' and my Thornett archive was exposed to light for the first time in many years as we set out to write this biography.

Of course, it is impossible to write about Richard without some reference to John and Ken because as you will read, their lives were strongly linked from growing up at Bronte, where they excelled at swimming and Water Polo, through to the two codes of rugby where the Thornett name is revered.

However, this is Richard's story and by any measure, his was an extraordinary life.

Stephan Wellink

CHAPTER ONE
A Time of Change

It was the best of times, it was the worst of times, it was the age of wisdom, it was the age of foolishness, it was the epoch of belief, it was the epoch of incredulity, it was the season of Light, it was the season of Darkness, it was the spring of hope, it was the winter of despair.
Charles Dickens *(A Tale of Two Cities)*

1960, and Australia was on the cusp of something special, although it was often held back from greater things by its own insecurity, conservativeness and a wayward belief in its own ability. However, it proved to be a transformative decade for the nation, characterised by significant social, political and cultural change. It was a time of immense progress, challenging traditional norms and fostering progressive ideals that struck the heart of the Australian psyche.

The concept of "cultural cringe" – first introduced by Australian critic A.A. Phillips in the 1950s – refers to a perceived inferiority complex or lack of confidence in one's own cultural identity and achievements. It suggests a lack of self-assurance and an inclination to look externally for validation and approval. Across so many contexts, Australia sat within this mindset in the 1960s, while amid it all, its people yearned for individuals or groups who might lead the way in proving Australia's identity is its own, and a mighty one at that. This era was when Australia began achieving this, and the pride and belief in our country began to emerge as our heroes and leaders proved themselves to the world.

Esteemed journalist Norman Tasker gave a different take. He felt it was more a "lack of opportunity… there weren't many people in the country, opportunities were limited," although he added that in the 1960s, "Australia started to get on top, around Dick

Thornett's era, and once they got on top, they stayed on top." Richard Thornett represented his country in three sports at the top level, across nine of the ten years in this decade, perhaps the most transitional and life-changing of any decade in recent history. He and the teams in which he played helped Australia emerge from the shadows of insecurity that had beset the nation for so long.

Consider what a significant time this was for Australia and the world: Harold Holt, elected Prime Minister in 1966, initiated several policies aimed at modernising Australia, while the country's involvement in the Vietnam War escalated and led to social unrest, dividing the country from a moral and ethical standpoint. The post-World War II baby boom resulted in a large youth population during the 1960s, also leading to cultural shifts and generational conflicts. Continuing to be influenced by global trends rather than having confidence in its own, Australian youth embraced aspects of the international counterculture movement, advocating for peace, love and freedom of expression.

In June 1964, The Beatles played to packed audiences in Adelaide, Melbourne and Sydney, their only tour to Australia, but Australia counter-punched with our own, among them Johnny O'Keefe and The Easybeats, striving to set our own stage amid a musical world dominated by overseas artists. The 1960s also saw a diversification of Australia's population, with increased immigration from Southern Europe, Asia and the Middle East, generating a new directional shift in our demographics and with it, a cultural shift. Meanwhile, significant local and global events stepped into the lounge rooms of Australians as the popularity of television grew, becoming a significant source of news, sport, entertainment and cultural influence.

The 1960s was marked by several significant assassinations that had global repercussions. While these events did not directly occur in Australia, they had an impact on the country's culture and mindset. In November 1963, US President, John F. Kennedy was assassinated, while in 1968, Martin Luther King Jr and Robert F. Kennedy were also victims of the assassin's bullet. A year later, as the decade drew to a close, man landed on the Moon, capturing the world's attention and fuelling interest in science and technology as the Space Race accelerated and the Cold War continued apace. It was a triumphant conclusion to one of (if not the most) dynamic decades in the history of mankind but typified the uncertainty that thread its way through the lives of those who lived alongside these remarkable events.

Norman Tasker has a fabulous story that he recalls from these times: "It is May 24, and back in the day, May 24 was Empire Day. When I was at school on Empire Day, we were herded into a movie theatre where we watched the Queen ride a horse as the national anthem played (*God Save the Queen* in those days) and then we all sang *Rule Britannia*. We were, to all intents and purposes, British, and this was the world into which the Thornett brothers were born. May 24 was cracker night. Bonfires lit up in backyards all over town (we all had backyards then) and bungers and double bungers and skyrockets and Catherine wheels burned and fizzed everywhere. Eventually it was stopped when the hospitals couldn't cope with the burns incidents.

Don't know that it was (cultural) cringe necessarily, but we were certainly told we were part of an Empire, and Britannia ruled the day.

Many years later, I got to spend an hour or so with the Queen in Buckingham Palace. I found her the humblest of people. She liked a gin and tonic and chatting with her brought back all those days of Empire, and by today's standards the incongruous nature of the world in which we lived.

One rugby example ... back in those days (1959, I think) it was the practice at Chatswood Oval at least, to play *God Save the Queen* as the players left the field after the fulltime whistle. As they walked off, all players would stop and stand rigidly to attention when the anthem began, as we all did in those days. On one occasion, the Gordon flanker Ken Yanz, a Wallaby but a notorious physical combatant of dubious discretion, found himself standing rigidly at attention beside a University centre with whom he had had some dispute during the game. Unable to help himself, Yanz threw a sharp jab which felled the University player. Yanz immediately resumed the rigid attention stance as the anthem played out, and nobody else moved. Certainly not the guy who had been poleaxed. Once the anthem finished, some retribution was sought, but nobody had moved until it was over.

Different world, different time."

David Maraniss, in his book **ROME 1960**: *The Olympics that changed the world (2008),* makes the point: *"Change was apparent everywhere. The world as we know it was coming into view."* The events of the 1960s had a significant impact on the Australian psyche and contributed to a cultural and social transformation. It is within this context that a great many Australians looked upwards to their icons who might steer them safely and inspirationally through such precarious waters.

Richard Thornett was one of them.

CHAPTER TWO
Sunrise 1940-1957

It (our sporting ability) didn't really come from our parents because they weren't sporting people at all. I really put it down to the fact that we lived near Bronte Beach and my father used to enjoy swimming, so every morning he'd take us, even through winter.
Richard Thornett

Richard Norman Thornett was born at Waverley War Memorial Hospital on the 23rd of September 1940, one year and 22 days after the start of the Second World War. He was brought home from hospital to Bronte, New South Wales (NSW), Australia, the third of three sons for Harold and Marge, and a brother to John and Ken. It was a tumultuous time, with the world reeling from the chaos and uncertainty that filled the hearts of its people, both here and abroad. Yet, amid this backdrop of darkness and conflict, a spark of extraordinary talent, joining those of his brothers, would soon emerge, and in the years ahead he would provide something special for a nation so in need of it.

Richard's mother, Marge, was a country girl, born east of Coonabarabran, although she didn't have many fond memories of rural life during the 1920s on the family property, "Koronga". She was from a large, reasonably affluent family and contracted polio at 14 years of age which rendered her unable to play sport, although she never complained about her condition. Marge was a modest, unassuming woman, regarded as a splendid lady who was never known to brag; she did not exist in the reflected glory of her sons. She was a great cook and hostess who provided for the many people who used to regularly drop by, for the Thornett house was often a refuge for friends of the boys who would always find a friendly welcome there and never leave hungry. In those times, a mother's lot was to be a good homemaker and Marge would always wash the boys' muddy football gear by hand, until the arrival of a Hoover twin tub machine which made her life a little easier. Marge unashamedly doted on and spoilt her boys; she was a gentle and caring mother who lived for her family.

Childhood friends and Randwick rugby teammates, ex-Wallaby Peter Johnson and Warren Hurt, who both spent much time at the Thornett household, spoke of Richard's parents fondly. Johnson said, "Mrs Thornett, she was just, she was just the mother to all of us. To virtually all of us. She was, she was quite extraordinary. Everyone ran everywhere. Just, you never, ever walked. You ran… and she would, she would say to me… 'You look hungry.' So, you'd have to have something like a piece of fruit or something and go."

Warren Hurt added, "You couldn't go to the Thornetts without Mrs Thornett saying, "You've got to stay for dinner, for lunch. And the thing is, she'd serve up these lunches that were just phenomenal. I mean that they'd almost feed Napoleon's retreating army, in terms of their size. She'd say, 'Are you going home now?' And after I'd tell her I was, she would reply, 'Well, you better have something to eat before you go. It's a long way to go.' It was all the time." Peter Johnson added, "Actually, Mr Thornett told me that when Richard left home, he saved $1.2 million on bananas alone."

Richard's father, Harold was born in Canada but lived his early life in England and migrated to Australia in 1904 when he was 12 years of age. One of seven children, he worked as an engineer at the railway. Harold was a keen swimmer and could be found every morning at Bronte Beach or Bronte Baths, a practice which could be traced back to his swimming sessions at Powell's Pool in Birmingham. He was a good man, a strong Christian, unassuming, stoic and quite conservative (he was known to not be a fan of the liberated 1960s) who gave his boys anything they needed – he was totally dedicated to them. Harold was tall and lean, a height he passed onto his sons, although it seemed they skipped the leanness.

Richard's parents were of modest means. They were both very dedicated parents, having no luxuries themselves but dedicating their lives to striving to provide the best upbringing possible for John, Ken and Richard. Neither parent had a sporting background, both because of Marge's affliction and due to a lack of opportunity in part because Harold had come to Australia as a 12-year-old and settled in an unfamiliar world in Hanwood, near Griffith, NSW. Whilst Harold swam regularly later in life, enjoyed sailing and had played a bit of suburban cricket as a fast bowler, none of his sons had ever seen or heard of rugby in their younger years; it was never discussed at home. Most of the boys' success can be linked to their environment – surf, sun, sand, physical fitness and supportive, nurturing parents.

Although growing up in the seaside suburb of Bronte, Richard's love of the land sprouted (excuse the pun) early in life through a childhood hero, Uncle Gus Attwood, his mother's brother. Gus lived on a property at Ungarie, near West Wyalong, NSW, and was a good farmer who had a strong influence on all three brothers early in their lives. He sparked a life-long passion in them for the land which remained strong throughout their lives. They visited him regularly on school holidays, taking long train trips on the Temora Mail to visit Uncle Gus on school holidays. Ken recalled, "Gus working his eight-horse teams and sowing wheat with his two lead horses, Bob and Nell. We spent many a day out rabbiting with horse and sulky accompanied by his greyhounds and by night they sprang rabbit traps. We enjoyed helping with the lamb marking and drenching and would often come back to Sydney with ten shillings or perhaps a pound for our efforts, particularly when Gus had a win at the races. Other fond memories of his visits to the country included playing the card game 500 in the evenings, Tilley lamps and kerosene, milking cows, the smell of the cypress pines and Pepper trees, and big tennis days." Upon returning to Sydney, Richard and his brothers felt so much more privileged than their mates to have had that experience, which struck a spark for a life on the land that never left them.

The three brothers trained at Bronte swimming pool in their younger days and at the age of four or five, they joined the Bronte Swimming Club and competed in the inter-club carnivals. Their proximity to the beach and regular outdoor activities were factors in their physical development. They were out and about early and often, and then after school until late in the evenings. Almost every day saw the Thornett brothers swimming in the morning before school or during the day, or both, at Bronte and in swimming competitions every Sunday. As they grew older, this lifestyle contributed to both their fitness levels and physical well-being required to achieve at higher-level competitive sport. Water Polo and touch football helped to establish skills, timing and anticipation. Former Randwick Rugby Union teammate, Stan Sparrow, also remembers not just Richard, but all three brothers having superb ball skills, honed through their sporting prowess in the water. "All three brothers were superb handlers – the Water Polo certainly helped and achieved and maintained fitness from swimming; all three were excellent swimmers."

Life in Bronte in the 1950s and '60s was uncomplicated; the Park, the Gully and the surrounding beaches would draw the local young folk together from all over. It is interesting to consider the strength of sportspeople and teams who were based in Sydney's Eastern Suburbs around this time, such as Murray Rose, Ken Catchpole and Michael Cleary (another triple-Australian representative from Randwick). Rugby League club South Sydney were premiers or runners-up in six of seven years from 1965, while Randwick Rugby Club won four from nine Shute Shields from 1959–1967; in 1967, both clubs won their respective premierships.

In summer, the brothers often went fishing for eels at low tide or caught waves at the Bogey Holes west of the baths when there was high tide and good surf. Winter would see Bronte Park (also known as 'the Gully') hold 20-a-side tackle football every afternoon until dark when dinner would be waiting when the Thornetts returned home. Richard was about ten and would often give away five or more years to his opponents in those games.

Those were the days when there were no agendas and children played outside for the fun of it. Local parks, beaches and pools were melting pots of children from different (but close-by) suburbs and schools – they would play with or against one another in the park during the week and do the same again on weekends. It spawned a wonderful era of sport throughout the country, long before sporting academies, outrageous playing contract sign-on fees and sporting scholarships.

Former Socceroos' captain, Johnny Warren, described the environment in which he was raised in his book *Sheilas, Wogs and Poofters: An Incomplete Biography of Johnny Warren and Soccer in Australia*. *"The setting of my upbringing was classic post-war Sydney. Extended and close-knit families, sun-drenched summers playing cricket, grazed knees from tarred playing fields, 'six 'n' out' and broken windows. A city rebalancing after the turmoil of the war, a society looking to redefine its mores and holding fast to what it knew to be true. My brothers and I were products of people who had lived through the Depression. The Depression taught my parents not to take anything for granted and always have a contingency or escape plan. They firmly believed that education and sport were an integral part of life."*

Norman Tasker added, "It was the post-war thing, everyone was into sport. Everyone. Everything was cheap, schools, all the schools had mostly male teachers. So, sport was a thing that was a very important part of life. And that naturally developed some very good players who were the sort of people you're talking about in the early 1960s."

Triple international, Michael Cleary, remembers the time well when asked how growing up in that era may have lent itself to people being so multi-talented across a number of sports (consider names like Thornett, Brass, Lisle, Cleary, Heinrich and Hawthorne, to name a few), "Well, it was because we weren't disciplined in any (one) sport. We just participated in whatever sport was available. We used to run the streets running bare feet and a pair of shorts and a T-shirt, or you'd have a school uniform. You'd get in it and you go running. And if there's a game of touch football on, you played touch football. If beach football, you played beach football. Handball, you played handball; tennis, you'd play tennis... you just adjusted to what was available at the time... Also, (I'd see Richard) a little bit at the Coogee Aquarium. I saw him around those times, but I thought that brothers Dick, John and Ken, they were all pretty close together. And we all wandered the streets of Bronte in those days. (We) just looked after each other and had a lot of fun. Dick, I found was a gentle giant with a turn of speed and at times a jovial fella with a bit of sarcasm in his voice. He always had a smile on his face."

Rugby League international, Kevin Junee, who like Cleary played with and against Richard, also remembers the simplicity of the times, the uncomplicated rituals and traditions, and the way of life. "I used to walk to school; I can't remember if I had shoes or not. Life was a little bit tough back then. Paddington was a tough area. Every parent seemed to be struggling. It was a working-class area. Your biggest honour was to wear the district football jumper, an honour to wear the red, white and blue. During winter we'd pull the timber off the fences and every backyard had a couple of palings missing to try and stoke the chip heater in the baths. We had the clothes prop man walking down selling clothes, and then there was the rabbit man (who) used to come around selling rabbits. The vegie man who had his horse and cart, and my mother used to send me out to scoop up the horse manure to put on our little backyard garden which was about a metre square. Yeah, life was pretty simple but tough."

Journalist Norman Tasker remembers the Thornett family. "Well, the thing that struck me (about Mother Thornett), as is the case with most sporting mothers, was the meticulous records; they kept the scrapbook. It was just voluminous, as you can imagine. But so far in covering pretty much all their lives, from the time they were kids playing Water Polo down to Bronte to John Thornett, leading the Wallabies to Dick being a multi-talented international. It was just voluminous. And she was obviously a very doting mother, as most mothers of good sporting people are. She treasured that scrapbook. She was a very proud mother. I met the old man once or twice. He was a taciturn sort of guy, but he was obviously pretty devoted to them too, I'd say. It seemed to me to be a pretty strong family."

The three boys attended Clovelly Primary School. John left in 4th class to attend Woollahra Opportunity School while Richard and Ken left in 6th class and went to Paddington Central Junior Technical School; Richard until 1955. After his first three years at Paddington, Richard left to attend Randwick Boys' High School to complete his Leaving Certificate. Unfortunately, he wasn't the academic that his brother, John, was and after failing his Leaving Certificate, he set his compass towards a life of sport, concentrating on Water Polo and Rugby Union in those early days.

Richard remembered. "Probably, the first competition game I played was when I went to Clovelly Primary School. I played Rugby League in the 6 stone-7 category when I was in 4th class because of my size. Even at that age I couldn't make the 5 stone-7 pounds where most of my classmates were. (In fact), I only just made the 6 stone-7 pounds but after a couple of years at Clovelly Primary School I went to Paddington and played Rugby League. As Paddington didn't play Rugby Union, I played (Rugby Union) with Bronte RSL Club while playing Rugby League with Paddington."

Perhaps as a nod to the future, at 13 years of age, Richard was a dual-code sportsman. He was playing First Grade Water Polo for Bronte at 14 and the recipient of three Combined High Schools (CHS) Blue awards in his three years at Paddington. Elsewhere in the school, two year groups behind Richard at Paddington was future Rugby League international, Kevin Junee. In Paddington's 1955 school magazine *Tricolour*, the football report detailed that by season's end, the 1st team *"... was undefeated, scoring 276 points to 4, Bondi being the only side to score against us."*

At the end of his third year at Paddington, Richard truly launched his sporting career when he transferred to Randwick Boys' High School in 1956. Their school magazine reports in both years are filled with praise for his sporting achievements. He excelled in swimming, Water Polo and football (Rugby League), both captaining the school and representing CHS in each sport. Richard's outstanding representation was recognised with a Combined High Schools "Blue Award" for all three sports in 1957. The New South Wales Combined High Schools' (NSWCHS) Blue Award is an extremely prestigious award that is only presented to students who have excelled on the sporting field, displayed outstanding sportsmanship and made great contributions to both their school and sporting communities. In all the years that the Blues have been awarded, only one other person has been awarded three in one year – David Woods, the Olympic Water Polo player, who was awarded for the same three sports in 1961.

Interestingly, 37 years later, the Sky High Room at Canterbury Racecourse held an evening that honoured past and present CHS sporting champions. It was a who's who of Australia's sporting royalty and included such names as Kay Cottee, Marjorie Jackson, Betty Cuthbert, Dawn Fraser, John and Ilsa Konrads, and John Henricks. Richard Thornett and then CHS sports association president, Dave Woods, were remembered for their feats in having achieved Blues in three different sports.

Award-winning journalist Adrian McGregor knew Richard well. Apart from his talented work as a wordsmith, he played rugby with Richard at Randwick Boys' High School in the 1st XV. His biography reads, *"Adrian McGregor's first trail-blazing bestseller "King Wally" created a new readership for Rugby League books. It was followed by the popular "Wally and the Broncos". His biography of Greg Chappell has been acclaimed as one of the finest contemporary contributions to the history of cricket while his account of the 1990 Kangaroos' tour of England, "Simply the Best" was described as the Rugby League book of the year. Adrian's biography of Cathy Freeman – "A Journey Just Begun" – was also highly acclaimed. Adrian is a writer with wide experience on Australian newspapers and he has won several journalism prizes, including a National Press Club award for best sporting feature."*

THE NATURAL

In an interview for this book, he remembered Richard Thornett vividly. "He was sort of a man amongst boys, really, because he was about 15 stone and I weighed about 12 stone. They put me as the other prop and a physical Ted Syme, who was a very good Water Polo player and swimmer from Bondi, came into the side as hooker. I can tell you it was a shock of my life to suddenly go into a scrum because Dick was holding up his side and the scrum was screwing badly. I was going backwards. When he first arrived, he was a Water Polo player as much as he was a rugby player, and he was enormously strong. My conversations with him were, basically, that he was a gentleman and he was observant. He was a very trusted person, you know, around the team.

I remember once we had a scrum (which) we lost. We're about the halfway mark and the ball went dead along the Sydney High School backline to their winger who went down the sideline. Just a yard or two from the sideline was Dick who had broken from the scrum as he was the prop and diagonally went across, anticipating what was going on and crashed him to the ground. It was amazing, you know, the performance, because he was such a big man. But he was fast. Once he got a bit of speed up, he was fast across the ground."

More than a decade later, Richard was still displaying his remarkable speed across the ground in cover defence. John Rhodes was born in Brisbane, Queensland and played wing and centre, including 63 times for Canterbury between 1968 and 1972. He played for NSW in game 3 of the interstate series alongside Richard in 1968 against Queensland, his old state, with NSW winning 29–11. Rhodes also played with Richard in the 1968 Rugby League World Cup, including the Final against France. When asked about Richard's playing strengths he said: "(Richard's) strength was his running but his defence was very, very good as well. If you got near him, he'd clobber you. I can remember we were playing against Great Britain and Clive Sullivan was on the wing. He was playing his first Test match and I marked him. We had a drop kick from the goal line and I missed him (Sullivan). He'd come inside and he easily beat me, (but) Dick was covering in defence and he grassed him. (Thank goodness) because we were the only two that were on that side. For a big man, he could cover a lot of ground and he was very fast for a big man, too."

The football report in the 1957 Randwick Boys' High School magazine stated: *"DICK THORNETT: Captain of the team and outstanding at lock forward or breakaway, represented C.H.S. against Duntroon, Associated Schools and Greater Public Schools. A brilliant attacking player and cover defender, and probably the best footballer in the competition."*

In 1957, he gave a year away to his opponents because he was young for his year group, Richard represented the CHS representative rugby side that played against Combined Associated Schools (CAS), Duntroon College and Greater Public Schools (GPS). In the game against the highly-fancied GPS side, a newspaper article prophetically read:

"Two brilliant schoolboy breakaways today will follow in the footsteps of their brothers.

The breakaways are Ted Heinrich (St. Joseph's College) and Dick Thornett (Randwick High).

They are rivals in the annual Combined G.P.S. V Combined C.H.S. Rugby Union match at the Sports Ground.

Heinrich captain of G.P.S. emulates his brother, Vince who led G.P.S. in 1952.

Dick Thornett follows in the footsteps of brother John, who played for G.P.S. in 1951.

Vince Heinrich and John Thornett played for Australia after their schoolboy Union careers.

Union's keenest judges believe Ted Heinrich and Dick Thornett could also become Australian representatives.

School officials expect a crowd of 10,000 to watch the match."

The crack GPS team won the day with a score of 22-6, helped by tries to the outstanding St Joseph's winger, Jim McCann, and another to one of the greatest Wallabies to play the game, Ken Catchpole. Another future Wallaby and Kangaroo, Michael Cleary represented Combined Associated Schools. CHS defeated them 29-5 with Richard scoring a try and kicking a goal to help secure the win. Ted Heinrich and Richard proved the newspaper prediction correct and did play together for their country in Rugby Union, as well as teaming up in Rugby League at Parramatta for four seasons from 1965-68.

Ken Catchpole recalls the game, and the first time he laid eyes on Richard; "(In the game) against CHS, I was in the GPS side and Dick was in the CHS side.

As we were running into the field, I thought, 'Gee, that's a big bloke. Really is big, (must be) a lock or second rower.' And then, as we took up our positions and the first scrum set, (I thought), 'God! he's a flanker!' He was really very impressive."

Years later, Roy Masters wrote, in a piece for *The Sydney Morning Herald (SMH)* on August 28, 1999, that Catchpole regarded Richard as *"... the best ball-handling forward I have ever seen."*

Four years after that CHS/GPS clash at the Sydney Sports Ground in 1957, Richard Thornett, Ken Catchpole, Ted Heinrich and Michael Cleary ran out in the same side – the Wallabies' first Test against Fiji in Brisbane on June 10, 1961, all as debutants. To emphasise their brilliance, Richard, Ken and Michael scored tries in an emphatic 24-6 victory. A few weeks later, all four boarded a plane bound for a two-Test tour to South Africa, with Richard joined by his brother, John, and Ken Catchpole was captain/coach of the Wallabies at the age of 21.

When Cleary was asked to sum up Richard in three words, he said, "Powerful, happy, good bloke." The future was looking bright, brighter than even Richard expected, although not necessarily in the way he thought it might.

CHAPTER THREE
Randwick 1958-1959

He took me under his arm and showed me how to live...He would get me into trouble and I was quite happy getting into trouble as far as I was concerned because I was there getting into trouble with Dick.
Rob Heming (Ex-Wallaby)

Richard entered his 18th year in 1958 having just left school with the world at his feet and the tide at his back. These narrow timeframe windows between school and career are often critical touchpoints in a person's life, as they consider which direction to take once the somewhat sheltered existence of school disappears in the rear-view mirror.

Richard decided that he would join the police force straight out of school in 1958, based primarily on two factors. He explained, "Well I suppose I didn't give myself much of a chance to be a good academic because I was spending all my time swimming and running around the (rugby) park. I failed the Leaving (Certificate) and then I thought I'd join the police force, and that was very good for my sport at that stage… It was a good job to have. I met a lot of good people from when I joined in 1958 until I resigned in 1965. I graduated through the cadets and then (progressed) into the main (section of the) police force, working mainly in the fingerprints section." Australia's star Rugby League lock forward, Johnny Raper, must have had a similar plan; he was one year ahead of Richard in the force.

Journalist Norman Tasker added how different the times were, "… rugby players were completely amateur and even the league players didn't get much. They'd work on a garbage truck or a big truck or something to make ends meet. I remember blokes like Norm Provan, who played Rugby League for many years, won ten premierships with St George. He would go to work on a Saturday morning at 8:00 or something, work through till about 1:00 and then move onto the (Sydney) Cricket Ground to play the match of the day. It was that sort of world; sport was just sport. I think when Dick started playing, the trams were still running in Sydney. You could buy a house for about 15 grand."

Now, whether or not Richard's academic prowess, or lack thereof, could be put down (as he claims) to the interference of his sporting pursuits might be up for some debate. The 1956 Randwick Boys' High School's *Pegasus* magazine report on the football season perhaps offered another reason, written over a year before Richard failed his Leaving Certificate. The editor of the football report liked to refer to his players by nickname: there was "Mad Jack" Turtle, "Irish" Ower, "Chook" Hawkins, "Caesar" Thompson. Richard was "Simple" Thornett – make of that what you will.

Brother Ken confirmed John's status as the academic of the family (and Richard's status in other areas) when he said that "John was the model child. He was gifted academically and never any trouble. Richard was somewhere between John and me in temperament and was Mum's favourite." Ken also mentioned that John would often miss those 20-a-side tackle football games as he was at home studying, so perhaps that might explain why eldest brother John went to Sydney University to study engineering and science – and was good enough to receive a Commonwealth scholarship. Furthermore, it might explain why Richard and Ken were the ball-runners in the family.

Richard also expanded on his comment that the police force was "...very good for my sport..." when he explained "I was looking for a reasonably secure position and I believed at the time that they were good with sportsmen. The police force encouraged sport and was supportive of me taking time off for training or even physiotherapy. I was very lucky to have good bosses all the way through and they were very keen and fanatical Rugby League and Rugby Union supporters, so I had good people behind me. If you were touring, you would have time off without pay and there was always a position to come back to. My parents also helped me financially; I lived at home with them during my earlier football and Water Polo career rent-free, they gave me a bed and food, and it was one of the reasons I was able to afford to tour in those days. We would be given 10 shillings a day, £3.10 a week, which just covered living expenses on tour."

Even on tour, Richard had to keep his guard up with his employer. On the 1962

RANDWICK 1958-1959

New Zealand tour, his boss, Inspector F.B. Whitehouse, in charge of Australia's Central Fingerprint Bureau, dropped into the third Test in Auckland to see that he was getting his money's worth!

At the age of 17, and "straight out of school, I joined Ken at Randwick in 1958," continued Richard. "I played three second grade games and was then promoted to First Grade, playing on the side of the scrum. Randwick, at that stage, had no real personalities because after the 1957/58 tour of the British Isles, of which Randwick had six players, all six retired in 1958. Randwick started forming a younger team of players such as Teddy Heinrich, myself, Bruce Judd, my brother Ken and Michael Stynes, Donnie Ford. I think at that stage the average age of the players in the Randwick First Grade side was about 20 years old. In my next year, 1959, virtually the same team went on to win the Sydney First Grade premiership (Randwick's first in eleven years). We beat Northern Suburbs in the grand final, 16-0. My brother, Ken and I played against John who was captaining Norths. John was not overly happy with the result but he managed to get over it and congratulate us. It was quite a thrill."

An interesting sidenote to this game was the brotherly physical confrontation that *almost* happened. It goes to the heart of Richard's relationship with his eldest brother, John. Richard remembers it like this: "I don't think we ever confronted one another in any sort of way. (Nevertheless,) I know he got a bit upset in the grand final when I had a bit of a wrestle with him. John Carroll was the Northern Suburbs second rower and I had him on the ground and was ready to hit him and I could see John sort of standing there with a 'Don't do that' look on his face." Richard didn't. John was probably the only person in the world, except perhaps his mother, Marge, who could have pulled that off!

To reach the grand final in 1959, Randwick had to defeat Manly in their semi-final, which they did, 16-6 in front of a crowd of 9,000 at North Sydney Oval. Esteemed journalist, Phil Tresidder, reporting on the game in his *Telegraph* column, wrote that *"Randwick set a tempo of play that overwhelmed the older, heavier Manly side... Richard Thornett, a 14½-stone second-row youngster who carries the stamp of a future Wallaby forward, played a splendid part. Two conversions he kicked also helped to give Randwick the ascendancy. Randwick led 5-0 at halftime through a try by Dick Thornett, which he converted from the touchline."*

In the *Sunday Mirror*, well-known sports reporter Dick Tucker opened his article on the grand final with *"Randwick yesterday won their first Rugby Union premiership for 11 years after a gruelling, brawling grand final against Northern Suburbs at Sydney Sports Ground."* Punches were thrown early and Norths' star fullback, Rod Phelps left the field with a deep gash to his face and neck. It was a huge blow to Norths' chances, with Phelps being instrumental in their charge up the ladder in their quest to win their first premiership in almost a quarter of a century. Tucker wrote, *"The match was a personal triumph for the Thornett brothers, Randwick's two, Ken and Dick, and older brother, John, of Norths. Fullback Ken was always a danger when in possession, running strongly and linking up with his backs. Dick capped a fine, all-round forward display by kicking two goals and a penalty goal from six attempts. John was outstanding in a courageous Norths pack which never wilted."* The crowd was posted at 10,460 and the gate takings were £1,168 – a cheap day out at the rugby for spectators. Four days after this remarkable fortnight, Richard would be able to celebrate with a beer at his 18th birthday.

"The first year I went to Randwick; Catchpole was there too and Wally Meagher, who was an all-time great… pulled Catchpole and myself aside as we were trialling for Randwick and starting the first season (of rugby) out of school," Richard remembered. "Wally said, 'I'd like you to have a couple of years in the juniors, in the Colts,' but I said, 'Well, I don't want to. If I did, I would go and play with my Bronte RSL side.' So, he didn't say any more to me but Catchy had another year in Colts before he came to grade in '59. So, they did try to keep the younger blokes out of it, yeah, but I didn't want to. I was down there to play. I didn't go down there to play colts." This was from a 17-year-old youngster, straight out of school, letting his thoughts be known to one of Randwick's great players and identities. If nothing else, Richard knew what he wanted.

Harold Rowe Thornett was conflicted whenever his sons opposed each on the rugby field. If he had one wish, it was to see them play for the same team; Randwick. After interviewing Harold in 1959 for *Sports Magazine*, journalist Alan Hulls wrote an article headlined **The Code's Family Affair**. It appeared in the June issue. *"Despite their liking for Water Polo, winter or summer, it is Rugby Union that is discussed constantly in the Thornett home. This strikes a sad note in the heart of their father, Mr Harold Thornett, who finds his loyalties divided.*

It was a disappointment to him when John joined Norths Club. He had cherished the thought of his three sons playing in the one team. Mostly he follows Randwick, but he saw Norths play Eastern Suburbs in the first round of this season. He was so enthusiastic with the open brand of football Norths played that he said in future he would have to divide his interest between Norths and Randwick, a tremendous decision for an ardent Randwick supporter to make."

Two years after Randwick's grand final victory and that small sibling altercation with his brother, Richard found himself on the same side as John in the third Test against Fiji in Melbourne. This time though, John was defending his little brother. Richard recounted, "We were probably lucky to get a 3-all draw there; they (Fiji) had improved so much on their tour that we just got away with it. The only recollection I have in that game is running around the front of the lineout and having a big Fijian fist come out of nowhere and hit me in the nose. I can't recall any other part of the game as I was concussed but I believe my brother John got quite upset about it and for the first time I could remember he threw a punch in a game of rugby. So, I suppose brothers do stick together."

Rumour has it that John only threw one other punch in his career (against the French). Norths only had to wait one more year to raise the trophy, winning the 1960 premiership, defeating Manly 21-3 in the grand final. Richard, while regarded as tough, was never one to seek to intimidate through his fists. Nonetheless, there may have been the odd occasion when he felt it necessary to provide some physical cover for a teammate or in retaliation for ill-discipline on the part of his opposition. *SMH* reporter, Malcolm Brown, reminiscing in his newspaper column the day before Richard's funeral, reflected that *"In a rugby Test against the All Blacks, an opposing forward saw Dick Thornett aim some well-directed retaliatory blows and asked, 'Were you an Olympic boxer as well as a Water Polo player?'"*

Richard rested from rugby in 1960 as he prepared for the Olympic Games, having been selected in Australia's Water Polo team. "I didn't play any football because we trained for the Games during winter. In 1961, I went back to Randwick again and was lucky enough to force my way back into First Grade," said Richard.

In 1961, Richard and John squared off once again in the South Harbour v North Harbour game at Manly Oval. In an article written by Stan Baxter in *The Telegraph*, John said, *"I will treat Dick as just another player and there will be no easy going for him as far as I am concerned."* Neither need have been concerned because both were selected and packed down in the NSW pack, and then for the Wallabies games against Fiji, South Africa and France. They were both in the City 1 team that defeated Country 1, 13-6 and then the NSW team that demolished Queensland, 45-0. They didn't play in the same row for either game, with John playing front row in both and Richard playing second row for City 1 and in the back row for NSW. They then paired up again in NSW's defeat of the touring Fiji side at the Sydney Sports Ground, 17-13, with John moving back to the second row and Richard playing at lock. The result was perhaps unsurprising to some degree, given the calibre of the NSW team. It contained 13 of the 15 Wallabies who ran out against Fiji two weeks later on June 10. As such, the South Harbour v North Harbour square-off between the two brothers was a bit of a non-event, as they played different positions to one another in each game. Perhaps it was just a case of trying to fit two of the best players in the state and country into the same team.

Legendary Wallaby hooker Peter Johnson said about Richard upon his return to rugby in 1961, "Dick Thornett had returned from the Rome Olympics, rated as one of the world's top Water Polo players. His impact on club rugby was immediate. Rather in the manner of the very best All Black forwards, Dick paid no regard for the efforts of opponents, almost to the point of ignoring them, except in defence when his attention to their welfare was complete. What caught the eye most of all was the way he, a huge man, could move with such speed and grace. Add to this his handling ability, hardly surprising in an Olympic Water Polo player, and the result struck terror into the hearts of all but the most stoic or stupid. On reflection, there was little shortage of either category on the Sydney scene."

Early in 1961, when Randwick still had their representative players, they jumped out of the blocks, winning their first six games consecutively, and things were looking bright indeed. They had defeated eventual premiers, Sydney University 10-6 and overcome Gordon for the first time in three years, 22-6, scoring six tries to one at Chatswood Oval (back when tries were only worth three points). Meanwhile, in *The Sun-Herald* Union Player Awards (given to best club performers each week on a 3-2-1 point basis), Parramatta's second rower, Ivan Mann and Richard, moved to the lead of the contest to find the "Best and Fairest" player of the year. Mann would not have been unhappy when the Fijian national rugby side landed soon after and things turned a little more favourably for him with Dick away on representative duty.

The Wallaby team that toured South Africa in 1961 contained six Randwick players, which contributed somewhat to Randwick's falling short of the semi-finals that year. There were trial and representative matches stretching over four months from April to August, which certainly had an impact on their win/loss ratio; Richard was only available for eight games, Heinrich seven and Catchpole and Cleary six. In fact, in *The SMH* on May 3, 1961, Stan Baxter wrote that the NSW Rugby Union barred any player chosen for the NSW team from playing club football in the next round as the risk of injury was too great. Randwick had a third of its First Grade side affected, including Richard. Something that came to mind for Richard was Michael Cleary's seven tries on the right wing for Randwick in their first club game back after the South African tour – oh, what might have been... Randwick would certainly have been in the frame for another premiership, and Cleary left Rugby Union soon after to join South Sydney Rugby League team for an illustrious career, although he would run out onto the field again with Richard in 1963 as his Kangaroo teammate.

From a sporting context, most would say that the true gauge of any sportsman's ability comes from the opinions of those who stand in direct opposition to them, engaging in combat with them. True understanding comes not from those who stand on sidelines, sit in grandstands or watch on screens. The opinions of those combatants hold more significant weight than even the sportsman's own teammates and his coaches, more than rival coaches, journalists and supposed experts. As we traverse the battles and journeys undertaken by Richard Thornett, you will read from these people's experiences and encounters both from a physical and relational perspective.

One such person was Rob Heming, a Wallaby veteran who played 21 times for Australia between 1961 and 1967 who is regarded as one of our greatest lineout forwards ever. Apart from playing alongside Richard in the Wallaby forward pack in 1961/62, he played against him as a member of the Manly Marlins Rugby Club, where he played 132 First Grade games. Heming marvelled at Richard's sporting talent because it spanned sports that were largely unconnected; water sports and rugby. He should know, as he himself narrowly missed out in selection for the 1956 Olympic swimming team. Heming said, "To think that he had his Water Polo and then moved to Rugby Union and league. To me, it's totally different.

Water Polo and running are miles apart."

He went on to say, "Dick was one of the best players that I have played with. The ability to run the ball, do everything, he could do it of course, and he was a joy to play with. In 1961, when I made my first tour, he was 20 and I was 29 and he took me under his arm and showed me how to live. I was playing not in the second row; I was playing Number 8 at that time and I enjoyed it immensely. All the games I had with Dick; I became great pals with him. We shared a room together and he always had that wickedness about him. He would get me into trouble and I was quite happy getting into trouble as far as I was concerned because I was there getting into trouble with Dick. Seeing it was my first tour and I knew nothing, but it was his first tour too. (Nevertheless) He seemed to know everything; I really admired his abilities so much and he was such a fun guy."

Fellow ex-Randwick player, Stan Sparrow, agreed that while Dick was the "toughest" and always willing to mix it in the "tough stuff", he was also "a joker with very dry wit."

Heming continued, "When we came back the next year, we (Manly) were playing Randwick and I was apparently too close to the ball (on the ground) and Dick promptly kicked me in the ribs, breaking two of them. Afterwards he said he did not realise it was me. I said, 'Well, I suppose I was fairly close to the ball,' and he said, 'Yes you were quite on the ball, I had every reason to get you.' It is always about the fact that we were such good mates and here he is breaking my ribs. I must say, I enjoyed being with him on and off (the field) all the time. He was really a delight… a worry, but a delight. Dick was always trying to lead me astray but John Thornett being around stopped me from going around the bend."

These were the days when lying on the ground in a ruck, close to the ball, rendered you a target, and no one was off-limits, not even a good friend. Unfortunately for Rob, it was his turn that day, but as was so typical, no grudges were held. Regardless, what a lovely story; the older player being led astray by the young pup, but loving every minute of it, and only being prevented from further trouble by that young pup's older brother, who seemed to be always on hand when trouble was brewing, to keep things in check (such as in that grand final game three years earlier).

Randwick underwent a similar experience in 1962 when several players were again away from club duties, including a five-Test series against the All Blacks, with two matches in Australia and three across the ditch. Nonetheless, Randwick did manage to make the grand final, going down at the last hurdle to University, 14-0, although they did manage to beat them earlier in the season. In his regular *SMH* newspaper article, respected journalist Jim Webster reported on that Randwick triumph over University, the previous year's premiers and eventual 1962 winners as well, 14-6 at Coogee Oval. Commenting on the fact that the Randwick side was depleted in numbers, including two players of international standard, he opened by lamenting a *"sad day for the University forwards who saw no dividends for their relentless scrummaging."* He went on to say that *"individuals from both packs gave fine performances, including (Richard) Thornett and Heinrich,"* before expanding further, *"Dick Thornett, the international, engineered the try that pushed the score along to 9-3. From loose play, he broke out with a surprise turn of speed..."* Randwick would be back in the winner's circle three years later where they would win three premierships in succession from 1965-67.

The Randwick District Rugby Union Football Club was formed in 1882 and admitted to the New South Wales First Division in 1889. In 2010, it announced its greatest team ever. This Hall of Fame team was announced at the Hilton Hotel Ballroom in Sydney, with Richard's name called out, joining Warwick Waugh in the second row. For a player who only had three seasons at Randwick, to be selected among such distinguished company was a magnificent achievement.

The criteria for selection in the Hall of Fame team was as follows:

The inductee must have been a distinguished Randwick First Grade player, have made a considerable contribution to the game of rugby and to Randwick, and finally he must have enhanced his and Randwick's reputation by his ability, sportsmanship and character.

The selected team was simply magnificent, and, if it were possible to have them on the field at the same time, at the height of their powers, this club side would have defeated most international sides at any point in history. This is the team:

Sir Nicholas Shehadie
Peter Johnson
Ewan McKenzie
Richard Thornett

Warwick Waugh
Colin Windon
Simon Poidevin
Arthur Buchan
Ken Catchpole
Mark Ella
David Campese
John Brass
Cyril Towers
Alan Morton
Russell Fairfax
Jeffrey Sayle (coach)

Legendary commentator Gordon Bray gave a phantom call of this team playing against the 2010 All Blacks at Coogee Oval in front of 15,000 people, with Randwick claiming victory 12–7 (two tries to one).

In Peter Jenkins' 2004 book, *The Top 100 Wallabies,* four of this team made the top 10. Richard's selection in Randwick's Hall of Fame XV was a worthy and deserved nod to an outstanding member of one of the finest clubs in the world.

A 3-kilometre walk north-east from Coogee Oval sat Bronte Baths. Richard was moving closer to his first taste of international representation, and having not yet turned 20, The Eternal City (Rome) beckoned. But first, there was work to do.

CHAPTER FOUR
Rome 1960

There is a tide in the affairs of men
Which, taken at the flood, leads on to fortune;
Omitted, all the voyage of their life
Is bound in shallows and in miseries.
On such a full sea are we now afloat,
And we must take the current when it serves
Or lose our ventures
    William Shakespeare (*Julius Caesar*, IV.ii.270–276)

You would be forgiven for thinking that Richard would have had his hands full enough playing First Grade rugby with Randwick, all the while attracting interest at a representative level as well. The warmer months, though, drew Richard to the pool where he proved himself to be an outstanding swimmer and Water Polo player, as well as a prodigy on the rugby paddock. It must be remembered that Richard was the swimming champion at Randwick Boys' High, captained their rugby and Water Polo 1st teams, represented CHS in all three and won a CHS Blue in all three as well, so he had form. Richard's brother, Ken, believed that had he persevered, he would have been a very successful, possibly Olympic-standard swimmer.

    It may surprise you to learn that Water Polo is the longest-standing team sport in which Australia has participated at the Olympics, starting in 1948. Richard's skills in the water, crafted from all those years in the Bronte Baths and at the beach, among other places, saw him rise to rapid prominence whilst still at school. Richard recalls, "About five years before I left school, (my brother) John was instrumental in forming the Bronte Water Polo Club. Bondi was the champion Water Polo team at this time and… John managed to get some players across to form the Bronte club where Ken, John and I played together in First Grade. I was playing First Grade Water Polo there from 14 years of age. In those days we used to train a lot, never distance swimming. We all did mainly sprint work; the furthest we would swim would be half a mile. At the age of about 18 I would have been about 15 stone and six foot, probably the same weight and height as I was at school the year before."

John and Bert Vadas, an ex-Hungarian Olympian, were instrumental in establishing the Bronte Water Polo Club in 1952. John, Ken and Richard played significant roles in propelling the club to the success they enjoyed in the Sydney competition. Having been runners-up in the Sydney First Grade competitions of 1953/54 and 1954/55, they claimed four First Grade premierships in a row from 1958/59 to 1961/62. Under the leadership of his brother John and the expert coaching of Vadas, Dick became an excellent Water Polo player with a legendary shot at goal and was a member of that inaugural First Grade winning team in the NSW Amateur Water Polo Association (NSWAWPA) Premiership season of 1958/59. John Thornett said of his brother, "As soon as Dick handled a Water Polo ball, he was an instant success and possessed a shot so powerful that it made most goalkeepers shudder just at the thought of it. At the Olympic Games, he gained the respect of seasoned internationals by his vigorous play and scoring potential. Dick became an excellent Water Polo player with a legendary shot at goal…"

John continued, "Incredibly, he was a marvellous thrower of the ball; he was a big swimmer, he was a very fast swimmer too, but he could throw the ball harder than anybody I had ever seen. Many blokes had a big circular action, but he just threw it straight, exactly straight and whacked them there; they couldn't believe how hard he could throw it." Ken was Bronte's goalkeeper, supported by John's affirmation that "He (Ken) had the reflexes; he was a fast swimmer, but he had terrific reflexes, and he was very good in the goal."

Richard's power was on display in one game against rivals, Balmain. Remembered Richard, "Bronte was playing Balmain and the Balmain goalkeeper was Herman Baykell… a very big man. I got a penalty, which was on the four-yard line, where you shoot for goal and the goalkeeper remains on the line. A lot of times you shoot around their head, or just above the shoulders, which is the last position their hands will get to. So, as he came up with his arms, my shot was a bit misdirected and hit him square in the face, and the poor guy actually went down. He didn't go under, but it knocked (him out), and stunned him for a while. I had to push the ball through the net to make sure it was a goal first, and then I went and helped him. But yes, I guess you might say, I had a pretty powerful shot."

Mick Withers played goalkeeper for Victoria and represented Australia in three Olympic Games, in 1960, 1964 and 1972. He was inducted into the Water Polo Hall of Fame. If anyone has an insight into what it takes to make it in the Water Polo game, it is Mick. In an interview for this book, the first thing he recalled was the bitter rivalry that existed between Victoria and NSW, although we suspect it may have been more so from the south, northwards. He recalled, "I was indoctrinated to hate those people from New South Wales. There was never any love lost between Victoria and New South Wales in the interstate Water Polo competition. (Each) team used to use its own change room and drank at its own pub. And so there we were, together for the first time. It was an eye-opener. This (feeling) was primarily because we only competed once a year for the honour of being the Australian champions, playing as a national team (only) every four years. (But in Rockhampton) I spent a lot of time with the team, so I got to know these folks from New South Wales who weren't all that bad after all."

He also remembers the powerful arm that jettisoned the ball towards the net, especially so as he was an opposing goalkeeper in their interstate clashes. As the only goalkeeper taken away to the 1960 Olympics, he was also (the only one) on the receiving end of the repeated tirade of cannon-ball artillery from Richard's right arm. He remembers, "Dick, in our team, was the fastest swimmer. The strongest player. Physically strong, he had the hardest shot or the fastest shot. He was very nice to have in your team, let's put it that way. I hated it (playing goalkeeper to Richard). In those days, the balls were leather and heavy, and they hurt. It was nasty having Dick Thornett throwing the ball at me at a thousand miles an hour."

Dick See was five years older than Richard and the same age as John. He played for the Bronte First Grade Water Polo side alongside John, Ken and Richard, and represented NSW in 1956. He was also a First Grade Rugby League player for Eastern Suburbs and Newtown between 1956 and 1964, so would have opposed Richard for two years in that context as well. See recalls, "We trained and transferred from Bronte to Rushcutters Bay Baths in the city, in the harbour, because of the deep water there, (whereas) in Bronte, you could stand up anywhere in the pool. It was a pretty stupid place to learn but that was where we learned to play. Most of our games were played in the Northbridge, Manly, Drummoyne pools and the famous old Balmain pool. Dick was a very talented boy, a great swimmer, a fantastic Water Polo player and very good footballer. Dick was a bit younger; he is like John in many ways, and I think Ken is the most different of the three boys. They all have their own attributes; I think John was more intellectually based than the other two but none of them were fools in any sense of the word."

Bert Vadas, the ex-Hungarian Olympian, was a leading figure in the Bronte Water Polo Club for many years. Dick See remembers, "Vadas left Hungary during the 1956 uprising. He was a great Water Polo player and that became our sport then for the next 15 years, and the Bronte Water Polo Club became one of the prominent clubs in the Sydney competition. Dick played for Australia and was the hardest throw of any Water Polo players at that time."

Famed journalist, Adrian McGregor remembers this legendary throw from his years back at Randwick Boys' High School, even when used in the playground. "I remember, some boys were ... people were (giving him a hard time) in the schoolyard once. He had the Water Polo ball in his hand, and he just turned around; he would have been at least ten metres away from whoever was doing it. He just lifted his arm up and threw the ball at this bloke who had turned his back. He hit him in the back, winded him and knocked him to the ground. It was just enormous strength and power. He was a man not to be trifled with in the schoolyard."

As Dick See suggested, the Bronte pool was a less-than-ideal setting for Water Polo, but it wasn't the only pool that posed problems. As Richard explained, "We played schoolboy stuff and also competition Water Polo at Manly and, yeah, the waves used to come through the pool, and you'd lose sight of the ball between the waves which was quite unique. Yeah, that was one tidal pool. There were very few Olympic pools that we played in in those days."

"In those days a lot of funny things happened in Water Polo. We used to play in tidal harbour pools at Rushcutters Bay, Balmain and Northbridge, which were a bit muddy on the bottom and became slimy and dirty at low tide. But you could do a few things under the water that you could get away with. So, yeah...

it was a hard game, but also a fun game."

"At Bronte, all the facilities there were pretty ordinary. It was a pretty small pool, and it was shallow, and we were losing balls out into the surf all the time, so you spent half the time retrieving the ball."

John Thornett had similar memories. "The far side of it was tidal, in the Manly Bay where the ferries come in and the far side was marked by rope, the old rope with the corks on them, so often Richard got sent out – as was common in those times – and he was standing over there beyond the rope and the ball was thrown at Richard but he moved the rope in quickly so it came out but I didn't see him do it. He's up to tricks like that. And that's right, another time, it might have been Rushcutters Bay – we played there a lot, and he went over there, he could get on the far side of the pool, and he'd be kneeling --- he'd kneel there and trick the referee and get the other blokes sent out… he was a great trickster."

Representing Bronte at the age of 17, Richard was chosen in the NSW Water Polo team in 1958, making him the youngest NSW state representative ever selected, equalling Olympian Ray Smee. Richard competed at the Australian Water Polo Championships in Sydney and was selected to represent NSW on three other occasions – at the Australian Water Polo Championships in Perth (1959), Melbourne (1960) and Adelaide (1961). He beat his brother, John, by a year. John first represented NSW at the age of 18, and did so on another three occasions in 1955, 1959 and 1960; sharing the last two years in the pool with his brother, Richard. Interestingly, John Thornett had the opportunity to be a dual Australian international as well, in rugby and Water Polo. He was well on course for selection in the 1956 Olympic Games in Melbourne but forewent the opportunity by electing to tour Japan with the Australian Universities rugby team!

Richard said, "John and I used to spend a lot of time together away from club training. We'd go down to the Bronte pool and pick a deep part of the pool, not the shallow parts, and tread water and pass with two balls, left and right hand, for an hour or so on end. And that created timing and I was only sort of 18 or so then, so it started early in my life, or probably earlier. And that's where I think your timing and coordination and ball skills all go back to that… anticipation. And I was reasonably fast for a big fellow too, so I suppose that goes down to all the early touch football. Yeah. I always relate back to the early Bronte days and I think there was a reason for it all." Good friend, Wallaby team-mate and neighbour, Peter

Johnson concurred. "Saturday afternoons we'd go down to Rushcutters Bay and train for Water Polo for hours and hours and hours until it got dark."

The fame of the Thornett brothers mirrored the development of Bronte Water Polo, where the three brothers became the backbone of the club. As their sporting prowess and reputations developed, other talented sportsmen like Ken Mills, Dick See and Vic McGrath gravitated to Bronte and the club became legendary in its own time. In many ways, the development and success of Bronte Water Polo Club ran parallel with the sporting success and achievements of the three Thornett brothers.

As Wally Meagher learnt when he suggested that Richard ease into his post-school rugby career at Randwick, Water Polo officials would not be spared Richard's frank and unfiltered assessment if he felt that they had a case to answer. It was often to his detriment; with Richard, you never die wondering. The end of the line for Richard and Water Polo was chronicled in *The History of the Bronte Water Polo Club*. *"It was at the end of the 1962/63 summer season, when Dick Thornett had a brush with Water Polo officialdom which severed his connections with Water Polo forever. There had been a lot of publicity at that time about Dick, his possible changeover from Rugby Union to Rugby League, and his signing with the Parramatta Rugby League Club."*

Richard explained, "It was before a semi-final at Drummoyne Pool and I, and this official, he walked up to me asked me to sign a statutory declaration to say that I was still an amateur. And I told him where, what to do with it and, I walked out, and I never saw another game of Water Polo for years. And I could've been of more benefit to keep on playing the game with younger kids than being treated like that. And there were a lot of Rugby League players playing Water Polo then, so it was a terrible precedent."

"I was so disappointed that that was the end of my amateur career, other than those times in the future when I was privileged enough to catch up with my old Olympic colleagues."

It was reported that in *"about 1959, Dick See ran for a seat on Waverley Council and was elected, but he couldn't stop Bronte Baths being filled in. Later, both he and Dick Thornett were banned by the peak body when they became professional Rugby League players. Despite playing league for Newtown RLFC, Dick See was able to quietly slip back into playing Water Polo. However, Dick Thornett was too high profile and was never re-admitted... which was a huge loss to the sport."*

The rules and regulations surrounding amateurism and the suspicion of payments made to players and competitors affected many athletes who were in the process of transitioning across from amateur to professional sports. Another triple-Australian representative, Michael Cleary, who ran for Australia in the 1962 British Empire and Commonwealth Games and played both Rugby League and Rugby Union for Australia, had to contend with similarly strict adherence during his career. He recalls, "I played for nothing, and a lot of people said my father got the money, but he didn't. I won a Seiko watch from Frank Hyde, worth £25, but I couldn't accept it because I would have lost my amateur status. Anything over $38 was money received. So, I couldn't take that." Cleary couldn't take a cent for playing for South Sydney in 1962 either, the year he transferred from rugby, as it would have jeopardised his athletics representation at the Games that year, so Souths got a great deal to snare one of the stars of the time for free.

Another bizarre sidenote concerns Richard's final appearance in First Grade Water Polo for Bronte in the 1960/61 season grand final. The match against Bondi finished in a draw after extra time had been played. The drawn result occurred because the two teams played on for so long and went so late that the pool manager had to turn off the lights! This has (unsurprisingly) never happened before or since!

The Olympic Games hold a special place in the hearts and minds of Australians. Along with Great Britain, Switzerland, Greece and France, an Australian team has competed at every modern-day Summer Olympics from 1896 to the present day – and won at least a medal at every single one. No Summer Olympic Games team sport stretches back further in history than Water Polo, with men's Water Polo first played at the Paris 1900 Games and at every Games since.

In what would be his first international appearance for his country after competing for NSW on three occasions in the National State Championships, Richard was selected in the 1960 Australian Water Polo team to compete in the Olympic Games in Rome, Italy. He recalled that "It was quite an experience to hear your name being called out in the side at the age of 19."

"Well, it was a bit of a surprise. I didn't really think I'd make it. It was after the Australian Championships in Melbourne... in January of 1960, I think it was and

John was there, and we were at a barbeque after the final of the Australian Championships. They had a barbeque, and they announced the Australian side… and yeah, it was a big thrill… and that's where it all started."

Richard was Bronte's first Australian Water Polo representative, a momentous moment for the club. Richard's good friend and playing partner, Vic McGrath, with whom he had an almost telepathic game relationship, was selected as first-reserve and attended the pre-Games camp in Rockhampton, but he didn't travel with the team to Rome.

Richard recalled, "Before we flew off to the Olympics, we had a training camp up at Rockhampton, which lasted quite a long time. It was supposed to be for the warmer weather, but it was still bitterly cold in the local pool there. The water temperature was about 58 degrees Fahrenheit (14 degrees Celsius), which was pretty cold, and every day was a real nightmare to try and get in the water for training."

"There were ten of us and we all got on very well together, although of course there was always some interstate rivalry between the New South Welshmen and the Victorians. We left Sydney (for Rome) which for me was such an exciting day, to be farewelled by my family and friends as I prepared to travel overseas for the first time. Other Olympians on the plane included primarily the rowers and some of the swimmers."

The Australians trained in Rockhampton with the Olympic diving team from June 17 to August 18 – not the warmest time to jump into a pool every day for a month, regardless of how north of home in Australia you might be. The Australians stayed in the *Three Crowns Hotel* in Rockhampton for the entirety of their stay in the city, nicknamed "Lousy Dots" by the players. From 'Rocky' to Rome – quite the lifestyle change.

Tom Hoad is a four-time Olympian in Water Polo – 1960, 1964, 1968 and 1972. In 2023, Tom recalled his frustration with the Rockhampton training conditions. "Rockhampton days were then a balmy 25 degrees, but the nights got down to near zero and the pool wasn't heated, it was bloody freezing. It was just so badly organised. We were the first Australian Olympic team to travel by air to an Olympic Games. My first ever flight was actually coming back from Rockhampton into Sydney, as we had initially driven up there, but flying to Rome was by Qantas Boeing 707, and of course, it took three separate jets to transport the entire team.

ROME 1960

We left early as we had a few trial games organised prior to the start of the Olympics, as our biggest problem in those days was that we didn't have any international competition. It was only in an Olympic year that we would play against other countries and, of course, our style of Water Polo was always about three to four years behind the Europeans. We weren't playing against these teams regularly enough to pick up on their new style, so we were always behind. When we arrived in Rome, we noticed a completely different technique used by the Italians and most other continental players. Our opponents weren't playing Water Polo the way they had done in 1956."

It would have been daunting, if not devastating, for the Australian team to land in Rome to this realisation after a three-month camp and four years since its last Olympics campaign on home soil. They had been training to play and defend against a style of play that was now four years out-of-date and they had no time to correct or adjust it.

Mick Withers remembers the Rockhampton days where the locals didn't always appreciate the presence of a few fit and handsome outsiders suddenly becoming fixtures at the odd local event or fixture, challenging perhaps their social connections with the opposite sex. He recalls, "In Rockhampton, directly opposite (the pub), there was a shop where we used to go and buy pies and stuff. The local girls were interested (in us) but the local guys were not all that keen to have these new blokes in town. But we got invited to a number of parties (and at one of the parties) these young guys came and started on us. Dick just stepped forward and said, 'We're not here to cause any problems. We're here to enjoy ourselves while we're up here and we're here to train hard.' I thought it was just fantastic. (It would have) been so easy to show your strength and put this bloke down. What a nice thing to say to that bloke, because you just saved him his life. He (Richard) was only 19 but he was a gentleman who was polite."

Tom Hoad recalls, "In 1960, Italy was the strongest side and won the gold medal. They were a lot smaller side than we were and a lot faster through the water. We probably had relatively bigger players and they were just too fast around the water for us... I was predominantly playing as an attacking forward or half because of my speed, and as a big man, this was probably unusual. There weren't too many big fast swimmers in those days, and I was the goal shooter. The bit of extra size gives you more strength and more speed through the water when moving towards the goals."

The Australian team, while relatively competitive, were ultimately outgunned by their more experienced and game-hardened opponents, finishing equal 13th in the 16-team competition. Regardless of the result, the Games provided many lifelong memories for Richard who was still not out of his teens during the competition. Many of these were positive experiences, while others not so, as suggested even before the squad left Australia. In a May 6 *Sun-Herald* article written by Les Ryan headlined **Water Polo a Costly Proposition**, the costs attached to the training alone were estimated at £1,000, while the *"preparation of the team and the trip to Rome and return will cost more than £12,000."* This meant that they had to raise most of the money themselves as Ryan claimed, *"They knew they could expect little financial support from the Australian Olympic Federation and set about raising what money they could."* Ryan went on to say that *"Officials expect to raise £6,500 in selling a trip to Rome to see the Games. A limited number of tickets will be sold for £1 each."* In commenting further on the national squad selections, for which he noted there were *"no surprises,"* Ryan went on to say, *"The two most promising players in the team are...West Australian Tom Hoad and... Sydney police constable Richard Thornett. In the recent Australian Championships and the Olympic elimination match against New Zealand in Melbourne, Hoad and Thornett were the two outstanding players in the water. Thornett, 6ft. 1in. and 15st. 7lb. is the ideal swimming back. He is easily the fastest swimmer playing Water Polo in Australia, capable of holding the Australian sprint champion John Devitt for at least 50 metres. He can also throw the ball with lightning pace and accuracy."*

Champion swimmer, Murray Rose, in his book *Life is Worth Swimming*, spoke of the flight over to the Olympic Games. *"The flight from Sydney to Rome was a disaster verifying Murphy's law. Initial engine troubles caused us to break down in Karachi. After about eight hours there, we finally got up in the air. Then we broke down again in Bahrain. We arrived in Rome at around 4 a.m., and the temperature was over 38°C. We were then held on the plane for several hours because there had been a cholera epidemic in Karachi. Once the red tape was cleared, we were allowed into the terminal building, which was basically just a box. It was several more hours before we were taken downtown to a little hotel that was air-conditioned very poorly. We were given some exotic food that tasted good but perhaps was not exactly the type of diet we should have been having before an Olympic competition. This journey was a difficult situation for the whole Australian team and one from which it took us a while to recover."* Richard's Water Polo teammate, Tom Hoad, concurs: "How we won *any* medals in swimming (I just don't know)."

Tom, when asked to describe Richard said, "Two words – enormous ability, but let me just expand on that a little bit because he was so involved in rugby, (that it's understandable) he never achieved his true potential in Water Polo. He virtually ceased playing in Australia a year after the Rome Olympics. He was a huge man, strong as a bull. Threw the ball like a rocket and could have had the ability to really go on… he was direct, just strong, when he kicked back and had such an enormous shot, he was dangerous."

A newspaper report after the trial against Japan suggested that Richard may have been calling upon his rugby skills when things in the water started becoming physical. **ROME**, *Sat. — "Sydney footballer Richard Thornett, 16 stone, today inspired the Australian Olympic Water Polo team's 6-3 victory over Japan. Thornett, in a powerful display, scored three of the Australian goals. He was out of the water for a few minutes in the first half when the Japanese coach, who refereed the match, put him out for a foul. The game was fiery early. The Australians resented the Japanese grappling tactics."*

The Games of the XVII Olympiad attracted a record 5,348 athletes from 83 countries. More importantly, it was the first Summer Games covered by U.S. television. CBS bought the television rights for US$394,000.

Information held in Water Polo Australia's archives articulate the conditions under which the Australian team prepared for competition. *"After checking into the Olympic Village, the training facilities and equipment were found to be first class, however, the supply of Water Polo balls was non-existent and Hermie Doerner, the team manager, was required to purchase balls from a number of different sources. Once all the competing teams arrived, the pools available for training became very crowded and each team was allotted only one hour per day (between 8 a.m. and 11 p.m.) for training. Eight trial matches were played against other nations, prior to the commencement of the Olympic Games, with Australia winning four and losing four. Wins were recorded against South Africa (3-2), Japan (6-3), Egypt (5-3) and Brazil (6-3) with losses against the USA (5-8), Russia (2-10), Hungary (2-6) and eventual champions Italy (28)."*

Whilst Australia failed to reach the semi-finals, perhaps their most impressive result was a preliminary round 2–6 loss to Water Polo heavyweights, Yugoslavia.

It's worth taking a moment to consider what had transpired against the Australians after the team was first announced, early in 1960. In the lead-up to and within hours of their arrival in Rome, before a ball was thrown in anger, the Australian team had already traversed many tricky paths that tested, to extremes, their resolve. They had trained in chilly waters in a Rockhampton pool for weeks on camp and struggled to raise enough money to even get to the Olympic city. They then grappled with the difficulty of finding the necessary basic equipment to train and play upon landing and were, frighteningly, confronted with the realisation that their game-playing techniques and strategies were significantly outdated. At least they had the Opening Ceremony to enjoy, striding forward in the Olympic Stadium betrothed in their national uniforms with their compatriots, marching proudly behind Australia's flag-bearer, yachtsman Alexander Stuart "Jock" Sturrock, MBE.

The hits, though, kept on coming. Pope John XXIII welcomed 4,000 athletes to St. Peter's Square prior to the opening of the Rome Olympics, but Richard lamented not being one of them. "Because our Water Polo team had a match on the first night of the Games, we (understandably) weren't allowed to march in the Opening Ceremony, which being my one and only Olympic opportunity, has always been one of the biggest disappointments of my sporting career."

An anecdote to this unfortunate decision followed a typical Australian storyline, which was published in *The History of Bronte Water Polo Club*. "*As a consequence, the team decided to arrange their own march in the Olympic Village, appropriately dressed in swimming trunks and towels, befitting of their sport. There was no chance that the boys from Australia were going to miss out on marching for their country at an Olympics, even if it didn't meet the dress code.*"

West Australian journalist, Ken Casellas, in covering the Games for *The Herald*, reported that "*Australians created another commotion at the Olympic Village yesterday with swimmers and Water Polo players staging a shocking protest march... the men, wearing shorts and ties without shirts, and the girls, in shorts and blouses, brandished 'flags', their swimsuits tied to sticks. They marched in a straggling group behind the official team of marchers as they left the village for the stadium. The assistant team manager (Mr Jack Howson) angrily asked them to stop behaving like fools and to return to their quarters. The trouble began when the team manager (Mr Syd Grange) told the swimmers and Water Polo players that, because they would be competing today, they would not be allowed to march – or even to leave the village to see the opening spectacle. Grange argued that the strenuous march and long stand in the airless stadium would sap vital energy."*

Mick Withers didn't seem so bothered. Looking back, he recalls, "I don't know that we were all that disappointed. Rome was like 35 degrees every day and they dropped you outside the stadium to stand in the sunshine for maybe two hours. Then you would be in the sun again for another hour at least while you're marching. Then you would march back to the bus compound. Then you'd go home. And then the next morning we're playing our first game. I didn't want us to march, and it wasn't sad. The fact that we did do something in the village did sort of half compensate for it. If I was a coach now, I wouldn't let the team stand in the sun for two hours."

Australians and Opening Ceremony controversies seem to court one another. Four years later, in Tokyo, Japan, Australian swimmers were banned from marching if they had competition in the first three days. The great Dawn Fraser and fellow teammate Marlene Dayman smuggled themselves out of the village to the ceremony to march with the team, risking being sent home. This was the same Olympic Games where Dawn was caught stealing an Olympic flag near the Emperor's palace.

Richard Thornett and controversy dalliances didn't end there. Australian ex-Olympic swimmer and journalist, Judy Joy Davies, writing for *The Sun*, began her article with the opening: **ROME**, Thur. — *"Two Australian athletes — champion miler Herb Elliott and Water Polo player Dick Thornett had their passes confiscated by gatekeepers at the Olympic Village tonight. Elliott, unperturbed, said later, 'I'd given my pass to my wife when she discovered she'd forgotten her visitor's card. But we got caught. Thornett… said a gatekeeper accused him of not being the man whose picture appeared on his card.' Thornett was on his way out of the village to take part in Australia's Water Polo match against South Africa. When his pass was taken, he appealed to Australian team manager, Mr Syd Grange, who immediately stormed down to the gate and demanded the pass back. But, without an interpreter, Mr Grange made little progress and Thornett is still without his card. Tomorrow morning, Mr Grange, plus an interpreter, will try to untangle the muddle."*

A Case of Mistaken Identity. Again.

Richard's identity being mistaken in 1960 Rome wasn't the only time that he was claimed to be someone else, although on this occasion, it wasn't a source of bewilderment and frustration as it was back in that Olympic Village. True to his cheeky side, I remember Richard sharing an incident with me that occurred one evening at a sporting function. Being a triple-Australian representative was no guarantee that you would be automatically identified as the name behind the face. That evening, while Richard was enjoying a beer with his own company in some corner of the room, (as he liked to do), a stranger sidled up next to him in an effort to engage in some friendly conversation. The stranger began with:

"Hi, John. It's great to see you again. I'm really good mates with your brother, Richard."

Richard didn't miss a beat and spent the rest of the conversation pretending that he was indeed John, entertained not only by how the situation was unravelling but also by listening to the many stories about his (and his brother's) sporting career, social times out and all the many friends they shared in common. This was typical Richard, and you will hear from his friends later who will say that getting an accurate read on Richard's thoughts wasn't an easy thing. And, like this scenario, he would often never give a hint as to which side of the ledger he was standing. Richard went on to say that he never revealed his true identity to this gentleman, so the night would have ended in one of two ways. Either the stranger would have left the function deeply satisfied at having spent the evening with one of the great Wallaby captains, or he would have told another member at the function that he'd just been chatting with John Thornett, only to be awkwardly and probably embarrassingly corrected from the other side of the room.

Brendan Morris, Author

The 1960 Olympics hold many significant memories, not just for Australians but the world. Events such as an Olympic Games generate such unifying, joyous emotions, although there are, of course, times when the stage is beset with tragedy. These Games will be remembered for Australian triumphs with

Richard watching on. He remembered, "The fact that we didn't make it through to the finals had one saving grace and that was that we were able to watch Olympic sports all over the place."

"After being eliminated, we had two weeks to follow and support the rest of our Olympic colleagues. I was so fortunate to watch the likes of John Devitt, Dawn Fraser and Tony Madigan, who many of us in the stadium that night felt had defeated Cassius Clay. We also saw Herb Elliott win the mile and afterwards I met brother Ken in Paris where we spent some time travelling. Ken was then at Leeds and took a long leave of absence to enable this to occur." Richard also stopped off at Leeds on the way home to watch Ken play at Headingley. It was a remarkable way to see the world at such a young age.

Mick Withers remembers the Games for similar reasons. "The Australian Water Polo team was part of the Australian Olympic swimming team; these days with Water Polo Australia running Water Polo in Australia, they are a completely separate entity to Swimming Australia. I am sure Dick, like me, was very proud to be part of the Australian Olympic swimming team with famous teammates like the Konrads, Dawn Fraser, Murray Rose, Johnny Devitt, etc."

Other unforgettable highlights of these Games, other than Clay's victory and charismatic presence, included former polio patient, Wilma Rudolph, winning three gold medals in the 100m, 200m and 4x100m sprint events, and Ethiopia's Abebe Bikila winning the marathon barefooted. There was sadness too though, when Danish cyclist, Knud Jensen, collapsed during the 100-kilometre (km) team race because of heat stroke and later died in hospital. It was suspected that he had been under the influence of *Roniacol,* a blood circulation stimulant. South Africa also appeared in the Olympic arena for the last time under its apartheid regime. It would not be allowed to return until 1992 when apartheid in sport was being abolished.

One of the beautiful outcomes of this one-in-four-year event are the stories of connection between competitors outside their sporting platforms. Richard told of meeting up with the South African team after competition in a bar in Rome. The players from both teams bonded so well and were having so much fun that the local residents, mostly in high-rise buildings, showed their 'appreciation' by throwing flowerpots and other material down at them. "Alas, no money was thrown, which is a good thing because it would have jeopardised our amateur status," said Richard. "Yeah, and the bloke couldn't shut up shop quick enough. When that happened, he pulled all the shutters down; we turned 'round to get another drink and it was all locked up."

After the Olympic Games finished, Richard, Mick Withers and two other Water Polo Olympians, John O'Brien from Victoria and Allan Charleston from Western Australia, jumped in a car for a four-day odyssey to London. The 19-year-old Richard, three years out of school, would have hardly believed the world into which he had been cast. As if Rugby Union and the Olympic Games weren't enough, a stop-over in Paris would offer another memorable chapter in his brief life journey thus far. Mick recalls, "We drove to London and had a very funny 4 or 5 days driving up through Europe. Dick was going over to see Ken, so we all had lunch together in London. It was the one and only time I ever met Ken. I went down to (see my brother in) Bath, and Dick went to see Ken. Then we got the plane back (to Sydney) that was picking up the team in Rome, so we were already on the plane (when the rest of the team boarded)."

"One night, we went to (cabaret venue) Moulin Rouge, Paris. After the show, we were out in the street and two or three of the girls came out. They were talking to Dick, and we said, 'We should spend more time with this bloke.' He was attracting all these girls that you wouldn't believe. We were saying, 'What's wrong with us? There are three girls and three of us,' but they all wanted (to speak with) Richard."

Mick Withers fondly remembers Richard. "A guy who was very, very pleasant to be with. Now, when you spend four days in the car with him, you sort of get to know him pretty well. He was a tough gentleman. Very cordial. He was never at the forefront of anything a bit rowdy. He was never one of those outlandish types."

And so, Richard Thornett returned to Australia an Olympian – a representative of Australia on the world stage at the highest level. For most, this would be, understandably, the pinnacle, the zenith of sporting achievement. To represent your country in one sport is such an honour, such a privilege, yet Richard's blazer still had two pockets upon which to sew, and the seamstress was just warming up.

On Richard's decision to leave Water Polo after such an illustrious introduction, Mick Withers looks back with great insight, his thoughts coming from a man with tremendous experience and perception. He struggles with the idea of Australia having lost such an influential figure in the sport at such a young age. "When he actually left the sport, we were all, Australia was, very, very disappointed because we'd lost not just an individual with a real ability to swim. The interesting thing about Water Polo is that the better players in the world are all 25, 26, 27. It's a game where you've got to know what's happening all the time. Usually, the better players have played longer and understand where the ball is all the time. And Dick, at 19, had all the natural ability (to do that so early). It was disastrous for Australian Water Polo when he dropped out. He was the best junior young talent we had. He was outstanding in 1960, blessed with his ability. Can you imagine Dick taking a backward step?"

CHAPTER FIVE
1961 – Fiji in Australia

We few, we happy few, we band of brothers;
For he today that sheds his blood with me
Shall be my brother;
    William Shakespeare (*Henry V*, IV.iii.60–2)

Back on home soil after an eventful time in Italy, to say the least, Richard's world was still spinning as he grappled with many balls in the air, both figuratively and literally. It was approaching the end of 1960 and summer was calling, so he dived straight back into the pool for Bronte's First Grade Water Polo side and won consecutive premierships with the club in the 1960/61 and 1961/62 seasons. He also had one more tilt representing NSW at the Australian Water Polo Championships in Adelaide.

In addition to recommencing his job with the police force, Richard's Water Polo commitments were book-ended with his First Grade Rugby Union career with 'the Wicks' at Coogee Oval. Randwick's First Grade side continued to be very competitive in the competition, even given the fact that they continued to lose a swathe of players to representative teams across those two years after Richard returned from the Olympic Games.

The journey to dual-Australian representation began in earnest in 1961 when the City 1 team was selected for their May 6 fixture against Country 1. The city boys ran out winners, 13–6 at North Sydney Oval, with Richard joining his brother John for the first time representatively; Richard packing down in the second row behind John in the front row. Both joined up once again when the NSW team was selected, enjoying success with a huge win over the Queensland side as well as a victory over the touring Fijian national side, with Michael Cleary scoring three tries before having to leave the field injured. In the lead-up to the Fijian match against NSW, one newspaper report certainly felt that the visitors were travelling in the right direction when it spruiked that *"The Fijians not only are spectacular footballers but they are showing how to promote the Rugby Union game and build it up as an object (sic) lesson for Australian administrators as well as players."*

The Test series approached and selections both individually and positionally were being debated off the back of the domestic representative season. NSW's dominance over its interstate rivals put its players in the box seat as far as national selection was concerned, but the relative inexperience of many of those in the frame was still cause for concern for many pundits. The Wallabies had not played a Test in two years, with 1959 offering up a winless two-Test series against the British Lions. As far as this year's first rivals, Fiji, was concerned, they had toured Australia twice prior to 1961, both two-Test tours, finishing one win apiece on each occasion; one series in 1954 and the first two years earlier in 1952.

1961, after that Test void the year before, looked an exciting prospect; three Test matches against Fiji, a two-Test away series against South Africa before a one-off home Test against the French. The selectors' first Test side, with John Thornett unavailable because of injury, contained only four men who had played Test rugby before, up front with Jon White, Peter Johnson and Tony "Slaggy" Miller, and at fullback, Rod Phelps. The 11 players in between were all debutants, a daunting prospect given the itinerary that year. To add to the intrigue, 21-year-old Ken Catchpole, playing his first Test match, was also appointed captain.

As the team came together after the halftime whistle, things looked dire as the local team was under pressure on the field and on the scoreboard. Many, the country over, were questioning the wisdom of those in charge at headquarters. But what happened in the ensuing 40 minutes not only changed the course of the match itself, but some thought may have shifted the course of Australia's rugby mindset from that point forward. The little general, Catchpole, dictated and controlled play between his bruising forwards and will-o'-the-wisp backs, took the game by the scruff of the neck, and continued to do so for many years to come.

Richard Thornett heard his name read out on the radio as a Wallaby to take on the Fijians in that first Test. Less than 12 months earlier, he was preparing to represent his country as an Olympian. It was a surreal development in this young man's life who now turned towards another path of wonderment in his country's colours. Respected sports journalist, Dick Tucker, wrote as the team selection drew close: *"Dick Thornett, giant 'baby' of the famous footballing brothers, today seems certain to become Australia's second dual international in recent months. Dick, an Olympic Water Polo representative at Rome last year, looks a certainty for the Australian Rugby Union team to meet the Fijians in the first Test at Brisbane on June 10. Australia's other dual international for 1961 is Brian Booth, now in England with the Australian cricketers. Booth played hockey at the 1956 Olympics in Melbourne.*

John, eldest of the Thornetts, is just as certain to be vice-captain of the team. Though the youngest, Dick at 20 is the biggest member of the family, standing 6ft. 2in tall and weighing a massive 16st. 5lb. If he and John earn Australian caps today it will climax a wonderful period for the family.

Brother Ken starred for Leeds when they won the English Rugby League Championship last weekend."

Back to that first Test at the Brisbane Exhibition Ground, and the Wallabies were down 6–3, two penalty goals to a try, but overwhelmed by a suffocating defensive unit that was shutting down (almost) every opportunity to break free and establish ascendancy. The second half began, and Australia's fortunes swung in an instant. All of a sudden, they began to find a rhythm and continuity that had eluded them for the first half of the game. Passes began to stick, space began to open up and players began to grind their way over the advantage line when beforehand, every hole had closed in front of them. They scored five tries to nil in the second half, sprinting to a 24–6 victory, securing a 21–0 shutout in the last 40 minutes, a point every two minutes and a try every eight. Five of the six tries in the game were scored by backs, the sole try by a forward scored by R. Thornett in his debut game. Of the six tries scored in the match, three were scored by players who, unfortunately, would be lost to Rugby League soon afterwards, including two (Cleary and Lisle) within months. It was also noteworthy that Rod Phelps was the only try-scorer who had played for Australia before, and bizarrely, his was the first try scored by an Australian fullback in Wallaby history, which had been 63 years at that stage. It says much about the way the game has changed since.

The press reports after the game were glowing, enthusiastic and optimistic. One newspaper article that challenged the words of those spruiked before the match said, *"The illusion of Fiji's spectacular greatness in the world of Rugby Union was rudely shattered by Australia's rousing 24-6 win in the first Test at the (Brisbane) Exhibition Ground today."* It went on to say, *"Australia's pack, led by torrid bullockers, Tony Miller and Dick Thornett, had the visitors really worried with territory winning movements, made in open play and in scrums. Four minutes after resumption, Thornett's aggressive attack paid off when he led the 'pigs' in a forward run after receiving the ball infield from down-the-line running Magrath... Thornett proved too tough to topple and he went over unopposed."*

Wallaby hooker Peter Johnson remembers. "By the time we reached Brisbane for the opening international, both Rob Heming and John Thornett had cried off with injury. Dick Thornett moved to number 8 and John O'Gorman took the vacancy at number eight while Graeme Macdougall, from St George, filled in for John Thornett. In the view of most, Dick Thornett was the player of the Test. He surpassed the Fijians in energy and enthusiasm and did so in such a constructive manner as to take the fight out of them. The fact was that every Australian player turned in a disciplined display which ultimately prevailed over brute force. The final scoreline of 24-6, six tries to nil was a fair reflection of the relative merits of the sides."

The second Test against Fiji beckoned, as did Australia's wonder as to whether this first Test performance was a 'one-off' or a sign of things to come.

Prior to 1961, Australia had not won a Test series against any nation since their remarkable two-out-of-two away Bledisloe Cup series victory just after the Second World War in 1949, 12 years prior. They were to win only seven more games from 35 Tests between 1949 and this first Test win in 1961, so the interim had seen barren times indeed. Beres Ellwood returned to the Wallaby lineup for the first time in three years, replacing Harry Roberts. Winger Ted Magrath injured himself in the first Test and was replaced by Bob Potter. Lineout specialist Rob Heming made his debut for the Wallabies in the second row, going on to become one of the first picked for his country in another 20 Test matches over the next six years. Of particular note was the return of John Thornett after injury, who came into the side replacing John O'Gorman. This was Richard and John's first Rugby Union Test together, with Richard at lock and John crouching into the pack as Heming's second-row partner.

Fiji arrived in Sydney for the second Test desperate to reverse the result of the first. They had played against Australia in Sydney on three previous occasions, winning twice, so they must have approached the game with some level of confidence.

The game was a much closer affair then the one played a week earlier in Brisbane, with the Fijians once more ahead on the scoreboard 11–9 at halftime and going even further ahead after the resumption with a penalty goal. They were gaining on the Australians with each game and this would continue right up until the final whistle of their last match in the country. The game featured the extraordinary talents of winger Michael Cleary, but also his toughness, something sceptics questioned when he first rose to the highest level of the game in Randwick's First Grade side and then through the ranks of representative rugby. Cleary scored a double in this game, taking his international career tally to three from two matches, but it was what happened in between the two tries that was just as significant. After scoring his first try, and a little over 20 minutes into the game, Cleary was knocked unconscious by Joe Levula and carried from the field. Amazingly, he returned, and scored his second try in the match, a brilliant one. This try was some retribution for Cleary, for one of the players he tore past on his way to the line was the same winger who had caused the head trauma to him in the first half.

Richard Thornett was highly involved again, ranging up in support of five eighth Jim Lisle's break to transfer off for centre Beres Ellwood's try. The 20–14 victory meant Australia had won the series, its first home series triumph in 27 years. 32-year-old prop, Tony Miller, was the only Australian on the field who was alive when it last happened. Nonetheless, there was one game left in the series. Beres Ellwood said of the rugby-playing Thornetts, "They were always gentle giants but, on the field, they were always tough, they always stood their ground... probably Dick had a little bit more venom in him than brother, John, but not in a bad way, no."

Stan Baxter, writing in the *Sun Herald* after the game, said that *"It was one of the most thrilling and hard-fought matches played in Australia in recent years... Fiji yesterday were ahead with only 20 minutes of play left and this lead was held from the start of the match."* Elsewhere, EW Kann wrote on the day of the second Test that *"another good display from the Australian XV today will make them practically South African tour certainties..."* He went on to comment on Richard's

1961 – FIJI IN AUSTRALIA

play thus far, *"Dick Thornett was the star forward of the Brisbane Test last Saturday. An intelligent and mobile forward despite his youth (he is only 20) and weight (16½ st.), he had a strikingly successful Test beginning."*

The third and final Test in the Fijian series was played two weeks later at Olympic Park in Melbourne. It was a bruising, brawling game as often happens in dead rubbers. Australia was ahead after a Jim Lisle try with less than ten minutes to go but Fijian winger Joe Levula, back in the news and right in the middle of the action, levelled the scores with a try of his own and the 3–all score remained for the rest of the match. Many observers considered Fiji the superior side on the day and unlucky not to have come away with the points. They enjoyed most of the field position as well as opportunities to score points throughout. Levula's try was a wonderful display of well-orchestrated risk after his captain, Orisi Dawai, kicked across field near Australia's quarter line. It was another example, among many, of Fiji's unorthodox yet spontaneous attempts to open up the field of play when in possession. It wasn't an unusual sight during the series to see Fijian players, on the attack, throw 30 metre passes across field, NFL quarterback-like, to players running in the outside channels in an attempt to just skirt the defence.

This was the game, mentioned earlier, where big brother John came to little brother's defence from flying fists. The game was a spiteful affair where there were many high tackles and other unsavoury events marring what was otherwise an enthralling game of rugby. The game and series actually ended with a brawl between the two forward packs, whilst the injury list included Josua Vadugu who cut his eye badly, requiring stitches. On the Australian side of the ledger, Richard Thornett suffered concussion from a Fijian fist, whilst Australian fullback Rod Phelps broke his nose when struck by Fijian winger Joe Levula towards the end of the game. Ironically, this Test was the first of the series that the Fijians were behind at halftime, yet they also came home over the top of their opponents for the first time.

In his book, *A Rugby Memoir*, Peter Johnson wrote, *"At the final whistle we could but limp to the dressing rooms clutching our hard-earned draw. The room was like a frontline aid station. Dick Thornett was mumbling incoherently, though, as John White observed, this was not extraordinary. We were terrified that an injury might be detected by selectors and affect our chances of making the squad for South Africa. The Melbourne Test was the most continuously dirty match, international or otherwise, in which I ever took part."*

In *The Daily Telegraph* in March 2003, rugby expert and writer, Peter Jenkins, selected his top ten Waratah 'hardmen' of all time. He mentioned some ferocious characters preventing the likes of former Wallaby backrower Steve Lidbury, dual-international centre Stephen Knight and nuggety halfback John Hipwell from getting a run. Not surprisingly, Steve Finnane came in first, followed by Tony "Slaggy" Miller. Richard Thornett came in eighth, just after Willie Ofahengaue. It was interesting to note that three of the top 10 – Richard, Rex Mossop and Ray Price – all eventually switched to Rugby League.

Norman May and Richard Thornett – a Friendship that Endured for Decades

"Dick was always my great friend. So, just about everything I touch, I've been somewhere with Dick Thornett."

"Yeah, 1961 and it was a match between Australia and Fiji in Melbourne. It was a Test match, and Dick was playing in the Australian team, and he was actually playing club football for Randwick at the time he was picked for Australia, and he was playing I think breakaway or second row, one of the two, for Australia. And I remember the match because the Fijians were supposed to be spectacular players, but this was their second tour and they played very tight football – second or third tour – and it was only the three points each and there wasn't much of a game, but we had a big party afterwards and Dick came along. I'll never forget, the party was at – we were staying at one of the pubs in Melbourne and Dick Healy was with me, he was my boss in the ABC (Australian Broadcasting Corporation), and we invited all the Australian players into our room for a party. And just imagine a room which was a pretty small hotel room and all the Australian players, and some women came, and we'd pass them across the top, bodily, to get them into the room. Anyway, Dick was there, and we ended up in the Albert Hospital in the doctors' quarters and finished the party there. It went till about five o'clock in the morning, and that was my first experience with Dick. And of course, I went on from there and I had more to do with him later on when he retired from football."

1961 – FIJI IN AUSTRALIA

On the back of a successful home series against our Pacific neighbours, the Wallaby squad took off for South Africa brimming with confidence; they had favourable results, a new generation of players who were starting to gel as a unit and an upcoming opponent regarded as, if not the best in the world, in the top two. 22-year-old Ken Catchpole was again given the captain/coach role, quite remarkable when you consider other players with the calibre and experience of 32-year-old Tony Miller, (on his second South African campaign, the first Wallaby to do so), Johnson, White, Phelps, Lenehan and John Thornett. Richard remembered, "After the Fijian series, they picked a team to tour South Africa in a three-week short tour, six matches. Again, much the same side as that which played in the Fiji series was chosen. They only took about 20 players. The first Test was played at Ellis Park in Johannesburg, one of the great rugby grounds in the world and a big thrill for me. The very high altitude meant that we found it very difficult to breathe and it did affect our performance. The second Test in Port Elizabeth was a little different. We could have won that game, even though the score of 23–11 to South Africa suggested otherwise; we had our chances and we looked the better side at times, but South Africa got out of it at the death. We had another four games against provincial sides. That was my only tour to South Africa but such an exciting one, even though it was for only three weeks."

The Australians played a couple of lead-up games in Australia on the way over to South Africa, very easy affairs against South Australia (47–3) and Western Australia (77–0). These two fixtures, before they had even left the country, resulted in injuries to Tony Miller and Jimmy Lisle, while a question was raised not long after about the suitability of those games in terms of preparation (the weakness of their opposition), given what they were about to confront. John "Sparrow" Dowse, a mate of Richard's right up to the end, scored 35 points against Western Australia, a world record for a first-class match at that point in time. This equalled his entire tour point-scoring account, where on South African soil he kicked four goals, eight penalties and a drop goal. Michael Cleary remembers. "We hopped on the Constellation (aeroplane). We went to Adelaide, played there. We played in Perth and (then) went to Cocos Island. We went to Mauritius and we landed at Jo'burg with 4,000 people."

The ill-tempered third Test against Fiji had also produced a number of injuries, and the worst affected was Ken Catchpole, who received a burst blood vessel in his left thigh. Frantic physiotherapy by Viv Chalwin got him as far as Mascot air terminal where the Australian captain proved his fitness by sprinting up and down the tarmac before boarding the flight. Plane delays saw the Wallabies arrive late in South Africa and according to rugby historian Ian Diehm, *"...almost immediately, (they) were whisked off to Windhoek, capital of a vast territory two-thirds the size of South Africa. Once there, the Wallabies were soon initiated into the custom of having a Klein/Kleine, which is a beer followed by a chaser."*

Richard Thornett was never, ever one to volunteer his memories of games that he played or his achievements on the sporting field or in the pool, but every now and then he would offer those closest to him a glimpse into a world that surrounded his physical, sporting conquests. One such story is about that trip to South Africa on the plane. Bjarne Halvorsen, one of famous boat builder Lars' five sons, was appointed manager of the tour, a man well-respected and liked by Richard and the other players. On the flight over, the captain or one of his crew had to address a passenger at one stage during the flight. This passenger was Richard Thornett, who was wrestling with someone on the aisle floor of the aircraft. The uniformed flight crew member was unimpressed, and addressing Richard, demanded to know the whereabouts of his manager, Mr Halvorsen. At this point, an arm squirmed out from underneath Richard's upper torso and a meek voice was heard to confirm, "I'm here." Richard duly returned to his seat, as did Bjarne, and the flight continued uninterrupted (except for the fact it was late). Michael Cleary recalls. "Dick liked sleeping on the floor of the plane, because we're in economy, three in a seat, and he was on the floor sleeping (as it was the only place a man that large could sleep in a cabin that size)."

These were the stories Richard did enjoy sharing. Those cheeky moments that offered a glimpse into the private world that he and his teammates lived, even if it was thousands of feet in the air.

CHAPTER SIX

1961 – South Africa

Do not send boys to do men's work.
   Wolfe Wolfaardt (Journalist, Afrikaans newspaper, *Suid Afrika Se Stem*)

Australia accepted a most formidable challenge when it sent the 1961 Wallabies under youthful Ken Catchpole to South Africa to tackle the mighty world champion Springboks. A tour of South Africa is a tough enough mission on a full-scale basis. But a flying three-weeks tour in which the touring side finds itself pitted against the Springboks in the space of a fortnight, and in the high altitude of Johannesburg at that, is asking a little too much.

Noted rugby historian, Ian Diehm, expressed the question posed by a leading player of the day: *"What country would take on a six-match tour of South Africa, including two Test matches against the world champion Springboks, with only 19 players, some of whom were crocked after being belted by the Fijians, plus a couple of passengers from Queensland?"*

Indeed, the answer was Australia, whose poor international record then included the failure to win a home Test against an International Board country since 1934! Tough assignment that it was, the tour was gratefully accepted by the Australian Rugby Football Union (ARFU). The Wallabies had not toured since 1958 and these tours provided an attractive counter to the continued ravages of Rugby League, and the premature retirements of leading players.

The first tour match was against South-West Africa, and given the timeframe and the rigours of the flights and transport taken just to get to the ground, it was little wonder that the Australians were under-prepared. Nonetheless, they ground out a 14–all draw to kick-off their campaign, a nice settler to acclimatise but there was still much work to do.

Ian Diehm wrote, *"The Wallabies had never played South-West Africa before.*

Their captain, Frank Greeff, a veteran lock forward from Otjiwarongo, played against the 1953 Wallabies for the Transvaal XV. The Wallabies failed to overcome Windhoek's high altitude, jet lag and the enervating heat to produce a lethargic display against a lively side and, in the end, the tourists were more than happy to see five-eighth John Dowse goal a vital penalty right on time for a timely 14-14 draw."

The Wallabies then travelled almost 1,500 km to Wellington, Western Cape, not far from Cape Town, and three days after the game against South-West Africa, they fronted up to Boland. After a scoreless first half, the Australians overcame a strong forward pack to take the match honours, 11–3. Again, Dowse's goalkicking had a vital bearing on the result.

Ian Diehm captured the atmosphere surrounding the game when he wrote, "There was a buzz around the ground when Dr Bertie Strasheim signalled the first scrum. The buzz became a roar as the Wallabies were pushed back 10 metres. This was the first time that John Thornett packed against an international prop and Chris Koch, with the national selectors present, gave the unfortunate Wallaby a thorough going over. On the other side, Piet du Toit, a prop with Herculean strength, made life difficult for Jon White." The Australians' scrummaging became a real problem for them throughout the tour.

After the Boland game, the South African selectors named the Springbok side, making five changes from the team which thrashed Ireland a few months earlier. Even though there was still one Wallaby tour match to go, the Springboks were forced to select their side – including the return of greats John Gainsford and Jannie Engelbrecht – at this point to get some time to work on their combinations, as there would only be three days before the Australians' match against North-Eastern Districts and the first Test at Ellis Park.

The Herald reported – **JOHANNESBURG**, *July 30, AAP (Australian Associated Press) Reuters* – "Ken Catchpole brilliantly led the Wallabies to a 11–3 victory against a strong Boland team in the second match of their six-match tour yesterday... Locks Dick Thornett and McDougall had a good game in the second half – especially in lineouts – and Thornett's try, which gave the Wallabies a 6–0 lead, was outstanding. He went up to collect a cross-kick by Ellwood after the Australian line moved left, and forced his way past two Boland forwards to score under the posts."

A.C. Parker, writing for local newspaper *The Cape Argus*, detailed that

1961 - SOUTH AFRICA

"The Australians had an advantage throughout at the lineouts, where McDougall often got the ball back cleanly with good wedging support from Dick Thornett in particular. Dick Thornett, who scored the only try in the match, was one of the outstanding forwards on the field."

Another highlight of this match for the Australians was the report that *"the non-White section of the crowd showed their pleasure at this result by chairing the Wallabies off the field."* The Cape Times reported, *"Wild enthusiasm and roars of applause by hundreds of Coloured spectators greeted the Wallabies' victory over Boland at Wellington on Saturday. They flattened the wire fence barriers and swarmed over the field. The victors were hoisted shoulder-high and chaired to the entrance of the dressing rooms. The police stepped in, and they good-humouredly sauntered back to leave the ground by their own exit."*

Michael Cleary remembers it too. "The coloured (spectators) were at one end and in the other three areas were all Afrikaans, white people. And I remember Catchpole said to me, 'Come round me, I'm going to put you in under the posts.' And he did. And one of the coloured fellas jumps the fence. He kept running over to me. 'Please, sir. Please, sir. Beat them. Beat them. That's what we're doing here.' And the policeman's got a baton, and he belted the *#@* out of him. Catchpole called us all together. He said, 'Come on, we mind our own business.' And I said to the fella (policeman) after the game, 'What'd you do that for?' He said, 'Well, that one fella came over (after) that try you just got. He said, the next try, the whole 10,000 would have come over the fence. So we have to stop it.' I said, 'Oh well, I don't understand it, but I don't agree with it.'" Cleary finished by saying, "(It was) something I've never experienced in my life. I mean, I'm 21 years of age then, as I said, just coming out of school and to see that. Oh, very hard to take, actually. Hard to understand."

This disparity between the two cultures would take many years to change. The Wallabies toured South Africa again in 1963 with John Thornett as their skipper. A member of that team, Mike Jenkinson, remembers. "(Peter) Crittle had become a favourite with one of the African hotel staff. When the team returned to their hotel after their historic victory in the Test at Ellis Park, Johannesburg, the euphoric Wallaby spotted the man, Hosiah, lurking on the outer edge of the all-white crowd in the lobby, trying to steal a glimpse of his Australian heroes in their moment of triumph. Crittle pushed through the crowd and gave

Hosiah a melodramatic hug. The African looked as if he was going to swoon with pleasure and the white fans were in such a magnanimous mood that nobody showed offence."

It is worth mentioning the significance of these comments. The Australians were extremely popular with non-white South African supporters, and other examples of this enthusiasm will be detailed later. When the Wallabies first landed in South Africa in 1961, they were handed a document from the South African media liaison officer. Among the information contained within it was the following:

TO THE MANAGEMENT AND MEMBERS OF THE WALLABIES TOURING TEAM OF 1961.

A FEW DETAILS AND SUGGESTIONS TO HELP MAKE THE TOUR RUN SMOOTHLY AND TO FACILITATE MATTERS FOR ALL CONCERNED.

1. *First of all a very cordial welcome to Messrs. Bjarne Halverson (sic) and Ken Catchpole and to all the other members of the Team. I wish you a happy stay in South Africa. May this Tour be a memorable experience to which you will always look back with pleasant memories and happy thoughts. I trust that we shall become firm friends and express the hope that life-long friendship will be moulded during your visit to our Country. With this in mind and in an endeavour to ensure the maximum benefit and enjoyment for all concerned I submit the following points the observance of which will do much towards the achievement of this aim.*
2. *I invite members of the Team to offer any suggestion, or make requests, within the framework of the Tour Contract... Every suggestion or request, however small, will receive our best attention and consideration.*

The list continues following usual protocol procedures regarding punctuality, rooming lists and the provision of a private lounge. Points 6 and 7, though, were not what most of the tourists might have been expecting:

6. *South Africa is a multi-racial country with two official languages. This may cause you some embarrassment at times, although we promise that everything*

1961 - SOUTH AFRICA

possible will be done not to inconvenience you unduly in this respect. If, however, you do suffer some unpleasantness, may we offer our apologies in advance and also appeal to you to bring such instances to our notice immediately.

7. *It is perhaps necessary to be quite frank with you as regards the South African colour problem. Social and other intercourse with the Non-whites of our Country is generally frowned upon and you are better warned against practices which may cause difficulties and unpleasantness. South Africa has lately suffered a very unfavourable and exaggerated overseas press in connection with its 'apartheid' (separate development) policy.*

During the Tour you will be afforded ample opportunities of forming your own impression.

The wild ride for the Wallabies that had the players continuing to zigzag their way across the country in 1961 continued. The next stop saw them fly to Bloemfontein and then travel by coach for the game at Danie Craven Stadium against North-Eastern Districts, a mere three days after the Boland match and three days before the next, the first Test against the South Africans. By now, you might be getting a clearer picture of how the itinerary would have tested even the most battle-hardened rugby types, let alone a (primarily) green and wide-eyed group of youths on their first tour for their country in perhaps the most challenging rugby frontier in the world. They played games on July 27, 30 and August 2 before their first Test on August 5.

After injuring themselves back in Australia on their way over, and in a desperate attempt to get some miles in their legs, both Tony Miller and Jimmy Lisle took the field for this third tour match. This meant that John Thornett dropped back to the second row, something which, after his experiences in the Boland match, would have been welcomed. Nevertheless, Piet du Toit would be chosen in South Africa's first Test team, so the nightmare wasn't over yet. Lisle's inclusion saw Rod Phelps move onto the wing, which was his third positional change in as many matches.

The Australians hit their stride in their final opportunity to fine-tune their teamwork before the big one at Ellis Park three days later. Playing North-Eastern Districts, they carved up their opposition with a 34–3 victory which would have put them in a good state of mind leading into what was about to confront them on

August 5. Michael Cleary, fast becoming a crowd favourite with some of the locals, scored three tries in an 8-try to one rout of a team, virtually the same team, that the All Blacks failed to defeat the year before (when they failed to score a single try). Leading only 3–0 at the break, the Wallabies piled on 31 points in an extremely confident and entertaining match. Local journalist Piet Wessels wrote, *"To my way of thinking, the performance of the Australian pack was the most impressive. In the lock pair, Dick and John Thornett, the visitors have two first-class lock forwards while the hooker Johnson can be compared with the best."* Even though the ground was still recovering after heavy overnight rain, the Wallabies were unafraid to run the ball whenever they had the chance, something that impressed even the most parochial of local supporters. The Australian forwards won six tight-head scrums to one and benefitted from about 80 per cent of the ball from the set pieces and in the loose.

Another local newspaper report ended with the following words: *"The morale of the Wallabies has been lifted since their 14–all draw with South-West Africa a week ago. They have now scored 59 points to 20 against and go on to Ellis Park and the first Test with plenty of confidence."* Reality and potential don't always align, and this would be severely put to the test as the whistle blew to start the match in Johannesburg.

To say that the Wallabies came back to earth at Ellis Park would be an understatement. Some suggest that it transpired because of an overconfidence that came after their fabulous display at Burgersdorp, but there was much more at play than just that, if indeed it was even a factor.

To avoid clashes with the Springboks' playing strip, the Australian Wallabies sported new playing colours on this South African tour. The now-familiar gold jerseys with green collar and cuffs and bottle green shorts made their appearance for the first time.

The Wallabies' selections surprised some when experienced prop Tony Miller was left out of the starting lineup. This meant that John Thornett would be packing down in the front row against the mighty South African pack, something that had presented its problems only a few days before against Boland. Meanwhile, Terry Reid was chosen over the uncompromising Ted Heinrich. Nonetheless, with names like Thornett x 2, White, Johnson, Heming, Catchpole, Ellwood, Lisle, Cleary, Phelps and Lenehan in the side, on paper at least, Australia still looked quite the formidable unit.

Things looked bright initially for Australia as they had the opportunity to run with the wind in the first half and use it to their advantage. There were nearly 60,000 at the game at Ellis Park, and it didn't take long for the Springboks to assert their authority, scoring after three minutes. Riding off the back of a menacing and extremely powerful forward pack, the Springbok backline was having a field day, playing a high-tempo game, much like the Australians had days before. Winger Hennie van Zyl scored three tries in the opening 33 minutes with the South Africans scoring four tries in each half. Australia's sole match points came from a John Dowse penalty. The 28–3 final score was South Africa's highest in a home international. Thankfully for Australia, the final result would have been a lot worse had South Africa's captain and goalkicker, Johan Claassen managed more than his two goals.

A.C. Parker wrote in *The Cape Argus*: *"As for the Wallabies, who fell too easily for simple scissors variations, few of them emerged with much credit. Dick Thornett, who battled hard throughout, was their best forward, and Phelps, Ellwood and Cleary showed occasional flashes of ability, while Catchpole covered well."*

Sports editor, Wolfe Wolfaardt in the Afrikaans newspaper *Suid Afrika Se Stem* was brutal in his assessment when he condemned Australia's performance, *"Do not send boys to do men's work,"* he crowed. In the *Johannesburg Sunday Express*, Ray Woodley was even more damning: *"We must face facts and so must the rest of the rugby world – the Wallabies are not up to international standard. This was not an international match. It was a club side playing a fully trained and highly efficient side from the greatest rugby country in the world."*

This gloating from the South African press did not impress Richard Thornett. Never one to boast, in fact if anything he was humble to a fault, Richard despised when success was cast upon the vanquished in any condescending or arrogant tone. He once reflected on his impressions from that tour, "John (Thornett) likes the South African guys but I thought they were arrogant. I remember when we toured South Africa in '61. I was only twenty, but our very first game was in Windhoek in the middle of the Kalahari Desert and after the game they had their normal reception... the South Africans got up and spoke in Afrikaans, the captain... I just thought, 'They've got a visiting Australian side there...' Anyway, I just thought that was not right."

A Man of Humility

There are countless stories of Richard's humility. It was difficult to draw any anecdotes from him on his career because he feared it would be misconstrued as boasting, something that horrified him. I remember teaching Jock Merriman, a young man from the NSW country town of Boorowa. He was a rather handy rugby player himself who represented Australian Schoolboys in Richard's good mate's position, halfback, later playing for brother John Thornett's first club, Sydney University. I had spoken/digressed one day in class about my father-in-law as a good sportsman and Australian representative, but that was as far as I took it. Later in this book, we speak about a school rugby jersey presentation in 2011 with Richard as special guest, where he is introduced by the MC as the sporting legend he was. Jock was halfback in the First XV that afternoon and in the room. He was also a boarder and the afternoon after that presentation, he looked from his window down to our steep driveway (I was a boarding housemaster who lived on-site) as Richard struggled to get out of his car. Jock ran from his room to help Richard from his 'ute', something typical of the fine man Jock was, and is. The next day, in class, I let Jock know how much Richard had appreciated his gesture, for he spoke of it when he walked into our home afterwards with his bags. Jock replied, "Not that it was a reason, but I didn't know what a legend your father-in-law is." I replied, "That's just the way he likes it to be."
Brendan Morris, Author

The Wallabies had three days off before another tour match against Border on August 9, and then they'd front up again for the second Test three days after that.

The relentless travel schedule did nothing to help the team and there must have been a travel agent or official back home running for cover when the Wallabies arrived back in the country. They played four games in ten days, including the first Test and had travelled thousands of kilometres by air and bus to get to each location. Ellis Park is about 500 metres shy of the peak of Mt Kosciusko, Australia's tallest, and so given the combination of playing at this altitude, an extraordinary travel schedule, and a growing injury toll (including Lisle who struggled with his injury from South Australia throughout the first Test), it is little wonder that they

1961 - SOUTH AFRICA

were ambushed. This wasn't the end of the problems that had beset the team, though, because preparing for the best scrum in world rugby was also proving to be a real issue.

It has often been said that success occurs when opportunity meets preparation. It is a wonderful sentiment, for while the opportunity was there for the Wallabies to take, the preparation left a lot to be desired, hence the result.

The problems for the Wallabies could be traced back to the raw power of the Springbok pack. "Scrums were their game," John Thornett recalled. "They were renowned for their strength, and all their loose play was blown up very quickly, so they had plenty of scrums to pack. Compared to the Springboks, the All Blacks were soft in scrums, and we went in ill-equipped to handle them. We had no scrum to practise in training before the game, and I was packing into the front row for only the third time in a Test. I was worn out, useless after 15 minutes. It finished up the worst loss I ever played in. Altitude, the scrums and some poor defence. They all combined to have an effect on the result."

Later, John Thornett expanded. "We hadn't experienced scrummaging (in training on this tour) before (because) we didn't have enough team players to make an opposing scrum for training. There were only 25 in the squad (it was actually 21), so we didn't have many scrummers."

There were actually only eleven forwards taken on the tour (and ten backs), so technically the Wallabies had three spare forwards for the Ellis Park game (front-rower Tony Miller, hooker Don McDeed and backrower Ted Heinrich). Miller's performance in the tour match before the first Test did not gain much positive feedback, with one newspaper account reporting that Miller *"...did not impress and was obviously short of match practice,"* perhaps as a result of still carrying the back injury he sustained in Western Australia on the way over. If Miller was indeed still short of match fitness and possibly injured, that possibly meant that the team only had a hooker and flanker upon which to call, and absolutely no scrum against which to practise.

Thornett continued, "We didn't have scrum machines available then and so we didn't do much scrumming. We went down there to Port Elizabeth and they lent us a police pack --- blokes to practise against. These blokes taught us a hell of a lot about scrummaging; they were big blokes and we learnt to get the scrum – get our feet back and really low... by actually holding the scrum so you couldn't be moved and we found we could do that. In the next Test, in that one week we learned how to hold a scrum, we played a holding scrum, and the next Test we almost won a week later. And I didn't play front row. Tony Miller came back, he had been injured, and I played second row with Dick that time and, yeah, we were very close to winning it; we were near the end and it was only ten minutes to go and we won the ball and it was a pass to Ted Heinrich, one of Richard's mates, and oh, the referee got in the way and Ted dropped the ball. He only had about three yards to run to score the try and we would have been in front. But (they were) pretty hard to beat in that situation."

"It was the worst experience I ever had on the field (the first Test). There was scrum after scrum and we were getting knocked back yards and yards every time. Peter Johnson was hooker and he'd win the ball and the scrums were going back. Catchy had to sort of jump aside to get out of the way of the scrum. After about ten minutes I was just about a write-off; I could hardly move – and I was reasonably fit normally – and the game went on and we lost it badly. I was just praying for the final bell to go so they wouldn't score anymore; we were just about helpless. I just tried to get off the field, walk off the field, and there were kids wanting autographs. Oh, they were amazing though."

It is quite remarkable to consider that a local Port Elizabeth police forward pack taught the Australian scrum how to scrummage in readiness for the next tour match and the upcoming second Test. Today, it is bemusing to hear Ted Heinrich point out, "My club, Randwick, might go through a whole season in those days and hardly pack a scrum because scrums were regarded as merely a means of restarting the game."

Once again, the Wallabies struck a gusting wind at the Border ground in their next tour match and had to overcome strong opposition from Nolan Flemmer's men before winning 17–6 with tries to left wing Ed Magrath and No. 8 John O'Gorman, Australia's best loose forward. Border's only try came from a great run by winger Ian Stewart.

The Australians now had the "luxury" of four days off before the next Test, their longest respite yet between games, in fact the longest on tour. They were the walking wounded, and they knew that beyond this next tour match they had to face up to the snarling Springboks, champing at the bit to grind the Wallabies deeper into the dirt. In four days, this squad of 21 had to pick themselves up and

1961 – SOUTH AFRICA

steel themselves, a task that most international sides halfway across the world with no one to turn to but themselves, would baulk at. To rub salt into injury (literally and figuratively) the game against Border at East London saw Catchpole and Ellwood out with injury, Richard Thornett struggling badly with a leg injury and Lisle out for the rest of the tour. The tourists fielded all six reserves, with John Thornett leading from the second row. Into the breach they went, with a depleted bench, a baying crowd and the South African national team licking their lips, watching on from the stands.

The Australians made three changes to their Test side, replacing Lisle with Phelps and bringing in Magrath and dropping Terry Reid and 'Butch' Macdougall. Ted Heinrich came in for Reid, while 'Slaggy' Miller was at tighthead prop, allowing John Thornett back into the second row.

There was an interesting development in the South African camp that mirrored exactly what Richard Thornett had endured not long before in his confrontation with Water Polo officialdom. The Springbok XV remained unchanged heading into the second Test, but as Ian Diehm noted in *Giants in Green and Gold*, *"as the Western Province players boarded the plane at D.F. Malan airport, a heavy-handed attempt was made to have John Gainsford and Doug Hopwood sign written undertakings not to turn professional. At their Port Elizabeth hotel, another of the team, Fanie Kuhn, was also tackled about professionalism. The players were rightly incensed and it required the intervention of the team manager, Boy Louw, to sort the matter out. Still, it was hardly the ideal preparation for the Test match, particularly as the press broke the story, and the South African Rugby Board (SARB) move was universally condemned by South African rugby personalities and old Springboks who gathered for the Test."* The similarities were uncanny, although unlike Richard's case, the players won the day and went on to play for their country.

In a display of pure courage and grit, the Australian team withstood everything their opposition threw at them, and while they may not have won the match at Boet Erasmus Stadium, they won something else; the admiration of many who had, only a week before, seen them as "boys..." and "...who were not up to international standard." The Wallabies lost the Test 23-11, but Ray Woodley, so damning in his summary after the first Test, was much more complimentary in victory this time, *"I salute the Wallabies display,"* he wrote in *The Sunday Express*.

Springbok centre Francois Roux, writing a column in *The Sunday Times*, added, "*The Waltzing Wallabies were very much in the game from start to finish ... and for long periods were actually doing most of the attacking.*" But South African Rugby Board president, Danie Craven, went further, describing the Australian improvement as miraculous. "*I have never seen such perfect handling,*" he said. "*Their performance shows they can improve even more before they visit us again in 1963.*" How true those words would be, and what sweet revenge lay ahead for the Wallabies who returned two years later.

Noted sportswriter A.C. Parker wrote in *Springbok Rugby Annals,* "*The Wallabies improved out of all recognition in this game and in all departments of play were more of a match for the Springboks whose attacks were blunted with fine, low tackles. In fact, the final score of 23-11 flattered the Springboks somewhat. Once again, open, attacking rugby was the order of the day and seldom has a game produced such long periods of uninterrupted play as was produced by both sides. The Australian forwards came into their own in the tight-loose... and here Tony Miller, Rob Heming, Ted Heinrich and John and Dick Thornett were outstanding.*"

South Africa started well again and got away to an 8-nil lead. The game opened up though when Michael Cleary crossed to bring the Wallabies back into the game. He went close earlier in the game but was brought to ground just short of the line. At halftime, there were many at the ground and listening on who were in some sense of disbelief, with the Australians trailing by a mere six points, 11-5, which shrank even further soon after the break when John Dowse's successful penalty goal closed the margin to three points.

Ian Diehm, in his book *Giants in Green and Gold,* noted, "*This was a particularly determined Australian team and big Dick Thornett cut loose with a rampaging run for the corner that was only just stopped by Engelbrecht. The Springboks ran on from this point but it wasn't easy for them, and their brave opponents won hearts with their gallant display. When the Springboks were penalised at a scrum 40 metres out, Dowse goaled to make the final score 23-11 to South Africa.*"

Diehm continued, "*The winning margin flattered the Springboks. The Wallaby improvement came from changed tactics and real scrummaging practice. With the Thornetts combining well in the lineouts with Heming, the backrow threw out a defensive mesh to thwart not only the Springbok backs but also the support play of Pelser, Hopwood and Van Zyl that was so effective at Ellis Park.*"

1961 - SOUTH AFRICA

Elsewhere, James Hattle wrote, *"The Wallaby forwards were lively right up till the end of the game, with the Thornett brothers, Heinrich, Heming and O'Gorman often prominent."* The SMH printed, *"Dick Thornett, Jon White, Peter Johnson and Rob Heming showed up the weaknesses in the Springbok pack."*

The publication *Wallaby Gold: The History of Australian Test Rugby* captured Ken Catchpole's honest appraisal of the Springboks and the tour. *"'We'd developed a bit more continuity,' Catchpole said. 'But at the time, the Springboks had the best backs, and the best forwards, in the world. Their scrummaging was beyond our experience. It was a wonderful tour, though. I remember flying into South Africa, at night, and being staggered by the number of people who had turned up to see us arrive. We had this fleet of cars at our service as well. They were like two-door Valiants. We'd never had anything like this laid on before.'"*

Manager of the Australian rugby team, Bjarne Halvorsen, proved why he was so likeable and held in such high esteem by Richard. His humility, generosity of spirit and honesty in his appraisal of the opposition were such great adjuncts to his character. In Francois Roux's summary of the Wallaby tour in his *Sunday Times* column, he reported that Halvorsen described the Springboks XV as the finest international combination he had ever seen. Asked to single out the Springboks who impressed him most during the two-match Test series, he said, *"It's impossible. They're all brilliant in one respect or another. I am amazed that players with such an exceptional flair for the unorthodox could have welded themselves into such a smooth working unit."* The genial Wallaby manager was justly proud with the performance of the Australian XV in the second Test. *"It is no disgrace to lose to this wonderful Springbok team. And nobody can say we did not give the 'Boks a run for their money on Saturday."* Halvorsen had nothing but praise for South Africa, its rugby officials and players. *"Except, of course, for the tremendous amount of travelling, I can honestly say that we enjoyed every minute of the tour,"* he said.

The players enjoyed it as well, as it gave them the opportunity to make some money while maintaining their amateur status. Michael Cleary explains, "We used to get two Test tickets, so you scalped these and got £40, £50. A lot of the blokes over there also bought diamonds. Yeah. And could also get Krugerrands (gold coins) and 51-carat diamonds over there very cheaply." It sure beat the 10 shillings a day they were receiving from the Australian Rugby Union.

Roux added, *"To me, the outstanding players in this touring team were their bully lock forward Dick Thornett and fullback Jim Lenehan. Both should be certain for the next tour. On Saturday, the young Thornett, who weighs a handy 230 lbs (pounds), was scrumming and rucking just as efficiently as the redoubtable Claassen and Du Preez. His lineout play was of top international class too. At times he even won the ball from the spring-heeled Du Preez, which certainly takes some doing. Equally impressive was his robust play in the loose. The way he stormed in and through the loose melees like a Sherman tank and broke away from the rucks with the ball tucked under his arm are the most lasting impressions I have kept of the Port Elizabeth Test. For a big man, Thornett is surprisingly nimble and mobile. He handles the ball like a back, and once he matures not even the roughest and toughest locks in and South Africa will be able to tame him."*

It's worth remembering that Richard was 20-years-old. If you are a parent of a son 20-years-old or not much older, think of him in this context – not just surviving, but thriving, even dominating. Even his brother John was in awe of his skills, which would certainly take him far in the years soon to come. "Yeah, he was big and he was strong but he was fast. He was a good rugby player in that sense. But yeah, he was fast and he was quick off the mark for a big bloke and he was strong and had good ball skills. That's why he was a great success in Rugby League, with those skills."

One needs to look beyond the simple task of evaluating success in terms of wins and losses for this tour. Its significant challenges across so many contexts made it a success in terms of establishing a foundation for what was to emerge in the months to come; in particular against the All Blacks the next year and the Wallabies' tour back to South Africa a year later again, in 1963. Their opponents had a genuine fear that the second Test in South Africa in 1961 may be a lightning rod of momentum that would push Australia forward against those who had stood over the nation in Rugby Union for so long. With a greater knowledge of the technical aspects of the game (a nod here to the police in Port Elizabeth, among others), of their opponents, of playing conditions and with a squad growing in confidence and cohesiveness, the future promised much.

At the baggage carousel upon landing back in Australia, the players bade farewell to one another, exhausted and eager to walk through the front door of home after a whirlwind tour of a formidable country, both from a playing and cultural perspective. They would have little time to rest though, because a mere

1961 - SOUTH AFRICA

two weeks after the Port Elizabeth Test, the Wallabies would play one more Test at the Sydney Cricket Ground (SCG) against France on August 26.

Australia had played France before but only on foreign soil. This time though, the battle would take place at home for the first time. France had won the Five Nations Championship three times in succession but their visit to the Southern Hemisphere had seen them fall to three successive defeats against the All Blacks.

The field on the day was completely waterlogged which scuppered plans by both teams to run the ball and play expansive rugby. The Frenchmen took the field in the slush against Australia at the SCG with pockets in their shorts, and in them they had a liberal supply of resin which they used on their hands to help their handling of the ball in the slippery conditions. It was a relatively simple yet at the same time masterful move by the visitors, who out-thought the Australians in more ways than one on their own turf. The French were too good for the Australians, scoring three tries to one, the game controlled by renowned Australian referee, Dr Roger Vanderfield. The Australians, though, did produce a magnificent try after the ball passed through a dozen pairs of hands in a 50-metre movement upfield, but it was too late to influence the result and France clinched the match 15–8. Three of the game's four tries, including Australia's sole effort, were scored in the final six minutes of the match.

Sadly, as the players dressed back into their formal kit for the post-match function, two of the party would be doing so for the last time with the team. For Michael Cleary and Jimmy Lisle, it was "Merci, adieu," walking off into the sunset with Rugby League contracts in their pockets and a new world before them.

CHAPTER SEVEN
1962 – The All Blacks

(Richard Thornett) was just a great athlete and a big, strong bugger and when he was charging at you, you bloody – you looked for your mate for a bit of assistance, put it that way. He was big, powerful and pretty bloody quick too, as I recall. And he loved running at you. We have a saying in New Zealand, it was a Māori side-step, let's run straight at them. And he was bloody good at that, I tell you. The biggest comment I reckon is he was like a real great New Zealand forward; he was just a great player.

Sir Colin Meads, Ex-All Black, New Zealand – interview

NSW continued their outstanding performances against touring national sides when they inflicted a 12–11 defeat upon the All Blacks a week before the first Test in Brisbane, their only loss on tour in Australia. It added to the victory against the Fijians the year before, and the British Lions two years before that. Richard was selected for this game but unfortunately had to withdraw because of broken ribs. For the first time in the history of matches between the two countries, a home-and-away series of Tests was played, the All Blacks in Australia for two Tests in May/June and the Wallabies flying to New Zealand in August/September for three Tests. New Zealand won four of these Tests and drew one.

Extra spice was added in this series as New Zealand's halfback was a former Wallaby, Des Connor, who went on to be regarded as one of the great All Blacks. Ken Catchpole had many fans back in 1959 who were calling for his inclusion in the Tests against the Lions, and this upset Connor. He said in 1998, "I did find the calls in the Sydney media frustrating... I felt I was the form player in 1959 and it was just coming down to NSW-Queensland rivalry. At the time, there were still five selectors, with one from Queensland, three from NSW and one from Victoria.

1962 - THE ALL BLACKS

I thought very much the writing was on the wall." Connor held on in '59 but moved across the ditch soon after and was teaching at Takapuna Grammar in 1960, and by 1961 he had satisfied eligibility requirements and was an All Black by July. There would be no love lost when he was presented with the chance to play against the youngster he felt his countrymen regarded more highly.

Before the first Test in Brisbane, Australia lost its captain, Jim Lenehan through injury. Rod Phelps moved to fullback and Lloyd McDermott became the second Indigenous Wallaby (after Cecil Ramalli in 1938) when he was called up to take Phelps' place on the wing. Peter Johnson took over the captaincy. Australia would also be without lineout expert, Rob Heming, who withdrew because he could not get time away from his optometry practice (which says a lot about the times), and he was replaced by Queenslander Paul Perrin. Surprisingly, after an impressive performance for NSW against New Zealand in the tour match, John Thornett was overlooked for selection. Catchpole returned after spending most of the season on the sideline, injured, but it was a gamble to play him against the All Blacks, such was his lack of match practice. It should be remembered, too, that over the off-season, Australia had lost the services of Michael Cleary and Jimmy Lisle to Rugby League – two huge holes left in a backline that was just starting to sizzle.

It was an extremely dour affair, especially given the promises of open running from both teams before the Test. It was all over bar the shouting when the New Zealanders led 17-0 at halftime. Kel Tremain scored the only try in a dreary second half while Australian centre Peter Scott kicked two penalty goals. It was a small consolation that the Wallabies won the second half, 6-3; New Zealand had shut up shop early. Richard was selected at the back of the scrum in this match and admitted, "I was selected at lock in this game but my cover defence wasn't there. It really wasn't my game – at that stage I was playing in the second row and probably not fast enough to cover the ground which a normal lock should."

Skipper Wilson Whineray expertly guided his team around the field and Colin Meads and Kel Tremain were Herculean up front for the All Blacks. The debut of Waka Nathan was remarkable while Don Clarke at the back always lifted his team, even if he was, thankfully, off with his kicking that day. In 2003, Sydney's *Daily Telegraph* chose its 100 Greatest Wallabies and also chose a similar list of All Blacks. Perhaps unsurprisingly, Colin Meads came out as 'Number One', and he was extremely praiseworthy of Richard, which we will hear later. Richard, too, loved his battles with "Pinetree", but he saved his greatest praise for two of his teammates, Tremain and Nathan. In an interview with Neil Bennetts for the National Library of Australia, he said, *"The bloke, Kel Tremain who was their number eight... he was probably one of the best players I've played against. And Waka Nathan was the other --- Waka Nathan was a back rower, they were just nice blokes off the field. You couldn't get boo out of Colin Meads. But they were good sportsmen on and off the field and I think that was one of the most important things in any sport or any facet of life."*

Between Tests, New Zealand scored 22 tries in its 103–0 defeat of Northern NSW in Walgett – what a venue for an All Black side! Winger Rod Heeps scored eight of them, a record for an All Black.

There were some changes to both sides for the second Test, although the visitors' pack remained the same. Jim Lenehan returned as captain and fullback, as did John Thornett, Rob Heming and John O'Gorman. In what was to be his Australian debut, Dick Marks dropped out with gastroenteritis, so Phelps slid into the centres and Beres Ellwood moved in to fly-half. New Zealand scored first but then Richard Thornett, part of the Wallaby pack going toe-to-toe with the tremendous eight men from New Zealand, crashed his way over from a lineout, and when Peter Scott converted, the Australians were up 5–3, a score they kept for most of the half. Then, on the stroke of halftime, Don Clarke, with the boos echoing around the SCG stands, elected to take a penalty from 6 metres on his side of halfway. The kick was never in doubt, easily sailing over the crossbar to plunge a knife in the hearts of the Wallabies as they trudged to the sheds for the break. Two quick tries early in the second half to the All Blacks perhaps confirmed what Clarke's penalty did to Australia's mindset, but it was, nonetheless, a sterling performance from the home side.

It was a significant shift in attitude and performance, a shift that didn't simply hover over this game, but a momentum that flung Australia forward for Tests and series to come. Max Howell's *Wallabies: A Definitive History of Australian Rugby* singled out certain players for praise, *"Flanker John O'Gorman had a splendid game, as did Dick Thornett and Slaggy Miller. Ken Catchpole at halfback was brilliant."* Hemings' return was also telling, if under-reported, for its significance. In the first Test, Australia lost the lineouts 45–11, but in the second Test Australia won the count, 33–32. New Zealand journalist S. B. Pickering wrote, *"Two magnificent forwards in a good Australian pack were the locks, the brothers Thornett, John and Dick. In the lineouts they were most effective, and in the general play they formed the hard core of resistance to the All Blacks forward endeavour, and were the dynamite in the Australian forward drive that brought Dick Thornett's try and nearly achieved others."*

Before the Wallabies left for New Zealand, there was one more local warm-up match to play –Australia vs The Rest at North Sydney Oval. It was one of those games where the underdogs had everything to play for and nothing to lose. In Phil Tresidder's newspaper article, he observed how *"Dick Thornett snatched victory for Australia against The Rest in the last few seconds of the Rugby Union Wallaby tour trial at North Sydney Oval. Thornett intercepted a loose pass and raced along the right-hand touchline for 40 yards to touch down. The try turned defeat into a thrilling 16-12 victory for the fancied Australia side. It was a dramatic turnabout. The fulltime bell sounded as Thornett walked wearily back to his delighted colleagues. The Rest, under the leadership of energetic Queenslander Alec Evans, had battled tenaciously. Dick Thornett's try capped a great game. He is now at the peak of his form. He formed a bustling partnership with his brother, John, in the second row. The tight, honest front row of Freedmen, Johnson and White gave them great support."*

Strangely, Australia's performances in the return series in New Zealand were even better than those played at home. Journalist and author Peter Jenkins wrote the following in *Wallaby Gold: A History of Australian Test Rugby:* "*The doyen of rugby writers, New Zealander T.P. McLean, even suggested Australia were unlucky not to win the first two games of the three in the Shaky Isles. One of the leaders in the pack this year was the tough Randwick number eight-cum-second-rower Dick Thornett. He weighed more than 16 stone but had speed, mobility and ball skills rare for a man of his size. Thornett, whose brother John took over the Test captaincy for the final three Tests, was earmarked for a long career – the damaging forward."*

Australia won all four tour matches leading into the first Test, against Poverty Bay (31-6), Counties (20-14), Wairarapa (43-0) and Horowhenua (28-6) before 'windy Wellington' greeted Australia for the first rugby Test of the three-match series on August 25, 1962. The change of country was accompanied by a change of halfback when, in a shock selection switch, Ken Catchpole was dropped and replaced by Wagga Wagga's Ken McMullen. McMullen found a newcomer in

19-year-old Phil Hawthorne outside him, the selectors bravely choosing a team with a brand-new halves-pairing. Hawthorne and prop, John Freedman, also making his Test debut in this game, would go on to illustrious careers with the Wallabies, Hawthorne switching later to a successful international Rugby League career. It may have been somewhat unlucky for Catchpole given the fact that he had had four fly-halves outside him in the previous four Tests, against three different opponents and in two different countries. In the previous Test, the last in Australia, his outside man at fly-half, Dick Marks (also making his debut) withdrew late and was replaced by Beres Ellwood, who had never played the position in national colours before.

John Thornett was chosen as captain as the Australians braced themselves to meet the might and force of the men in black, led by an almost World XV forward pack. A charge-down from a Jim Lenehan clearing kick by the brilliant Waka Nathan led to debutant winger John Morrisey scoring the first points of the game, the only points of the first half. Fifteen minutes into the second half, the score was unchanged until backrower Geoff Chapman, also making his Test debut, kicked two penalty goals to put the Australians up 6–3. Don Clarke evened the scores soon after, making it 6–all and then appeared to be the villain in the piece when he was penalised for foul play, striking out with his legs in a tackle. Chapman struck his third penalty to take Australia to 9–6.

With seconds left in the game and Australia ahead, fortunes swung once more, as Chapman, who had kept Australia in front for the much of the game, turned villain this time as he was penalised for a ruck indiscretion. Clarke, now the hero, calmly stepped up and slotted the equaliser, much to the despair of the Australians. The whistle blew; 9–all, the first draw in the history between the two nations.

T.P. McLean wrote in the *New Zealand Herald*: "*It was an unsatisfactory ending to a game of which the principal features were the swiftness and gallantry of the Wallabies in defence and the ineptitude of the All Blacks in attack... that control which New Zealand forwards are expected to develop could not be sustained. Well done, the Wallabies! There could be no other tribute...*" It was a quiet shout-out to the Australian forward pack that they were able to blunt the most potent national forward pack in the world. Another New Zealand newspaper report complimented the Australian forwards, who it said, "*...were particularly impressive and this has been at a department where the Wallabies' play had been most suspect until today.*

The Thornett brothers, Dick and John, led the Australian pack into the thick of the fight." The Herald's Jim Webster wrote that "O'Gorman was splendid in the Australian pack as was Dick Thornett and veteran Tony Miller..." Meanwhile, New Zealand manager, Jack King said, "I confess I thought in the first half the Australians were going to win. They played very well and their forwards were magnificent."

Australian hooker Peter Johnson remembers in his book, *A Rugby Memoir*: "Many of our team thought we had scored a 'moral' victory but despite such romantic sentiments the scoreboard read 9-9 and for me, and history, that was that. In New Zealand the media concentrated on analysing the performances of their own team, especially in defeat or, in this case an equally unacceptable draw. However, it was generally agreed the outstanding player of the match was Jim Lenehan. He had outgunned the mighty Don Clarke, with whom, it seemed to me, the entire Kiwi population had a love-hate relationship. Jim was superb but no more so than John Thornett who, by example, kept our pack focussed for the entire match. A few acknowledged our forwards had at least held the most powerful pack in rugby. Dick Thornett, I know from discussions in later years, was truly feared by even the greatest of that outstanding New Zealand team."

Another article in *The Christchurch Star* was headlined **One of the Strongest Touring Teams**. It opened with this comment from Mr N J McPhail, the convener of the All Black selection panel: *"The Australian rugby team at present in New Zealand is one of the strongest to visit these shores. They have a particularly fine pack of forwards. This Australian team is a much better one than people give them credit for and it is time people became aware of the fact."* When approached by *The Christchurch Star* on selection policy, he said, *"In all the newspaper criticisms bemoaning the performance of New Zealand, few have yet had the gumption to come out and say just how good these Australians are. Their forwards are very good indeed and they have a particularly fine one in young Dick Thornett."*

The Australians played three tour matches between the first and second Tests, losing two of them, (Canterbury 3-5) and (North Otago 13-14), and winning against West Coast-Buller (9-0). The second Test was their ninth game in a month. The three Test matches each came four days after the previous tour match, so there was little time to recuperate and prepare thoroughly, but that was the nature of tours back then and they had to adjust as best as they could. Ken Catchpole and Peter Crittle returned, and Dick Marks was selected in the centres.

THE NATURAL

The New Zealand selectors were brutal in their assessment of the New Zealander's performance in the first Test, wielding the axe by chopping Kel Tremain, Dennis Young and Ian Clarke. Like Catchpole in the not-too-distant past, reputations meant nothing and even the great Colin Meads wasn't spared the slaughter. It was a vicious response against such great players. As it turned out, Australia took full advantage and dominated the forward exchanges in the early parts of the match, with the home side turning to the mercurial Don Clarke to get them ahead on the scoreboard.

If the selectors were hoping for All Black dominance, they found none in the first half, with neither team scoring. Richard Thornett made a huge run that had the crowd on their feet, but it came to nothing, while Lenehan and Chapman missed shots at goal that were costly. Peter Jenkins scribed, *"Ken Catchpole was outstanding, as was the Australian pack. The Thornett brothers, Peter Crittle and Jon White were particularly solid, more than matching the All Blacks on this occasion."*

There was a significant incident that changed the course of the game when Catchpole found Jim Boyce in space and put him across the line for three points. It was disallowed, and Peter Johnson, incredulous, later wrote in his memoirs, *"The first Test decision that allowed Clarke to construct a draw was odious, but the penalising of Catchpole for passing off the ground to send Jim Boyce in under the posts... was absolutely ludicrous."* Richard was equally incensed. "A turning point in the game came when New Zealander, (winger) Morrisey held onto the ball and should have been penalised. I can recall Catchpole trying to pick it up but Morrisey wouldn't let go. Catchpole had Lenehan (it was actually Boyce) just outside of him and rather than Australia being awarded the penalty try, a penalty was awarded to New Zealand against Catchpole for hands in the ruck." Midway through the second half, who else but Don Clarke kicked New Zealand to victory through a penalty, the only points of the 3–0 match. Australia may have lost the game, but how far they had come, even from only a few months earlier in Australia, was remarkable.

There was sympathy, even from the locals, that the Australians were unlucky to lose a game in which they had outplayed New Zealand, particularly the manner in which it played out. The New Zealand Rugby Football Union (NZRFU) Chairman, Tom Morrison, said after the game, *"Apart from goalkicking, Australia must be called unlucky not to have won by a fair margin."* One of the most generous pieces of commentary came from ex-Wellington coach and New Zealand journalist Clarrie Gibbons in his *Looks at Rugby* newspaper column. He opened his article by saying, *"One could readily have been constrained to say to hundreds of people in Dunedin last Saturday night "Stop your moaning and give credit where it's due." He went on to say, "The Aussie forwards are all men. Sydney policeman 'Dick' Thornett is the best lock forward who has come to New Zealand for a long time. Woe betide the Sydney wrongdoer who thinks he can outrun him. On one occasion last Saturday he scaled up the right touchline like a pacy three-quarter and then centre-kicked to place Australia in a position from which, with a bit of luck, they could have scored."*

As was the case before the second Test, Australia played three tour matches before the third Test, once again losing two of them, (Thames Valley 14-16) and (Southland 11-16), and winning against Wanganui (29-6). Richard Thornett continued his good form, scoring in the Thames Valley match and, according to *The SMH* on August 19, against Wanganui, he, *"...had perhaps his best match to date."*

Before the final Test, renowned New Zealand journalist T.P. McLean wrote, *"... the Test today offers a test within a Test – an internal contest to determine whether within the two teams the natural ardour of youth, the irritation with performances or criticisms, the training since boyhood days, can be directed towards the production of rugby as it really should be played."* It was.

Ken Catchpole had to withdraw on Test eve with severe hip bruising, but that was the only change to the Australian team. Colin Meads returned for the All Blacks, joining his brother, Stan, in the second row. In the Australian second row were the two Bronte brothers, Richard and John Thornett. They knew what was coming for them; a raging 'Pinetree' Meads hellbent on proving the selectors wrong for dropping him for the previous Test as well as a demon desperate to regain some pride lost in his demotion. If it was the selectors' intention to motivate Colin Meads back into form, it worked, as he tore into the Australians from the first whistle. The home side moved to an 11-point lead in the first half. Many sides would have rolled over and capitulated. Not this new Australian side, who had come so far and proven so many wrong, and they set about grinding their way back into the game. The forwards, in particular, were outstanding, led by the Thornetts, but even a Chapman penalty and a brilliant Lenehan try after a

50-metre team raid down the blindside wasn't quite enough to staunch the flow coming in the opposite direction. The Wallabies were certainly not disgraced in their 16–8 defeat, winning the second half 8–5. They drew as close as three points adrift, 11–8 at one stage in the second half. Thinking back to two crucial moments in the first two Tests, and Australia were perilously close to returning home 2–1 series winners.

Waka Nathan recalled that the Australians were much tougher than people gave them credit for in the 1962 Tests. "We won four out of the five Tests (played across the two home-and- away series), but Australia was a tough side. John Thornett was a magnificent captain and his brother Dick played rugby, league and Water Polo for Australia."

Richard Thornett proclaimed, "That (1962 New Zealand tour) was a more successful tour for us, because being together for one year with that young side in 1961, we were starting to come together more cohesively as a team."

As stated earlier, the greatest critique that any person can be given, regardless of which field they traverse, is from those who compete in the arena against them. The very best of the All Black, were well aware of the presence of Richard Thornett whenever he took his place on the field. Captain, Wilson Whineray, in comparing his opposite skipper, John Thornett, to Richard, said, "Now Dick, of course, was a different kettle of fish altogether. He was a big guy and he was a very strong, powerful running fellow. You never forgot Dick was on the field on the other side; he'd be in your face a bit and over the top of you and in a manner that John wouldn't. John would be more – he'd be just working with others and building things and trying to work together to get one guy in the clear, whereas Dick would be right, straight up the middle at you."

The great Colin Meads had a similar mindset as he continued the fish metaphor. He shared, "We'd never come across Dick up until that stage, and hell, he was a different kettle of fish altogether. I suppose we got up to a few tricks and pushing and that sort of thing in lineouts but hell, he took no prisoners. He was playing for keeps, he was not the gentleman John was, put it that way. Every time I've gone back there are reunions, you meet up with John again but you don't see Dick and that was always sad for me 'cause he was a good guy to have a beer with afterwards and he was just a great athlete and a big, strong bugger and when he was charging at you, you bloody --- you looked for your mate for a bit of assistance, put it that way. He was big, powerful and pretty bloody quick too, as I recall. And he loved running at you. We have a saying in New Zealand, it was a Māori side-step, let's run straight at them. And he was bloody good at that, I tell you. He's not the front man or anything like that, he just keeps away to himself sort of thing ... he was a good bugger. John and Dick were --- they were great guys but they weren't similar – Dick was the aggressor, I don't know. John was the nice guy and Dick ... you'd almost think it was sort of planned that John would send Dick in, 'You go in and bloody fix these buggers up for us' sort of thing. I know it wasn't like that but he was just a great rugby player and the biggest compliment I reckon is he was like a real great New Zealand forward, he was just a great player."

Renowned rugby coach and sportswriter, Peter "Fab" Fenton observed, *"Well, Meads would be a good judge because he was one of the toughest buggers who ever lived. And he was ruthless, too. I mean, he was just uncompromising. He epitomised that All Black pack. So, if Thornett had impressed Meads, he was a bloody good player, because Meads wouldn't ever admit to being impressed by many people. But I don't think Australian rugby realised how much they missed him because they hadn't seen him for very long."*

Jack Pollard summed up Richard's abilities in his book, *Australian Rugby – The Game and the Players*. *"Few stronger men have played for Australia and he remained unruffled by the most torrid exchanges. Dick relished hard, tight forward play, which was John's strength and he had the ball handling skills of his brother, Ken. The Thornett coolness and ability to handle a torrid occasion was more obvious in Dick than in his brothers. He seldom raised a hand in anger. Scrummaging and mauling were his strengths although he was more than useful in the lineouts and was always there to back up. He was a loss to rugby, having proved himself one of Australia's great big forwards when he partnered Rob Heming and his brother to give Australia the solidarity it had needed for years."*

30-Test rugby veteran, and ex-Sydney Lord Mayor, Sir Nicholas Shehadie told the authors of this book, "Dick was a great athlete for a big man, he could do it all, actually. The three of them had great ball sense." As men, he went on to say about the brothers, "A very fine family... a great example to anyone. They were a fine family. So, much credit must go to Mum and Dad. But as I say – 'the Thornetts – what you see is what you get.' The Thornetts, they are great blokes to have behind you."

The third Test against the All Blacks was played on September 22. Richard Thornett ran onto Eden Park as a 21-year-old, although he would celebrate his 22nd year the next day. He had already played First Grade Water Polo for Bronte, won four First Grade premierships with them and represented NSW on four occasions; played First Grade Rugby Union for Randwick District Rugby Union Football Club for four years and won a First Grade premiership; he had been selected for the Australian Water Polo team that competed at the 1960 Olympic Games in Rome; and he had represented NSW in rugby and played Test rugby against Fiji and France in Australia, the Springboks in South Africa and the All Blacks both at home and in New Zealand. It had only been five years since he had finished school. In a few short months, he would be adding another line to his impressive CV.

An interesting article appeared in *The SMH* on September 19, 1962, curiously from Wellington, New Zealand. It said, *"Big Wallaby second rower, Dick Thornett said tonight he had no intention of switching to Rugby League. It was reported from Sydney today that Parramatta Rugby League Club might make a lucrative offer to Thornett when he returned from New Zealand."*

Well-respected journalist, Norman Tasker, reflected on Richard's ability as a Rugby Union player, "Well, he certainly was a fine player. I mean, I first saw him play, I think probably 1959, which was with Randwick when they won the premiership. I covered the 1961 season for *The Daily Telegraph,* which was his first Test-match season, along with about 12 others… he was a superb player, there's just no question about that. Most of his performances were fairly spectacular because that's the sort of player he was. I mean, his great strengths – he was a very big man, comparative to the time, but he was very, very quick. He could run like the wind. He went to New Zealand in 1962 and he was exceptional there, to the extent that Colin Meads wrote he was the finest second rower he had ever played against. I think his great strength was his ability to run at speed for such a big man. He was part of a remarkable family. He was a remarkable athlete, no question about that. And a great achiever, a very high achiever."

Loyalty Knows No Boundaries

Of course, teammates could be great yardsticks as well. Richard and I used to joust, verbally, whenever the Wallabies played, about coaching (the necessity of?), scrums (the pedantry of?) and players (across eras). I was a huge George Gregan fan, but nothing I would ever say could make a dent in Richard's assertion that his good friend and Wallaby, Ken Catchpole, was the greatest halfback ever to walk the Earth, if not the greatest player ever. In the end, I would just throw a comment in somewhere, sit back and smile as Richard unleashed. It was often more enjoyable than watching the Wallaby victory itself. Catchpole said this of Richard: *"He was a very good player. Well respected by teammates and opponents. It's possible my playing career might have been much longer if he was on the field when we played the All Blacks in 1968; my last game for the Wallabies."*

Brendan Morris, Author

In 1999, the NSW Rugby Union assembled a select group of historians, rugby writers and former Waratahs to pick the best NSW team of all time as part of its 125-year celebrations. A third of the Wallaby team who travelled to New Zealand in 1962 were selected in this greatest NSW team of all time. They were: Ken Catchpole, John Thornett, Jon White, Rob Heming and Richard Thornett. Peter Johnson and Rod Phelps were also chosen as reserves. It spoke to what these players had not only contributed to NSW rugby but also their role in revitalising the Wallabies and their international reputation, which many felt was reignited at the beginning of the 1960s.

In June 2001, *The Sun-Herald's* Greg Growden published his "Ten Greatest Wallabies". After John Eales, who topped the list, came Mark Ella, then David Campese. Ken Catchpole came in 4th with Richard rounding out the top ten, an amazing tribute given Richard's short, two-year stint in a Wallaby jumper. Growden commented that Richard, *"...was the most fearless of forwards, having a competitive drive that kept him hitting rucks like a runaway Mallee bull. Old timers can still show the marks from when they made the mistake of standing in front of that bull."*

CHAPTER EIGHT
Rugby League

Kick! He can kick like an army mule –
Run like a kangaroo!
Hard to get by as a lawyer-plant,
Tackles his man like a bull-dog ant –
Fetches him over too!
DIDN'T the public cheer and shout
Watchin' him chuckin' big blokes about –
    A.B. ('Banjo') Patterson (*The Reverend Mullineux*)

Phil Tresidder wrote in his newspaper column towards the end of 1962 under the headline **UNION FEARS LEAGUE BAIT TO THORNETT**, *"Rugby Union's champion forward, Richard Thornett, could probably name his own signing-on fee on the current Rugby League market. It doesn't take much imagination to envisage the impact his 16-stone frame would make in the league ranks. The league's current crop of collar-stud tacklers wouldn't relish his bumping runs."*

As the 1963 Rugby League season approached, there was blood in the water as frenzied league clubs chased rugby talent to bolster their ranks. Michael Cleary and Jimmy Lisle's transition the year before whet the appetites of scouts who were circling. Sydney journalist Dick Tucker wrote that North Sydney were chasing Tony Miller, 33-years-old and in the twilight of his career. Ken Catchpole was also in the Rugby League crosshairs, and even Boyd Blackburn was, the former NSW fullback who had retired from rugby several years prior.

Of the ten clubs in the 1963 NSW Rugby League competition, only Wests, Balmain and Easts were not interested (at least not publicly) in the race for Dick Thornett's signature.

However, North Sydney seemed certain to drop out of the race after Thornett said that he would delay his final decision on which club he would join until the end of the month (January). Norths steadfastly refused to wait for a reply to their huge offer, which was in the vicinity of £7,000. Harry McKinnon, Norths' president said: *"After today, they can forget about us. We are not waiting any longer."* In one rather humorous newspaper report, it was noted that *"A Souths official said last night, 'From what we hear, Thornett is talking in telephone numbers and we are definitely not interested.'"*

George Crawford wrote in his newspaper article that *"St George secretary, Mr Frank Facer contacted Mr J V Comans, who is handling Thornett's league negotiations. Mr Comans yesterday said representatives of Parramatta and North Sydney clubs also informed him they would bid for Thornett. South Sydney and Manly already had made direct approaches to Thornett. Mr Facer said: 'St George will talk football logic with Thornett and explain the advantages he would have in my club. I feel Thornett would like to play in a pack of forwards which includes Norm Provan, Johnny Raper and Ian Walsh. This would give him a big advantage for his start in the league game.'*

WF Corbett's newspaper article also reported that Newtown secretary Jack Carey was hopeful that Thornett's decision would be in favour of Newtown. Canterbury were also in the race.

In the aftermath of the 1962 New Zealand tour, Peter Johnson reflected upon what many Australians felt. "The tragedy of the off-season was the departure of Dick Thornett to Rugby League. (It) wasn't that Australia had no other big, able or powerful forwards, but rather Dick had such a concentration of these qualities (that) he was on the verge of recognition as a colossus of the game. His exceptional talents had already been identified by critics both in South Africa and New Zealand. One top Kiwi scribe, who was too ashamed to be named, admitted to me he already believed Dick superior to anyone in the All Black pack of the previous season and (I had to) contemplate who that encompassed."

Bill Mordey, in *The Mirror* on January 24, 1963, announced, **"Parramatta to get RU forward.** *Dick Thornett, the international Rugby Union forward, is certain to join Parramatta Rugby League Club this season."*

Eventually, Richard decided to join his brother, Ken at Parramatta for a reported £8,000. True to his word, Richard left it until the end of the month to finalise his decision, perilously close to the start of the pre-season. The Rugby League world seemed cautious, even sceptical at what the future held for this young recruit, and another newspaper article at the same time opened with, *"A word of advice to Rugby Union star Dick Thornett on the eve of his entry to league – 'Don't get offside with the players from the start.'"* It wasn't exactly an open-armed embrace welcoming Richard to the fold. He had plenty of doubters and would certainly have to work hard to prove himself.

Well-regarded journalist Jim Webster wrote in his *SMH* article early in 1963, *"Rugby League fans! Meet Dick Thornett, the hulking Rugby Union star who has now joined your ranks. Thornett has not reached football maturity. But last Rugby Union season, especially on the Wallaby's tour of New Zealand, he showed he was climbing towards it in leaps and bounds… Despite his massive frame, Dick is docile – off the field – and very quietly spoken. A bit stand-offish to those unknown to him, he is reserved and speaks in very low tones even when the friendship is made. But he does not need to talk on the football field. He makes his presence felt in his own way. He should make an ideal Rugby League second rower. Coupled with his immense size, his toughness and natural football ability, he has amazing speed and mobility."*

Australian Rugby League was also looking out for fresh blood in its forward pack. Alan Clarkson wrote in *The SMH*, *"England last year showed their superiority in thrashing Australia in the first two Tests. The forwards were our main downfall last season. They looked second-rate against the speed and skill of the English pack. A new crop of forwards must be produced or groomed for the tour. To match England, they must be intelligent scrummagers, tough, speedy and guileful. Australia does not possess this type of forward at present. The only new forward to excite any interest is former Rugby Union international Dick Thornett, a 16-stone second rower with a blend of speed, toughness and intelligence of the type needed."*

One of those who seemed to have question marks over Richard's ability to find his feet, at least early, was St George captain, Norm Provan. A news article that appeared in *The Daily Mirror* detailed that *"Immediately Dick Thornett signed with Parramatta, having rejected the terms offered by St George, Norm Provan, Saints captain coach, went on record with a statement that it would take the crack Rugby Union man a year to learn league. 'It's an open secret that some of the league forwards are going to try and give the newcomer the works. A word of warning* might be in order. The All Blacks, a set of men who would eat any league pack, made this mistake. Thornett left a few of them sadder but wiser men. Apparently, he plays hard all the time but becomes a holy terror if he is stirred up.'"

Provan's sentiments make you wonder; if they thought it would take a year for Richard to find his feet in league, why would they bother chasing someone who'd require 12 months of work to start getting some return for the investment? Not long after, Provan could not have been proven more wrong.

On the other hand, Richard had a huge fan in *The Sun-Herald*'s Alan Clarkson. Richard's first game of league was a pre-season "Craven Mild Cup" game against South Sydney. On March 1 in *The Sun Herald*, he wrote, *"Dick Thornett, the hefty former Rugby Union international, made a deep impression in his first Rugby League match last night before a crowd of 17,750 at Redfern Oval. His great speed and intelligent play helped Parramatta to a runaway 26-4 win over South Sydney in the first round of the pre-season competition. Thornett amazed the crowd with his great speed. On last night's display, he seems destined to be a force in representative matches this season. Rarely has a player switched over from union to league with such smoothness as Thornett did last night. They were amazed early in the match when the 17-stone second-row forward raced down the sideline with the speed of a back. He scored a try in the second half with excellent backing up and went to the ground only twice in the match with the ball. Other union forwards when they have switched to league have taken a number of matches to get the 'feel' of the new code. But Thornett fitted in as if he had been part of the team for several seasons."*

Sixty years later, journalist Norman Tasker also remembers Richard's debut. "I think it might have even been his very first game in Rugby League on a Wednesday night at Redfern Oval. I can't remember who they were playing, but he made a break somewhere about his own 25-yard line, ran the length of the field, whether he scored or not, I can't remember. But it was just such a spectacular run and people were falling off him, a big man running very quickly. And that immediately set him up as a Rugby League player of extraordinary abilities."

Elsewhere, Clarkson called Richard a *"Dream R.L. forward"* and *"... the most exciting Rugby League prospect Australia has had for years."* He went on to say, *"After the drubbing Australia's forwards took from England last year, Thornett's display came like a fresh breeze. Here was a fellow fast, tough and intelligent, who has the size to stand up to England's forwards. He could be an important part in*

Australia's quest for the League Ashes in England later this year." They were prophetic words indeed given how 1963 panned out, but this certainly was enormous praise for one who had only just played his first professional Rugby League match.

Parramatta Rugby League Club joined the New South Wales Rugby Football League (NSWRFL) competition in 1947 along with Manly-Warringah. Despite a succession of good coaches including Frank MacMillan, Vic Hey and Jack Rayner, success on the field was rare and the club struggled, finishing last ('wooden spooners') nine times between 1947 and 1961, including a run of six wooden spoons in a row. On rare occasions, Parramatta showed that they could mix it with the best teams in the competition; their biggest problems had been a lack of player depth and inconsistency. In 1962, and with a record of eight wooden spoons out of the previous ten years, Parramatta knew it had to enter the player market. In 1960, the residential rule was dropped and the transfer system was introduced. Winning had become an expensive exercise and Parramatta had to join in the mad race sparked by 'millionaires' Wests.

Let's go back to when things began to turn for this beleaguered club, with a Thornett right in the middle of things, although his first name wasn't Richard. When Ken "Killer" Kearney accepted a three-year coaching contract in 1962, Parramatta's long-suffering fans hoped he would bring a winning mindset as well as halfback Bobby Bugden and centre Geoff Weekes from the St George juggernaut that had won six premierships in a row under Kearney's leadership. Kearney's former teammate Billy Wilson said, "He must get a great deal of credit for setting up the pattern of success" (which enabled St George to ultimately dominate the NSWRFL competition for eleven seasons). In one sense, Kearney was coming home. He was born in Penrith, attended Parramatta High School and represented the Wallabies in seven Tests from the Parramatta Rugby Union Club. He served with the RAAF in Europe during World War II before switching to Rugby League with Leeds from 1948 to 1951.

When Kearney returned to Australia, he joined St George and from 1952 to 1961 achieved extraordinary success. He was captain of the 1956 premiership team and then as captain/coach, led St George to another five titles. Kearney was a dual International, touring twice with the Kangaroos to England and France; in 1952 and again in 1956/57, the second time as captain. His playing and coaching credentials were impeccable.

In addition to Bugden and Weekes, Parramatta recruited tough Newtown forward Noel Dolton, whose nickname was, frighteningly, "Tombstone", a young five-eighth, Leo Toohey, from South Sydney and two English wingers from Workington Town, Ken Foord and Mike Jackson. They joined Brian Hambly and hooker Billy Rayner, who had both represented Australia at the 1960 World Cup, and 21-year-old Ron Lynch, the captain of Parramatta and a freshly-minted Australian international after he played two Tests during the mid-season tour of New Zealand in 1961. The challenge now for Kearney was to meld the old with the new players to create a competitive team.

Kearney's team had an inauspicious start in 1962 and lost three of its first four pre-season matches – a new competition introduced by the NSWRFL. Of more concern was that Parramatta's win/loss record after the first six rounds of the premiership mirrored the results of previous seasons where they finished with the wooden spoon. It looked like the same old story.

Parramatta played well to defeat Easts 12–9 in round seven and then faced Balmain at Leichhardt Oval on May 20; this game proving to be a turning point for their season. The team 'clicked' from the kick-off. Bobby Bugden and Brian Hambly were inspirational as Parramatta raced to a 23–5 lead at halftime. It was also the debut of Leeds fullback Ken Thornett, who signed on to play seven matches with Parramatta during the English off-season. *The Daily Telegraph* reported, *"Parramatta fullback Ken Thornett played his first league game in Sydney following three successful seasons in England. Thornett took things quietly but showed his class as a player. He fielded the ball beautifully, brought off some solid tackles and showed a turn of speed in some strong breaks with the ball."*

Journalist Alan Clarkson wrote, *"He showed his reputation as one of England's best fullbacks had been earned. A trifle short of condition, Thornett made several strong and fast runs. Whenever there seemed the slightest chance of a break, he loomed into the attack."* Parramatta defeated Balmain 26–17. From there, the team grew in confidence and Ken Thornett demonstrated the skills that had made him a big name with Leeds in England. Ken was a superb ball handler and the Leeds fans named him "Buckets" because of it. At each game, bets were laid as to whether Ken would drop a ball. The bookies rarely, if ever, paid out.

After the first Test loss to the touring Lions on June 9, E.E. Christensen advocated for Reg Gasnier to be replaced as captain after *"playing the worst game of his career when Test skipper."* Christensen wrote, *"Australia could have solved her Rugby League captaincy problem had Ken Thornett been given a run in the State games in Brisbane* scheduled for 20 and 23 June". These games were selection trials for the second Test. Christensen observed, *"...a player with Thornett's knowledge of the Englishmen, plus the respect they have for him, would have made him an ideal leader."* Keith Barnes was skipper and fullback for the second Test and Ken would have to bide his time before making his debut in the 'green and gold'.

Ken Thornett's impact and influence on the Parramatta side were immediate and obvious. Kearney's team were undefeated during his seven games with them and Parramatta were semi-final bound when Thornett returned to Leeds to fulfill the final year of his contract. They were on their way with a renewed sense of purpose and vigour. Parramatta had good, accomplished players and were not a one-man band, however, Kearney's men proceeded to lose five of their last six matches without Ken Thornett at fullback as the wheels began to wobble. Fortunately, they had amassed enough competition points to enter the minor semi-final against Wests. It was to be Parramatta's semi-final debut.

The game was a tight and rugged contest. Wests centre Gil McDougall scored two tries as Parramatta went down 6–0 (back when tries were worth 3 points). Kearney said, "Lack of experience showed here and there when the play got hot. Wests' two tries would not have been scored but for the ball being dropped." Wests went on to meet St George in the grand final. Norm Provan had succeeded Kearney as captain/coach of St George and he delivered a seventh consecutive title with a 9–6 victory.

In his first season, Kearney had lifted the team from last to the semi-finals. He introduced new training methods and greater discipline. Importantly, he was creating an environment that encouraged his players to work closely together towards achieving success on the playing field. Parramatta were now a team to be respected and the humiliation of multiple wooden spoons was a thing of the past as Kearney and his team looked towards reaching greater heights in 1963.

Of all the coaches Richard had across the years in union and league, he probably admired Kearney the most. Richard was always a little wary of coaches as many players of that era were, but he admired Kearney's approach, his wisdom on the game and his forward-thinking. He said, "He really stuck it up me, but he was pretty switched-on to all the conditioning work for his season, and he made me do double the amount of all the blokes. He was a hard trainer and probably took great delight in training me harder as I was probably a little overweight and coming from a union background, I had to earn my stripes.... but it would certainly help me and benefit me in the long term and I admire Ken Kearney as a coach, he was a great coach."

CHAPTER NINE
Parramatta

You are mad if you don't get your full fare off Souths for your return...
Richard Thornett (in a letter to his brother Ken before the 1963 season)

Ken Thornett agreed to join his brother at Parramatta full-time in 1963. He was enjoying the many pleasures of Paris when "….my brother Richard had suddenly burst into the news. He had announced his decision to play Rugby League and had placed all his negotiations in the hands of Mr Jim Comans." Having not played together since the Randwick days, the last of which was 1959, Richard left one brother's side and joined the other in a Parramatta team hellbent on trumping their 1962 results, with the nucleus of a team well-equipped to do so.

While the 1962 season may have been an inkling of what might be coming the next year, given the dramatic turnaround of results and an appearance in the semi-finals, things were developing behind the scenes well before Richard signed on the dotted line with Parramatta. Souths were chasing Ken to join them, and up until very late in the piece were confident that they had him in their grasp for the 1963 season. As it turned out, it wasn't to be. Richard wrote and posted a letter, halfway across the world from Bronte to Leeds, to his brother, Ken. Dated 21.3.62, it said in part:

Dear Ken,
Just a short note, mainly to send you the paper clipping. It is the only time anything has appeared in any of our papers. Joe Maloney rang me (Souths) and told me that it was pretty definite that you were coming home towards

the end of April but it looks as if you are still undecided. This Joe Maloney said to me that seeing that you are going to play with them why don't I? It seemed pretty definite that you were going to play but after reading your letter it still looks very doubtful. Norths are a club that could be interested, but I don't know... The secretary of Norths rang me when he heard a rumour that I was turning so he may be interested in you. I don't know his name off hand. You are mad if you don't get your full fare off Souths for your return and I would go for big money because he was telling me that he had 30 thousand pounds to spend on buying players.

All the best for now,
Richard

Norman Tasker remembers the intricacies surrounding club loyalties, both from a player's and fanbase perspective. "Well, it was more loyal, players didn't hop about from club to club the way they do now. When I started writing (about) it (Rugby League), there was a residential qualification rule. A bloke like Frank Facer, the St George Secretary, would have about 25 people registered (as living at his) home. But technically they had to play within a certain area, all built around the old Sydney tram line. Basically, that disappeared over time, of course. But in that era, 50s and 60s, it was tribal because people stuck with the one club. They just stayed there. Now, they just hop about wherever the opportunity exists. But in those days they were a lot more loyal to their foundations."

Ian Heads, the great journalist, author and historian, painted a picture of Parramatta's home ground in the 1960s when he wrote:

"Uncertain memory suggests that it was on a Saturday afternoon in the late season of 1963 that I first covered a Rugby League match for Frank Packer's Sunday Telegraph. Of the venue, I am sure: it was Cumberland Oval, set in the beautiful Parramatta Park, a suburban ground of the old style, possessing a rickety wooden grandstand on the floors of which fans would drum their feet in rising crescendo to get their team going. In the depths below lay dark and primitive change rooms, where famous players of the calibre of the Thornett brothers, Ken and Dick, would have to settle for cold showers on winter afternoons, owing to the fact that the boys in the early grades had used up all the hot water."

Denis Fitzgerald, a Parramatta teammate of Richard's and ex-club administrator, including CEO, remembers well the tribalism from his time at the club as a player, "When you look back at Cumberland Oval, it was just disgraceful. You had a grandstand that was timber but only held 800 people. That was the only cover. And then there was just timber seating there, about 5 or 6 rows around the perimeter of the ground. The fencing, it sometimes had barbed wire there so that the mad fans wouldn't be jumping over the fence and getting onto the field. So that was just what you grew up with. And other than that, you had to stand up or if you got there early, you could sit down. Most clubs didn't like playing at Cumberland Oval because of some of the outrageous behaviour of the fans but… I think it was exaggerated a little bit."

Visiting teams did not relish the prospect of playing at Cumberland Oval where even walking from the field to their dressing room could be eventful. Mick Veivers joined Manly from Queensland in 1965. The Kangaroo second-row forward remembers the long wire cage on wheels at Cumberland Oval, which was rolled out to provide protection against missiles launched by fanatics in the crowd at opposition players as they left the field. Veivers also recalled being on the receiving end of outrageous behaviour from a fan when walking within the protection of the cage, "…a young fellow urinated on me. That's…. what should we say… that's supporters at the lowest level."

Peter Dimond, the tough Western Suburbs and Australian international winger also experienced the walk through the cage at Cumberland Oval after he had "cleaned up" Parramatta's halfback Robin Gair, dislocating his shoulder. Dimond recalled, "…when we came off at the end, the officials pulled the wire cage over the path to the rooms, but things were still thrown, and I was spat on and so forth." A police sergeant approached Dimond in the dressing shed and told him he should not go to the Parramatta Leagues Club for drinks, such was the safety concern for him and his family. Dimond added, "…by the time I got changed, (my) car and family were at the back door, surrounded by police officers and we drove out with a police car, front and back."

Tony Melrose played Rugby Union for Parramatta and Australia before switching to Rugby League with the Parramatta Eels. Melrose remembers, "…as a young kid, Dad used to take us down to Cumberland Oval." He added, "The old Cumberland Oval was the perfect setting because even then I knew it was like, '… no bastard wants to come here.'"

After that first pre-season game victory over Souths in 1963, Parramatta went on to win three from three of the next preliminary games before losing to St George in the semi-final, 8–3 at the Sports Ground. It was a fabulous start to the season, although there were even better things to come for the Eels.

As if handling a new sport and team wasn't enough, on top of the pressures and expectations that were coming from all directions, journalist, Norman Tasker reported that *"Former Rugby Union forward Dick Thornett is likely to become the main goalkicker in the Parramatta Rugby League team this season. Parramatta coach Ken Kearney said he expected the club to get extra value out of Thornett as a goalkicker... Thornett will take the field with Parramatta's goalkicking responsibilities when he plays his first match on February 28 (1963)."*

As it transpired, the duties were shared, with Ron Willey and Bob Bugden kicking significantly more goals than Richard throughout the season, but it was certainly another burden to carry upon his young, yet broad shoulders.

Parramatta enjoyed significant success in 1963, its greatest since joining the competition 16 years prior. Joining the club with Richard was former Easts centre, Bill Roney. A medical practitioner at Parramatta Hospital, Dr Roney had represented NSW in Water Polo alongside John and Richard Thornett at the 1960 Australian Championships. On Ken Thornett's recommendation, Parramatta paid Leeds a £3,750 transfer fee for Derek Hallas from Leeds. Hallas didn't enjoy Parramatta's "crash and bash" style of play and while he enjoyed living in Australia, he felt the way his new team went about their game plans stifled his abilities.

Fred Pickup, though, another Leeds/Ken Thornett Parramatta convert (although Fred went to Parramatta after a playing stint with Manly), said that "I enjoyed my time there. There were some great blokes. We had a great team. We had a great following, too. (We) weren't a team of champions but (we) were a champion team."

Ironically, this could have played in Richard Thornett's favour when he first took the field for Parramatta. One of the attractions of Rugby League that he would often espouse was its tendency to allow players space to run. This was exactly Richard's game, and run he did, introducing a style of play not often seen in many, if any, Australian Rugby League forwards. The pack also contained outstanding players in ex- or current Kangaroos, Bob Bugden, Ron Lynch, Brian Hambly and Billy Rayner.

A sluggish start, to say the least, saw them win and lose four games from their first eight. After taking an early 2–0 lead against eventual premiers, St George, they went on to lose 51–2 at the SCG on April 6. Nonetheless, in the return fixture on June 1 at the same ground, they went down by a point, 6–5. *The Sun-Herald's* Tom Goodman wrote the next day that *"St George were fortunate to beat Parramatta, 6–5, and so retain their Rugby League premiership lead, after a tense struggle at the SCG yesterday. Parramatta certainly wiped out the disgrace of their complete breakup in the opening round of the competition,"* going on to say that *"Dick Thornett had a splendid all-round game..."* Parramatta was starting to find their combinations at this stage and only lost once more before the finals, to Manly by three points.

Another who came to Parramatta on Ken's recommendation was Ivor Lingard, who played for Featherstone Rovers in England. Reflecting on Richard, he remarked, "Richard was very physical but the crowd wouldn't know it. He had a quiet physicality about him, often unseen, unlike some of the other show ponies. Socially, Richard was a little bit quieter than Ken, although he would always join in for a drink after a game. He would often give you a little side look and throw a comment with a little cutting edge like, 'Oh, you Pommies...' He'd like to have a bit of a go at you like that but it was always taken in fun..." Lingard was attributed with bringing from England and perfecting the famous Cumberland throw, the technique whereby the tackler would grab the arm (or body) of the ball-carrier at the same time as slinging them over their outstretched leg. Ray Price in the 1980s used it very effectively. Fred Pickup, who played with Richard in 1966/67 said, "He was a very intelligent footballer. I used to follow him around the park and scored many tries off (him). He was a thinking forward not 'a bash and barge merchant'."

Richard began attracting attention for his ability as the season progressed. He was no one-trick pony based on a pre-season game against South Sydney. He was a standout in their May 4 trouncing of eventual grand finalists, Wests, 15–4, which also marked his brother Ken's return to the team from England. Richard was also mentioned in Tom Goodman's *Sun-Herald* article, when he *"landed one long penalty goal in the second half."* Alan Clarkson in his *SMH* article on June 10 said of Richard's performance against Canterbury, *"If anyone was to be singled out in the Parramatta team it would have to be second-row forward Dick Thornett...*

PARRAMATTA

Thornett is improving with every match, but yesterday he had his best game since switching from Rugby Union at the start of the season. He played a major part in three of his team's tries and scored one himself after some quick thinking. In one of the scoring movements, he handled the ball three times before giving the final pass."

In Parramatta's July 14-3 victory over North Sydney at Cumberland Oval, he was praised by *The SMH*'s Tom Goodman (who, in April had called Parramatta's forwards "Galloping Clydesdales") for his *"outstanding constructive play which dictated to Norths' forwards."* Kearney later said Dick Thornett was going so well with each succeeding match that he could finish up player of the year. He was even playing like an extra back – in the Newtown game a week later, he raced 35 metres clear to score in their 21-6 victory at Henson Park.

During the season, Parramatta also played the visiting South African Rugby League side at Cumberland Oval on July 30 (only four days before their first semi-final clash against Balmain), but it was an anti-climax with the Eels running away with the game 39-18.

In the game against Balmain, in front of nearly 40,000 fans at the Sydney Cricket Ground, the gods were smiling on the men in blue and gold, with Parramatta the recipients of an almighty piece of fortune that literally fell into the hands of captain, Ron Lynch. Down 4-7, Bob Bugden took a difficult penalty shot for goal, his attempt hitting the upright and falling straight to ground, only for a fast-chasing Ron Lynch to scoop it up and dive over for a try. Bugden's subsequent conversion saw Parramatta the 9-7 victors and into the final against St George, who were still well-entrenched in the midst of their record-setting premiership dominance. Parramatta were regarded as the one team which could topple Saints from their lofty pedestal.

In front of nearly 60,000 fans, the final proved an epic struggle between two of the most powerful packs ever assembled. It featured bone-jarring tackles and Herculean defence, interspersed with flashes of brilliance from Reg Gasnier and the dynamic Ken Thornett. While Parramatta had an outstanding pack, their St George opponents; Monty Porter, Ian Walsh, Kevin Ryan, Norm Provan, Elton Rasmussen and Johnny Raper were world-class. In the end, "Puff the Magic Dragon", Reg Gasnier, proved the difference, slicing through twice to help the Saints grind their way to a 12-7 triumph. Parramatta was five points adrift of their first grand final appearance, a spot taken by St George and eventually won in a controversial match against Wests, 8–3. This was the game where photographer John O'Grady captured Norm Provan and Arthur Summons in a sporting embrace, the famous image, later titled "The Gladiators". Norm Provan, a week earlier, had to deal with that Rugby League rookie that he felt earlier in the season would not have been up to such a contest.

Parramatta's success was reflected in their fanbase, who were revelling in a purple patch in the club's history. The *Parramatta Rugby League Magazine* reported, "*Total attendances for the season were a staggering 374,267, sure-fire proof of Parramatta's great drawing power. The former "Cinderella" was now the belle of the Rugby League ball.*" Three players, Bugden, Rayner and McCall played 20 games that year, but Richard only came in one game behind, 19 games of Rugby League in his first season in the toughest league competition in the world. He also scored five tries during the premiership rounds, one more than his fullback brother, Ken. It said as much about his talent as it did about his toughness.

Fast forward to 1978. An infamous class war, for want of a better term, made its way into the hearts and minds of the Sydney Rugby League fraternity. Wests were losing players to rivals Manly, who were prepared to pay big money to secure the signatures of several Wests' players. Wests' coach, Roy Masters, whipped up a hysterical siege-mentality mind-game based on the script that the entitled Sea Eagles were raiding Wests' playing group, leaving them to struggle with a paltry roster and bank balance. It was a classic psychological "Us versus Them" story that *almost* worked. Roy Masters pushed the 'class distinction' theme at every turn and dubbed Manly "The Silvertails" and Wests "The Fibros".

Of course, the class distinction argument can also be made about Wests themselves during the first half of the 1960s. Wind back 15 years to 1963 and Wests were known as "The Millionaires" for the big money they could offer players to defect to them. They finished the 1963 season as runners-up, the third time in as many years to the same team (St George). The April issue of *Sport Magazine* that year had a special report written by Kenneth Raymond which had the headline **Australia's Costliest Footballer – 8,000 pounds for four seasons – is the latest signing in an all-out competition bid by THE MILLIONAIRES' CLUB.** "*In a military-like campaign, lowly Parramatta set out four years ago to win the Rugby League premiership in 1964. Now, the rich giant Parramatta – fielding some of the highest paid players in the sport – might even take out the premiership a* year ahead of schedule. Even without the reward of a premiership, Parramatta's emergence from the football doldrums would remain remarkable. Today it is among the wealthiest of Sydney Rugby League clubs. It is a real power in the league and its star-packed team draws crowds more than three times greater than those of four seasons ago."

Raymond continued, *"The football fraternity calls it 'The Millionaires' Club'. The latest member of this distinguished company is Dick Thornett, probably the most exciting and certainly the most expensive football 'buy' of recent times. He is a crashing, hard-running, smash-tackling front-row or second-row forward whom everyone confidently expects to prove a sensation in league."*

The list of player purchases continued under the watchful eye of coach Ken Kearney. Rugby League emerged in 1908 from the shackles of amateurism, but thanks to the poker machine revolution in the '60s and a more professional approach by boards at club level, the winds of change were soon to blow hard in terms of player financial negotiations that would change the game forever.

An article in *The SMH* on September 1, 1963, reflected upon the changes sweeping through Rugby League in a financial sense. The article began, *"As the Rugby League playing season ended yesterday, the gold rush to buy players for next season began. During the past week, club officials have been secretly conferring with many top players either to retain their services or secure their transfer from other clubs. One club official said, 'This is the biggest boom ever in league.' Altogether Parramatta are estimated to have spent £20,000 building up a team that went close to becoming this year's champions."*

At season's end, the same newspaper announced that *"Test lock forward Johnny Raper (St George) is the winner of The Sun-Herald's contest to find the 'Best and Fairest' Rugby League player of the season."* It was noted that *"Second-rower Dick Thornett's third placing was noteworthy as this is the first season in league of this former Rugby Union Test star."* It was an amazing first year in the game for the young Rugby Union convert. Ken Thornett was only a little way back in 7th place.

CHAPTER TEN
1963 - Representative Games

Back with my new club Parramatta, I soon adapted myself once again to Australian conditions. We had a strong team with internationals in Brian Hambly, Ron Lynch, Bob Bugden, Bill Rayner, and Derek Hallas from Keighley. Ron Lynch was team captain and Ken Kearney, coach. Dick had settled down well in the second-row position. His early Rugby League experience as a junior was making the transition much smoother for him. He had strong opposition in the selection for representative games from such seasoned players as team colleagues Ron Lynch, (and) Brian Hambly, Queenslander Ken Day and Balmain's Peter Provan. In the Tests against New Zealand, the second-row positions were shared by Ken Day, Brian Hambly and Peter Provan. I ran into the hottest lineup of fullbacks that had been around for some time. Keith Barnes, the former Australian Test captain, Les Johns the fair-headed Newcastle player, and Graeme Langlands, formerly of Wollongong and now with St George, all breathed heavily down my neck.

Ken Thornett *(Tackling Rugby)*

The 1963 representative season was atypical and hectic. Two international teams toured (New Zealand and South Africa) and then Australia undertook a long tour of Great Britain and France. The first part of the representative season was traditional – City vs Country then a step up to NSW vs Queensland, NSW vs New Zealand and then Australia vs New Zealand. Each game was a trial for Australian selection. The South African tour of Australia was an experiment which did not work. There were attempts to establish a competition in South Africa during 1962/63 but this came to nought. No domestic South African competition for Rugby League meant there was no way to develop players there; therefore, there

1963 - REPRESENTATIVE GAMES

was no future for the game. The South African representatives who toured Australia were drawn from ex-Springbok Rugby Union players who were playing for English Rugby League clubs or here in Australia, such as Fred Griffiths.

Phase two of the representative season was all about shortlisting players for selection to tour England and France with the Kangaroos. So, the NSWRFL finals series, City vs Country, two NSW vs Queensland matches and then selection of the team for England and France.

Three Parramatta forwards were chosen to represent Sydney vs Country at the SCG on May 11 – Ron Lynch in the Firsts, and Brian Hambly and Richard in the Seconds. It had been less than two-and-a-half months since Richard's Rugby League debut against Souths in that pre-season game at Redfern, so in context his selection was a remarkable achievement. The City teams were so strong that Richard's brother, Ken, had to be satisfied with a spot on the reserves bench in the Seconds, with Canterbury's Les Johns filling the fullback role in the Firsts and Graeme Langlands in the Seconds. To accentuate Sydney's glut of fullback talent, Keith Barnes was not even considered because of injury. Other members of the City Seconds side included Graeme Langlands, Michael Cleary, Johnny King, Monty Porter, Billy Wilson, Brian Hambly and Peter Provan – an amazing lineup and dignified company indeed for Richard's Rugby League representative debut. The City Seconds side defeated their Country counterparts, 30–8. Six of this City side, including reserve Ken Thornett, would be on a plane to Great Britain with the Kangaroos at the end of the year.

The month of May also held two NSW matches, neither of which featured Richard. The first was against Queensland at the Brisbane Exhibition Ground, a week after the City/Country matches. NSW won the game, 20–10, with Elton Rasmussen and Richard's Parramatta teammate, Brian Hambly, in the second-row positions. A week later, on May 25, NSW took on the touring Kiwi side in front of 50,000 people at the Sydney Cricket Ground, falling by a meagre 2–5 against a team claiming to be the best in the world at the time, with Les Johns kicking one from six attempts – it was close! Johnny Raper strained a quadricep muscle in the first half and *The Rugby League News* reported that if not for the injury *"...he would have picked up the low pass from Reg Gasnier late in the day that could have turned the match into a win instead of a narrow defeat. Brian Hambly came right back into his own and has regained the form which he mislaid after the World Cup tour of 1960. Hambly last year trained himself down fine, but this year has built up his weight and finds himself playing far better football. He had an excellent game against the Kiwis last Saturday and his Parramatta teammate Ron Lynch did likewise."*

The Rugby League News (June 1, 2 issue) commented that *"While the Kiwis can improve on their showing last week, Australia also should be stronger as those men who played last week for N.S.W. and go on to Test selection will have had that extra experience against the Kiwis. Both teams will go into next Saturday's Test with a first-class idea of how their opponents can play and the style of football they will need to match them. The ingredients are there for one of the greatest Tests ever seen on the Sydney Cricket Ground and for the best ever between Australia and New Zealand."*

The Kiwis came knocking as fine international adversaries. The Kangaroos team to play New Zealand on June 8 was announced, with Richard's name missing from the team list. Given his inexperience, this was not a surprise, even given the form he had shown in the three months leading up to the game. Australia won the first Test, 7–3, the mercurial Reg Gasnier crossing the stripe to give the Australians the game, with Bob Hagan adding the extras. Ken Day and Peter Provan were selected in the second row in the one-try-a-piece Test played at the Sydney Cricket Ground.

New Zealand split the first and second Tests with matches against four sides, including against Queensland at Lang Park on June 15, winning two tries to one, 14–10. Brian Hambly replaced Peter Provan in the second Test at Lang Park, Brisbane, but it wasn't enough as The Kiwis tied the series, winning 16–13. "Captain Blood," Billy Wilson, was favoured to lead the Kangaroos to England and France at the end of the domestic season. However, Wilson suffered a severe gastrointestinal disorder leading up to the Test and should not have played. He played well below his best and as a consequence of his poor form and the loss of the Test, Wilson was dropped. He did not represent Australia again. New Zealand scored four tries to three, with New Zealand winger Brian Reidy scoring a hat-trick. The other Kiwi try-scorer was co-winger, Ken McCracken, which said something of New Zealand's game plan that their four tries were all scored by their wingers. McCracken's son, Jarrod, captained the New Zealand Rugby League side and played at the top level in Australia and England, including a stint at

Parramatta from 1996–1999. In a relatively untapped market, by the end of the 1960s and at the start of the '70s, Australia started looking at New Zealand talent. Oscar Danielson, Henry Tatana, Bill Noonan and Bernie Lowther, among others, started taking the field each week in Sydney.

Changing Times

My father was the resident compere at Canterbury-Bankstown Leagues Club at this time, and I would often come home from school to sit with Noonan and Tatana. Funny, even as a youngster, I knew the Australian Rugby League landscape was changing from a relatively cloistered one to one that was more cosmopolitan, exotic and culturally expansive.
Brendan Morris, Author

The second Test result rang alarm bells for selectors. In Tom Goodman's article in the June 23 *Sun-Herald*, he said that in the second Test, *"New Zealand were clearly superior – most markedly in teamwork, with superb backing up and better use of the ball."* On June 23, in *The SMH,* under the headline **Australian Change is Likely**, it mentioned that the *"Australian performance suggested that changes would be made when the third Test team is picked here tomorrow night."* On June 29, the third Test team was announced and Richard's Parramatta teammate, Brian Hambly, was replaced by Richard himself. In addition, Eddie Lumsden replaced Michael Cleary on the wing and Arthur Summons replaced Barry Muir and was appointed captain. Second Test captain Billy Wilson was replaced by Noel Kelly.

Hambly was recalled though when Richard withdrew because of a knee injury sustained in a club match against Manly at Brookvale Oval the week before. As E. E. Christensen reported in *The Sun* on June 26, *"Big second-rower Dick Thornett today failed in his fitness test and withdrew from the Australian Rugby League team to play the third Test against the Kiwis at the Cricket Ground on Saturday. His place was taken by Brian Hambly, who had been dropped by the selectors on Sunday night."* In *The SMH* on June 26, 1963, Alan Clarkson wrote, *"'Dick's chances aren't terribly bright at this stage,' Australian coach-manager Clive Churchill said last night. Thornett and two other players, winger Eddie Lumsden and prop Noel Kelly, will have to satisfy Churchill of their fitness in a special trial... Thornett damaged his knee in Saturday's match against Manly at Brookvale Oval."* Australia went on to win the third Test against New Zealand, 14–0. The Kiwis were a tremendous touring outfit.

Two weeks after the New Zealanders left Australian shores, South Africa arrived with their first international Rugby League team. As Gary Lester highlighted in *The History of Australian Rugby League*, *"The decision to sanction official Tests might have been premature, but South African football was dominated by Rugby Union, and to have any chance of enticing rugby players to the professional code, organisers of the 1963 tour felt the chance to play for one's country would be an incentive. The South African Rugby Union vehemently opposed the introduction of Rugby League, as the late Dave Brown found when he went to Johannesburg in 1962 to help establish the game there. Although there was a sprinkling of players with Rugby League experience, most of the team was made up of former rugby players."* It was an overly ambitious undertaking, to say the least. To round up a group of sportsmen in one sport and try to mould them into players of another, in such a short space of time, was a stretch to begin with. To then fly them 11,000 km to play Test matches against the strongest-playing nation in the world and expect them to compete, was almost unfair.

After missing the New Zealand third Test, Richard was given another opportunity to press his claims for an Australian jersey when he was selected to represent Sydney against the South Africans on July 13 at the Sydney Cricket Ground. In the lead-up to the match, Alan Clarkson in July 9's *SMH* said, *"Performances in the Sydney team on Saturday, particularly (from) five-eighth Len Diett, winger Michael Cleary, second-row forwards Dick Thornett and Graham Wilson, and prop Kevin Ryan could have a big bearing on Test selection."* Of this list though, only one name appeared in the program the following week.

Sydney ran riot, winning the game on a rain-soaked ground, 49–5, with Ken Irvine scoring an amazing six tries. Richard, in his first Rugby League game against an international side, crossed the try line himself. It was a very strong Sydney outfit, more than half of whom would turn out for Australia a week later. South African manager, Mr Irwin Benson, blamed the boggy conditions (and some "pathetic" defence) for his team's demise, although they didn't seem to affect the Australians, and in particular Ken Irvine. Tom Goodman, in *The SMH* on July 14, 1963, wrote that *"Big second-rower Dick Thornett ran 70 yards late in*

1963 - REPRESENTATIVE GAMES

the day to score after Raper had sent him clear." Referee Darcy Lawler helped keep parity as best as he could, penalising Australia 15-2, an amazing statistic given the amount of attack the home side enjoyed. Richard passed his first test at representative level with honours. On the other side of the world, his brother John led the Wallabies in the first Test against the Springboks at Pretoria. It was another red-letter day for the Thornett family.

One week after the Sydney vs South Africa game, on July 20, Richard Thornett ran onto Lang Park as a Kangaroo and triple international in the first Test against South Africa. Richard was 22-years-old. He was Australia's 28th dual-code rugby international. Just as the Wallabies had changed their playing colours so as not to clash with the South Africans on their 1961 tour, the 1963 Kangaroos did similarly, wearing the traditional Australian jersey of blue and maroon (worn by the 1908 pioneers) to distinguish them from the predominantly green jersey of South Africa. After the Sydney demolition, there were fears that this match would be a complete mismatch, but Australia seemed to always maintain control without putting the foot down too hard, keeping the South Africans at arm's length throughout. Australia, captained by Arthur Summons, led 15-4 at halftime but coasted to victory, 34-6 in the second half, scoring eight tries to nil. Writing in *The Rugby League News* on July 27, Barry Muir commented that *"Australia's forwards ran well. Queensland's Ken Day and Peter Gallagher frequently split the South African defence. Dick Thornett, playing in his first league Test showed that he has ability."*

Another significant asterisk was placed against the Australian side that faced the South Africans in the second Test, played at the Sydney Cricket Ground on July 27. Ken Thornett joined his younger brother in the side, selected as a centre. This was not only another tremendous achievement from this remarkable family. *The Rugby League News* (July 27, 1963) heralded that they were *"...the first brothers to do so (play Rugby League for their country in the same team) since New Year's Day, 1912, when Viv and Billy Farnsworth were together in Australia's third Test team in England. The brothers Farnsworth were a real force for Australia, Viv in the centre and Billy at five-eighth as Australia swept to a 33-8 victory. The Thornetts could be equally dominant."* They certainly were, as we would soon discover. A nice sidenote relates to Denis Fitzgerald, which is that the Farnsworths were Denis' father's uncles, so the coincidental connections can certainly be very interesting.

In commenting on his connection with Ken on the field, Richard would recall that in Rugby Union, "Ken, you wouldn't know he was there; it wouldn't be any different, but in the league game, he seemed to be a little bit more --- he'd sort of understand that I'm not going to run the ball up like most of them do and he'd know if he was going to get a pass…he'd call the tune off me because if he saw a break he'd call it and he was more positive or more open towards me about calling. So, you'd hear his voice above everybody else's, and you knew he was there when something was on."

When questioned on whether he looked up to his eldest brother, John, Richard reflected, "I suppose I did. When I was still at school and he was playing First Grade at Sydney Uni, I used to go and watch University play most Saturday afternoons. I played junior rugby in the morning and then I would normally go and watch him play. I'd get public transport to the University Oval or wherever (he played)."

Richard's first Rugby League international with brother Ken, for the Kangaroos against South Africa on July 27, was significant among three other "brotherly" events for him over the course of three different years. In 1961, on June 17, he played his first Rugby Union Test with brother John in the second Test against Fiji at the Sydney Cricket Ground. The next year, 1962 at Eden Park in Auckland, New Zealand on September 22, he and John packed down in the third Test against All Black brothers, Colin and Stan Meads, with both sets of brothers packing into opposite second rows. In 1963, two weeks after Richard and Ken's duo act in Rugby League in South Africa, on August 10 John captained the Australian Wallabies team in the second Test against South Africa in Cape Town, winning 9-5. What a fortnight!

In their book *100 Years of Rugby League*, Collis and Whiticker wrote, *"Captained by Reg Gasnier, Australia posted a record 54-21 win over an outclassed South African combination in the second Test at the SCG yesterday. The aggregate 75 points scored is a Test record, but the match was a 'Test' in name only. In a farcical lead-up to the match unprecedented in Test football, champion Australian lock Johnny Raper trained with the opposition during the week in order to help them with their scrummaging. Australia led 28-3 at halftime with nine different players scoring 12 tries and Les Johns adding nine goals to his try for an individual total of 21 points."*

1963 - REPRESENTATIVE GAMES

Next, South Africa played four matches in New Zealand, losing the first three. They finished the tour on August 10 with a 4-3 victory over New Zealand at Carlaw Park, Auckland. This game is not given Test status because two Australians - hooker Fred Anderson (Canterbury) and second rower Graham Wilson (Newtown) played for South Africa due to the serious injuries the team suffered on the Australian leg of the tour.

The game was never given a chance to grow in South Africa. The influential South African Rugby Union closed every possible avenue, from threatening disqualification to players and teams to using their considerable influence to prevent councils from providing grounds for Rugby League use. Those South African rugby players from time to time switched to Rugby League clubs in England, as the professional game never grabbed a local foothold. The shunning of South Africa by the rest of the world from sporting contact because of their apartheid policy also ensured that Rugby League had no chance.

While all this was happening on the representative front, the NSW domestic season was continuing throughout August. It culminated in the grand final on Saturday, August 24 between St George and Wests, with the Dragons taking the premiership 8-3. There were some refereeing decisions made by Darcy Lawler that created controversy, but ultimately St George managed to win their way to their eighth title in a row following two close games at the end of their season. The very next day after Saints grand final victory, Sydney played Country at the Sydney Sports ground, with Sydney winning a hard-fought tussle 15-10. This game was used as a selection platform for the State side that would play two games against Queensland in the upcoming week. Parramatta's Ron Lynch was captain of the City side with Richard Thornett joining Graham Wilson from Newtown in the second row. Barry Rushworth (Lithgow), Earl Harrison (Gilgandra) and Paul Quinn (Gerringong - Parramatta great Mick Cronin's mother's cousin) impressed with strong performances.

The New South Wales side for the first Queensland match was chosen the night of the City game, and this time, unlike the two games back on May 18 and 25, Richard's name appeared on the team sheet. The day after the City/Country game on August 26, *The SMH's* Tom Goodman reported that *"Fullback Keith Barnes last night was chosen in the NSW team to play Queensland in the Rugby League match at the Sports Ground on Wednesday. Barnes thus will have the chance* to impress the Australian selectors who immediately after the return interstate fixture at the SCG on Saturday will pick 26 Kangaroos for the tour of England and France."

He went on to say that the selectors also *"preferred Dick Wilson to Billy Rayner as the hooker (and) Dick Thornett and Graham Wilson to Brian Hambly in the second row... new candidates are being paraded; some others appear to have forfeited hopes. Reg Gasnier, Ken Thornett, Graeme Langlands, Les Johns and Ian Walsh, who are all thought to be tour certainties, are being spelled. Among others not named last night are wingers Michael Cleary, who yesterday slightly sprained an ankle at the Sports Ground, and Eddie Lumsden, five-eighth Jim Lisle and halfback Frank Stanton."*

NSW were exceptional in that first game on Wednesday, August 28, scoring five tries to one, with Richard managing to score one himself in a strong display. Keith Barnes showed his worth with eight goals in a wonderful performance by the New South Welshman.

There would be changes for the return match on August 31 though, with the Kangaroos' touring side selected that night. In fact, there were nine changes for the second game. The four who retained their places were all forwards – the two props, Kevin Ryan and Paul Quinn, and the two second rowers, Graham Wilson and Richard Thornett. Again, some were rested or injured, while Ken Thornett came into the side as captain, joined by two other tour favourites – Graeme Langlands and Ian Walsh. The *SMH's* writer, Tom Goodman, wrote on August 29 that *"Dick Thornett was superior to Wilson with the ball in his hands: he positioned himself well in attack."* Queensland were much more competitive in the return match on August 31, falling 13-5 after being in arrears only 3-0 at halftime. Richard Thornett made it a double in the interstate series, scoring another try in the win at the SCG. He had done all he could possibly have done as he sat down in the dressing rooms after the match, hoping the selectors would have seen things in his favour when they deliberated later that evening.

CHAPTER ELEVEN
Perspectives

I have seen things you people wouldn't believe. Attack ships on fire off the shoulder of Orion. I watched C-beams glitter in the dark near the Tannhäuser *Gate...*
Rutger Hauer as Roy Batty *(Blade Runner)*

By 1963, Richard had played with both John and Ken in international teams, completing an incredible journey from their days as youngsters swimming in Bronte Baths and at Bronte Beach, playing First Grade Water Polo together for Bronte and football with the locals in Bronte Park. Sports journalist Norman Tasker is well-qualified to comment on the Thornett brothers. In 1960, he began an association with them when he covered either Rugby Union or Rugby League. "Well, I covered Rugby Union for *The Telegraph* 1960/61. Then I covered Rugby League for *The Telegraph* 62/63. Then I went back to Rugby Union (from) '64 onwards and then I was employed by *The Sun* as their Rugby Union man from that point on. So, I had associated with them in both codes through that era. Richard and Ken, I think probably because they played league... had a bit more freedom to run and were very dynamic running players. John was more of a technician – scrummaging, rucking and doing all the sort of unseen things that happen in rugby football. But John was a wonderful leader. The other two were just really dynamic players and Rugby League sort of brought out the best of that because it allowed them more freedom to run than Rugby Union did at the time."

Perspectives on my Father-in-Law

Richard was, at times, an enigma. *Even those closest to him, other than, I think, his immediate family, found him tough to read at times but not in a* *bad way. Personally, I rarely heard him say anything negative about others, but his acerbic wit or dry, straight-faced humour would lead to humorous interactions. As great friend Warren Hurt said as one of the eulogists at Richard's funeral on October 18, 2011, "Dick had a quirky sense of humour and sometimes it was hard to determine if he was joking or on the verge of becoming annoyed. He liked to keep people guessing but it was all a joke, of course!" Richard's brother, Ken confirmed this when he said, "Richard was mischievous and possessed a wry sense of humour."*

There was never any malice in his actions or words, *although I'd laugh sometimes when at his home in Millthorpe in older age, he would bang his fist on the table when my two young twin daughters would make too much noise. Sophie and I didn't even pick up on the fact that the noise was annoying him, but rather than shout (because he didn't want to say the wrong thing), a simple thump on the dining room table would silence the room, Richard would smile and a silent murmur would descend once more. Among many memories I have is Richard's humility and modesty, which bordered on a chronic reluctance to discuss his achievements. I feel this emerged out of a fear that he would be seen as gloating. His brothers, John and Ken, were exactly the same, a reflection of their upbringing; Harold and Marge's lessons had woven themselves into the very fibre of their sons, even into old age. As Kevin Ryan said about Richard: "He just liked (in others) decency, honesty and fairness, I suppose." When Ryan was asked for three words to sum up Richard, he replied. "Decency, Geniality, Dedication." Coming from someone like Kevin Ryan, that said a great deal.*

Three colossal men. *One day in the mid-2000s, not long after Sophie and I were married and staying in Millthorpe with Richard, we travelled to Broula, near Cowra, about 300 km from Sydney and an hour from Millthorpe. We were visiting John Thornett and his wife, Vivienne, on their property, Clarendon for the day. For me, an exciting day beckoned, more so than I had let on. Also joining us were Ken and Willeke Thornett. Of course, this was a chance for the three brothers and their wives to catch up, something I always enjoyed. Privately, though, I was yearning for the opportunity to chat but mostly hear from the three aging yet colossal men in the same room at the same time; of times of yore when the world was a different place. They had* experienced and confronted things I could only read (or dream) about and I wanted to hear it all.

Humility was a Thornett trait. Getting information from Richard Thornett about his exploits would come, if you were lucky, in an almost reluctant trickle, never a flood, such was his humility. His brothers, John and Ken, were exactly the same. Richard would rarely, if ever volunteer stories of his past, so you would have to pry them out gently, like an archaeologist afraid that one false move and the valuable artefact would break. From recollections and tales from the past, as the afternoon wore on, the brothers began to feed off one another's stories, bouncing ideas around as one memory would ignite another in someone else. What began as a bit of a Q & A on my part became a genuine heart-warming and beautiful exchange. Those men of yesteryear were warmed by the memories that came back to them, and it seemed, even just for a moment, that they were back together again, standing on the edge of the Bronte pool and holding once more the rusted chain that kept them from being swept into the sea. At the risk of sounding trite, their eyes lit up and they laughed at and with one another in a way more reminiscent of boys, of young men.

In terms of people I had seen or met, at that point anyway, they spoke of men who were strangers and places foreign to me – Ryan, Rayner, Lynch, Karalius, Tremane, Whineray, Ellis Park and Wembley Stadium, "Whacker" and "Freak" (whom I found out later were Waka Nathan and Frik Du Preez). The greatest, hardest, fastest? Answers came slowly to start, but the trickle became a stream as the sun set.

In the car on the way home, Sophie observed me looking silently out the window. Nothing much was said for the little while it took for us to wind our way out of the drive and onto the road towards Millthorpe, leaving John and Ken behind us in the dust. But we were only leaving them in the physical sense, for emotionally and spiritually, they were still sitting with us in the car, next to youngest brother Richard in the back seat. Sophie at last spoke as she turned and remarked, "You look pretty happy with yourself?"

"That," I replied in a daze, "was the greatest afternoon of my life. Top of the list."

She simply replied, "So, where would you put our marriage on that list?

THE NATURAL

She had me there, as she often did, and I knew that nothing I said at that point would have saved me, so I simply looked out of the passenger window and smiled as we drove on further back to Richard's home. The only noise came from the back seat – a small, almost indecipherable chuckle. I paused, not knowing whether to reply with a chuckle myself, or stay silent. I chose the latter. If otherwise, I was certain that those words, that would remain in her head for eternity, would come back again, more than once, whenever I was perceived to have said or done the wrong thing. As they say, "It is better to say nothing and be thought a fool, than to open your mouth and confirm it."

Brendan Morris, Author

CHAPTER TWELVE
The Kangaroos

When the play was at its toughest, Dick was always there in the thick of the action and with Brian Hambly, Noel Kelly, Ian Walsh and the other forwards on the 1963 tour, more than matched the Englishmen in toughness and skill.
Arthur Summons (Captain/Coach, 11th Kangaroos)

Between 1908 and 1994, Kangaroo tours were the pinnacle of an Australian player's representative career and these tours are part of Australian Rugby League folklore.

Kangaroo tours were tests not only of a player's skill on the field but also the resilience of his mind and body over long and often arduous trips. In the days when international travel was by ship, the Kangaroos would typically be away from home for at least six months; the subsequent availability of air travel shortened the trip to 4–5 months! Once on the ground, the players had to deal with many challenges. The playing schedules were tight with two or three games played in a week, and players would back up for games even when unfit to take the field. Refereeing tended to favour the home teams, and the accommodation was often substandard. And, in comparison to the climate in Australia, the winter in England could be freezing cold, wet and gloomy.

Kangaroo teams representing Australasia toured England in 1908/09 (45 games), 1911/12 (35) and 1921/22 (36). The Australasians – a selection of predominantly Australian players and some New Zealanders – secured the Ashes for the first time in England during the tour of 1911/12 when they won the first Test 19–10 at Newcastle, drew the second 11–11 at Edinburgh and won the third at Birmingham 33–8. The Kangaroos were captained by halfback and dual international Chris McKivat. In 1908, McKivat had captained the Australasian

Rugby Union team in 17 of their 31 games on tour and to a gold medal at the London Olympic Games. In 1909, *The Brisbane Courier*, dated September 2, reported that McKivat "... led the Wallabies in their famous series of matches against the Kangaroos." For agreeing to play against the Kangaroos under Rugby League conditions, McKivat and eleven of his Wallaby teammates were suspended by the Metropolitan Rugby Union.

It would be more than 50 years before another dual international (Arthur Summons), who also played in the halves, would lead the Kangaroos to England and then France.

Evolution of Australian Kangaroo Tours 1929/30–1959/60

- The first "all-Australian" Kangaroo team toured England in 1929/30 and played 35 games including four Tests against Great Britain and a game against Wales.
- During the 1933/34 tour, the Kangaroos played 37 games including three Tests against the Lions, one game against Wales, and one against England in Paris.
- The tourists of 1937/38 played 35 games including two Tests in New Zealand, three in England and two in France.
- After World War II, the Kangaroos toured again in 1948/49 and played 37 matches including three Tests against Great Britain, an international against Wales, two Tests against France and some minor games there.

The tours expanded further into France and the Kangaroos of 1952/53 (40 matches), 1956/57 (28) and 1959/60 (37) played three Tests each against Great Britain and France.

Ten tours of England from 1908 to 1959/60 yielded just one Ashes series victory for Australia. However, it is worth briefly reflecting on the efforts of the 10th Kangaroos (1959/60) before moving on to the path taken by the 11th Kangaroos (1963/64).

The 10th Kangaroos included future Australian captains Johnny Raper, Reg Gasnier, Ian Walsh and Barry Muir, who blossomed under the leadership of fullback and captain Keith Barnes and the guidance of their coach, "The Little

Master" Clive Churchill. Brian Hambly, who toured in '59/'60 and '63/'64, observed, "Well, in '59 we were all young, but we had Keith Barnes there, who was the captain; and Rex Mossop, the vice-captain. Rex had a lot of experience over there. But I found in 1959 – I always say this, and a lot would disagree, the 'Pommies' were a lot better unit then than they were in '63 and we'd just got it nutted out in '59, and in '63 most of us went back in because we were all young in the first tour in '59. I'd say fifty per cent of them went back again (in 1963/64) and we won the Ashes. But if you ask me, the 'Pommies' in '59 were a lot tougher than they were in '63, and we had their sort of style of game. We sort of adjusted to the style of game they played."

In his interview for this book, Keith Barnes described how close his team came to winning the Ashes in 1959. "We won the first Test pretty convincingly actually (22-14) at Swinton, and then we went to Leeds for the second Test and they just beat us there by a point (11-10) and there was a try disallowed from what they claimed was a forward pass….a controversial try that was disallowed, which would have given us the series. And then in the third Test at Wigan, we had the referee by the name of Eric Clay and there was never much chance of us winning that game." The Kangaroos were defeated 18-12 and the Ashes remained in England.

Seven members of the 10th Kangaroos – Reg Gasnier, Brian Hambly, Johnny Raper, Barry Muir, Noel Kelly, Ken Irvine and Ian Walsh – would make up more than half of the touring Test team in 1963. In 2013, Noel Kelly reflected on touring England for a second time. "Our bones had hardened," he said, "and the players backing up for another tour had learnt how to adjust to English playing conditions, which was an advantage in '63/'64." Keith Barnes was Kelly's captain in 1959/60. "The experience they gained playing in England certainly set them up for the '63/'64 side, but there were a lot of newcomers in that side including the Thornett brothers who really complemented the make-up of the team. They were great players, the pair of them."

The achievements of the 10th Kangaroos were a harbinger of things to come.

The 11th Kangaroo Tour of England and France – 1963/64

After Parramatta's successful season, three of its players – Brian Hambly, Ken Thornett and Richard Thornett – were selected to tour England and France with the Kangaroos. Parramatta captain and second-row forward Ron Lynch enjoyed a terrific season but missed the tour. Prop forward John Cleary, who played for Queensland in the 1963 interstate series, told why "... in the last game in Sydney, Queensland versus New South Wales, he broke his collarbone....he was a certainty to go on that trip. And I was very fortunate. I was like... I was a bloke who sort of took his spot." In fact, John Cleary was there on his merits and "Thirsty" Lynch, a lock forward, was replaced at the 11th hour by Kevin Smyth, the lock forward from Western Suburbs.

Ken Thornett, who had mastered English playing conditions when he starred with Leeds from 1960–1962, was impressed with the composition of the 1963/64 Kangaroos. "The Australian selectors performed a wonderful job in assembling this team, with experience, and youth being blended in the correct proportion." Five players from Queensland, three from NSW country and eighteen from the NSWRFL competition were selected for the tour. Barry Rushworth was the youngest at 20 and Kevin Smyth at 29 was the oldest. Richard Thornett was 22 and now a triple-Australian international. It was an extraordinary achievement by one so young.

Richard always did his utmost to look after teammates who needed help. He provided support for his new Kangaroos teammate, Rushworth, just as he had supported fellow Wallaby Rob Heming two years before. Rushworth said, "Dick, as far as I was concerned, was very caring. I was only 20 years of age and Dick was a big, big second rower. I was only about 12 stone (76 kilograms). Over in England, you had to be protected by your forwards. And Dick was wonderful at it." According to Rushworth, Richard was, "...very protective...", during their years together at Parramatta.

The captaincy of the Kangaroos was up for grabs. The leadership role had been akin to a revolving door from 1959–1963. Keith Barnes captained the 10th Kangaroos in 1959/60, at the World Cup (1960) and once each against France (1960) and the Lions (1962). Brian Carlson led Australia against New Zealand (in 1959 and 1961). Barry Muir also captained against New Zealand (1961), while Reg Gasnier and Arthur Summons led Australia for a Test each against the Lions (1962). Billy Wilson had 'C' against his name in the match programs for the first two Tests against New Zealand (1963). Stability at the top was needed – desperately.

At the start of 1963, Arthur Summons (28) and Billy "Captain Blood" Wilson

(35) were the favoured candidates to captain the Kangaroos. Summons became one of the favourites to lead the 11th Kangaroos when he captained Australia in 1962 to victory over Great Britain in the third Test at the Sydney Cricket Ground.

That third Test was filled with controversial incidents and three of them influenced the outcome of the game. First, Australian prop forward Dud Beattie dislocated his shoulder, and knowing he could not continue (no replacements were allowed), decided to take an Englishman with him. He targeted the Lions' fiery lock Derek "Rocky" Turner, who had been dishing out punishment mercilessly to the Australians. Mick Veivers, who played in that Test recalled, "I was there in the second row and was pushing up Dud Beattie, and he just said, 'Mickey, I'm steppin' out here,' and I'm thinkin', *'No we've got to bind,'* I thought, *'Come on! Front rowers!! What's he gonna do?'* And of course, I didn't know that his shoulder was out of its socket, and he stepped around and then with his good arm he tapped Rocky on the shoulder and Rocky came up (from the scrum) and, with his good arm he (Dud) gave Rocky a 'Hello. How are you?' Rocky turned into a seething mass of mad humanity. Dud hit the ground. Well, (referee) Darcy Lawler said (to Rocky), 'You're off,' and then he turned to Dud who had the crook arm, and by that time they'd realised that Dud had sucked him in, 'And when you can get up off the ground, you follow him.' That was it."

The second incident occurred just before fulltime when Ken Irvine scored a try out wide after taking Bill Carson's pass, which was clearly forward. In his book *Never Before, Never Again* Larry Writer mentioned the third incident in this passage: *"Australia squeaked home 18–17 in the third Test, thanks largely to a series of debatable refereeing decisions by Darcy Lawler, who, after sending off Sullivan and Turner for minor crimes, demeaned his supposedly impartial profession by offering advice on how to place the ball to Australian goalkicker, Ken Irvine, who was lining up what turned out to be the match-winning conversion."*

Under Summons' watch, Australia had saved national pride against arguably the greatest and the most menacing Lions team in the history of the Ashes.

Australia would play the Lions for the Ashes again in less than 18 months; this time under English conditions. At the end of the 1963 domestic season, the Australian selectors chose Summons to captain and, to his great surprise, also coach the 11th Kangaroos. Ian Walsh was his vice-captain. The managers were the deputy vice-president of the NSWRFL, Jack Lynch, a premiership winner in 1936 with the undefeated Eastern Suburbs team, and Arthur Sparks, an administrator from Queensland. Coach Summons felt some embarrassment as his coaching experience was nil and he believed it was a cost-saving exercise that led to his coaching appointment.

Summons would say of Richard, "Dick was one of the great second rowers in Rugby League history. In my experience of touring with the Thornett brothers, it seemed that nothing ever fazed them. There were never any disciplinary problems, breakdowns of communications, no disputes or 'blues'. That is not to say they did not enjoy themselves, because they did, like all players did. I am proud to say that John, Ken and Dick are my friends."

Summons was an astute individual and a good leader. He had toured the UK with the Wallabies in 1957/58 (with John Thornett) and knew some of the conditions his team would encounter. He also understood the importance of tapping into the experience of those players who had previously toured England and France with the Kangaroos, so Reg Gasnier, Ian Walsh, Noel Kelly and Johnny Raper formed the nucleus of Summons' 'brains trust' during the tour.

Included in the Kangaroo squad of 26 were five ex-rugby internationals – five-eighth Summons, second-row forward Richard Thornett, winger Michael Cleary, centre Jimmy Lisle, prop forward Kevin Ryan plus two former state Rugby Union representatives – prop forward John Cleary (Queensland) and fullback Ken Thornett (NSW).

For Richard, this would be his fourth international tour in four years in three different sports.

In the 1960s, some thirty years before full-time professionalism was possible in Australia, most players who turned out in the NSW Rugby Football League premiership held a job or multiple jobs that allowed them the flexibility to play at the highest level. In the mid-1960s, Manly-Warringah's Australian representative Mick Veivers worked for the department store FJ Palmer and Sons in Sydney, as did Les Johns. Veivers would go on the road to sell apparel and uniforms to private and public schools. Michael Cleary did well from the other jobs he tried. He recournted: "I was doing three jobs. I was doing Millers (Department Store). I was doing football. I was doing modelling. They'd call me Michelle, and say, 'Get your handbag, lift up your skirt and run,' and all that sort of thing. Well, I made a fortune."

The jobs held by the 1963/64 Kangaroo tourists included sales rep, clerk, driver, farmer and school teacher. Richard was a policeman. He was also the heaviest tourist at 16 stone, and one of the tallest at 6' 2".

Dual international Kevin "Kandos" Ryan was a life assurance representative, which may, or may not, have been of some comfort to his opponents. Ryan's nickname referenced the cement produced at Kandos in the central-west of NSW.

Michael Cleary explains why he was less-than-assured when he faced "Kandos" Ryan on the field of play. "In the '65 grand final, Jimmy Lisle said to me – and we're playing St George – 'Come 'round me. Come 'round me.' We'd only been on the field ten minutes. So, I went 'round him and when I looked up in front of me, it was Kevin Ryan. My head came out my arse when I met him. Five minutes later, Jimmy Lisle says, 'Come 'round me. Come 'round me.' I said, 'Get stuffed.' So, Jimmy had to do a pivot around himself, and he had to run into Kevin Ryan. I couldn't run into him again. But he was….. he was a tough fella, Kevin."

Noel Kelly was a three-time Kangaroo tourist (1959/60, 1963/64 and 1967/68) and one of the toughest men to play the game. When asked about tough men in Rugby League, he said, "Kevin Ryan was a tough man. One of those raw-boned bloody blokes; no matter where you tackled him, one part of his bone would hurt 'ya'."

Ian Walsh played with Ryan for several seasons at St George and saw the effect of his devastating defence. Walsh observed, "He liked to take a man high, ball and all. He'd come in with his shoulder and arms going 'Whack!' and down the man would go on the broad of his back, with Kevin's weight crashing on top of him. After this had happened to him once or twice, an opposing player would see Ryan coming and throw a stupid pass, or even drop the ball on the ground. In attack or defence, Kevin was one of the most feared players in Sydney."

Lions' international, Dick Huddart, who played at St Helens under the legendary "Wild Bull of the Pampas" Vince Karalius, and with Kevin Ryan at St George, said Ryan and Karalius were similar because "each was feared and uncompromising and had a strong mind, and both enjoyed success after football – Kevin as a barrister and politician, while Vince made millions in the scrap metal business." Both men were also devout Catholics. Karalius was described by Alex Murphy as "like having one of the Kray twins as your best mate, he was that hard."

Karalius would come face-to-face with the Kangaroos soon enough.

As Richard and Ken Thornett prepared to leave Australia, their brother John was a world away, preparing to meet challenges of his own. *The Rugby League News* reported, *"The Thornett family will enjoy a unique sporting distinction when the Kangaroos leave on Saturday. Ken and Dick will represent Australia at Rugby League in England while brother John is leading the Wallabies in South Africa."*

The brothers Thornett were on a quest for the Holy Grail of their respective rugby codes. The world was watching.

The arrival of the 11th Kangaroos was eagerly awaited in England. A newspaper article by Leslie Woodhead appeared in *The Liverpool Echo* on September 7 under the headline **Personalities Who Can Make Aussies' Tour A Success.** He wrote, *"There is no team quite like the Australians for whipping up interest, and this year's party is laced with personalities who look certain to be big favourites with the English spectators. Some have previously been seen in action over here; others are completely newcomers, and on the eve of their arrival it is an opportune time to introduce some of the men who will be wearing the famous green and gold of Australia this season."*

Woodhead went on to single out Richard and Ken Thornett, Mike Cleary, Ken Irvine, Peter Gallagher, Earl Harrison, Les Johns and Noel Kelly. Woodhead listed the jobs of the *"colourful tourists"* and ended with: *"But their main role during the next couple of months will be as public entertainers – a job for which they are well-qualified and very soundly equipped."* Woodhead's observation proved to be well-made. Western Suburbs winger Peter Dimond remembered, "By the time we got to England in 1963 we had experienced players and new thinking to go with the champions we had. What was really important was that with Arthur at the helm, we took over our own coaching and developed our own game; a game based on speed."

According to the managerial report, the Kangaroos were given an *"unforgettable send-off"* from a large crowd of family, friends, supporters and Rugby League officials, which *"made a deep and favourable impression on all members of the party."* The flight to England was long, stopping to refuel at Perth, Singapore, Bangkok, New Delhi, Karachi, Beirut, Cairo and Rome. The flights were uneventful, although the legendary radio commentator, Ernest "Tiger" Black, reported a close encounter during a stopover. "Some members of the party had a rugged 20 minutes when trapped in a lift at Singapore Airport. Jack Lynch, Mike Cleary, Dick Thornett, Peter Dimond, Kevin Smyth, Earl Harrison, Ken Irvine, Noel Kelly and I were in the lift with the temperatures well over 100 degrees. The boys all were hoping they were in England and they would not have cared how cold it was." Thankfully, the Kangaroos, Lynch and Black were freed from the sauna-like conditions in time to make their connecting flight. The aircraft carrying the 11th Kangaroo team touched down in London on Sunday, September 8, 1963.

The Kangaroos' playing schedule was 36 games over four months including three Tests each against Great Britain and France.

CHAPTER THIRTEEN

England

The sure way to miss success is to miss the opportunity.
   Philarete Chasles

Barely 18 months after the success of the Lions in Australia, *The SMH* reported on Sunday, September 8, 1963, that concerns were being raised in England about the makeup of their forward pack for the Ashes series. "*England's selectors will be more worried about forwards than backs when they meet in four weeks to name the home side to play Australia at Wembley in the first Rugby League Test. Britain's problem is the replacement of experienced men who have reached the close of their international careers. In many cases, their replacements or potential replacements have yet to prove themselves of Test class. Hardest man for Britain to replace may be Brian McTigue, the astute forward leader and ball distributor who is slowing to a walk these days. Little more than a year after the tour to Australia, where Britain's pack did so much toward winning the Ashes, the whole front row is expected to be replaced for the Wembley Test. Lock forward Vince Karalius is attempting a comeback to big football but may find his lack of pace now a handicap.*"

The stakes were high, as were the expectations, for both teams to deliver an Ashes-winning series.

Upon arrival, the team had a short stay in London. A press report on an early training session appeared under the headline **Kangaroos Train on Wet Ground**. "*The Kangaroos trained for the first time yesterday with rain on the ball, in conditions under which they will play most of their games in England. The English football is slightly smaller and more difficult to handle than the standard Australian ball. Wet grass at London's White City Stadium and a slight drizzle during the training period made it harder to control. Some of the newcomers, including five-*

eighth Earl Harrison, made handling errors. They snatched at passes instead of drawing the ball into the body in the correct wet-weather technique. The forwards ran and passed impressively in their first full-scale workout. Ian Walsh, Noel Kelly, Dick Thornett and Johnny Raper shone in crisp, short-passing bursts. Peter Gallagher and Kevin Ryan were a little behind them, with captain/coach Arthur Summons driving the big men to something approaching match tempo. This final training run in London has given the team confidence as they leave this morning for their Ilkley headquarters in Yorkshire."

This training session confirmed just how important it was to understand and adapt to the playing conditions in England. The experience of the Kangaroos who had previously toured England – Kelly, Raper, Walsh and others – would be a key factor in the team's success. Richard, a natural athlete, adapted quickly to the conditions as he did to most situations during his sporting career.

The team left London by train on Thursday September 12 minus Johnny Gleeson who was in hospital due to a severe reaction to his smallpox vaccination. Gleeson was expected to rejoin the team before the first Test at Wembley. The rail trip took four hours to reach Leeds in Yorkshire. The Kangaroos then travelled 18 miles by bus to Ilkley, which was to be their base in England.

Ilkley was little more than a hamlet for centuries until the mid-1800s when it rose to fame as a spa town. By the mid-19th century, there was growing belief in the health benefits of cold water and bathing that led to the development of grand hydro hotels, with wealthy visitors including Charlotte Bronte and Charles Darwin arriving by coach to 'take the waters'. Darwin spent nine weeks in Ilkley around the time his *Origin of the Species* was published. Ilkley started off being an ordinary Dales village but as the water cure became popular, it became gentrified.

In 1963, Ilkley had a population of more than 18,000 people, was 30 minutes by train from Bradford and Leeds, and its training facilities were excellent courtesy of the local council.

In his book *The Kangaroos*, leading journalist and author Ian Heads, wrote, *"There was some early awkwardness in Ilkley, the result of published criticism by a couple of players after the 1959 tour that the town was a 'dreary old place,' but the '63 Roos generally found the quaint Yorkshire village a happy operations base."*

The Kangaroos stayed at the hotel that lodged the 1959/60 tourists. Ken Thornett recalled, "We stayed at the Troutbeck Hotel, Ilkley, a quaint old stone mansion but not much heating. Beautiful views of the Moors and up to the Cow and Calf Rocks." Manly-Warringah's Frank Stanton shared the unheated attic room with Ken Thornett atop the Troutbeck Hotel. When interviewed for this book, he said, "Ken was a mentor to me and we roomed together at the Troutbeck, which was not far from Leeds. Ken had so many mates from his playing days there that I didn't see much of him (outside of training and match days) and when I did, he would spend time checking his share portfolio, which was an unusual pursuit for a Rugby League player at that time."

Not everyone was enamoured with the environment.

According to Michael Cleary, "Morticia from the Addams Family would have thought it was a palace." There was no heating until a coin was placed in the gas meter. Cleary said, "I knew how to rort the gas meter. They had gas meters in all the rooms. So, I bloody broke the locks and recycled all the pennies in there. So, I got free heat. Free."

In the foreword to Ian Heads' book, *The Kangaroos,* Stanton described the facilities that the team shared. *"The one bathroom and toilets available to our party of 28 was two floors below, a long cold walk on a winter's night. The times after training were the worst. You'd be freezing cold and very likely soaking wet, standing in a great long queue waiting for your turn in the shower, and praying that the hot water would last."*

Michael Cleary told this story. "I remember coming back from training one day – we were out of water and someone – it might have been Dick – said, 'There's never any bloody hot water in this place. What's wrong with it? Fair dinkum!' And the manager yelled out, 'If you didn't bathe every day, there'll be plenty of hot water!'"

Noel Kelly survived the Troutbeck Hotel experience during the '59/'60 and '63/'64 Kangaroo tours. When interviewed in 2017 on the *Rugby League Digest* podcast, he said, *"We were stuck at Ilkley, 22 miles out of Leeds while senior officials would fly in on first class and stay at an upmarket hotel. We all liked Ilkley. (But) We were just so far from everywhere. There were rats. We had 26 players locked up in a bloody room. Locked up in a pub with nothing in it."* Perhaps jokingly, he added, *"We had to burn a wardrobe one night to stop freezing."*

Another veteran of the 'Trouty' was Ian Walsh who roomed with Kevin Ryan. "Our first job was to summon the carpenter and have him force the window down. I don't think it had been opened in the four years since the last visit by the Kangaroos. Kevin was a fresh air addict and once the window was down it stayed that way, through the snow and sleet, for the whole of our three months in Ilkley."

On top of everything, Kevin Ryan took it upon himself to provide 'pastoral care' for his teammates by becoming their gatekeeper and challenging anyone who dared to enter the Kangaroos' sanctuary. Michael Cleary said, "Kevin Ryan at that time was very religious. He used to keep guard by the stairs and wouldn't let us take 'birds' up to our room. Kevin Ryan was a very straight shooter; a strong Catholic."

Michael Cleary's roommate, Queensland prop forward John Cleary (no relation), said he did not know whose idea it was to put a prop and a winger together in the same room. "A front rower and a winger wasn't a good proposition." Although John admitted that his namesake, "... had all the good gear, he had perfumes which they used to use and all the powder. Yeah, he was a good groomer. He had all the good clothes, and I wore a couple of his $1,000 coats. They were pretty good."

Richard roomed with his Parramatta teammate Brian Hambly. Their fellow Kangaroo, Peter Dimond, observed that Richard and "Grumpy" were inseparable both on the field and off it. Brian Hambly said of Richard, "Dick was always my second rower, and well, Dick was a good running forward and big bloke, had plenty of skills, football skills. I suppose that comes through with his Water Polo. Oh, mate, they (Ken and Richard Thornett) were good fun, good blokes, good to play football with, mate. You can play football and some blokes want to throw the towel in. Blokes like the Thornetts wouldn't do that, mate. If the game's tough they're in there doing their best with you. And he's laid back, isn't he, Dick?"

Ken Thornett was revered in Leeds, where between 1960 and 1963 he had established himself as one of, if not the, finest fullback/s in England. Christened the "Mayor of Leeds" by the Kangaroos, Ken facilitated the purchase of a fleet of cars for his teammates. "A few of us bought cheap cars from Brian Shaw, ex-England loose forward and Leeds teammate. I think I got the worst deal being an old mate. The car looked good with beautiful feather-padded seating and walnut instrument panel. It was 6 cylinders but shortly after fired on just 4!" He said it was common to see players pushing one of their clapped-out vehicles to get them started.

Michael Cleary took a different approach to procure a motor vehicle. "I remember I bought a Humber Hawk. I went to auction. Paid £23 for it. No one wanted a six-cylinder car; (but) petrol (in England) was only three shillings a gallon. In Australia it was eight shillings a gallon. So, I bought this Humber Hawk and I had it for three months. I sold it for £12.10 when I left. It got me around everywhere."

The Kangaroos settled into a routine of training, team meetings, physiotherapy and long bus trips to and from their games, a cycle which would continue throughout the tour.

They were ready for the opening game on September 14. Richard was included in the forward pack to play Warrington and when Australia kicked-off in front of 20,090 people, he chased hard and fast to make the first tackle of the tour. The Australians were getting the better of the fiery forward exchanges with Noel Kelly receiving a number of cautions before he was sent from the field after 28 minutes of the first half. *The Guardian's* correspondent Harold Mather proffered, "*The Australian Rugby League team started its campaign ...brilliantly and disappointingly.*" He wrote, "*Whereas it played much excellent football and fully deserved its victory, several of its members showed temper not in keeping with any side, especially one on tour.*" Richard and "Kandos" Ryan received cautions for tactics, which, "*...coming from players good enough to be selected to represent their country on tour, were unbecoming.*" The *Daily Mail* said, "*...the potential of the team in attack was clear...*" and the Kangaroos had "*...hurled down the gauntlet...*" adding, "*They are prepared to challenge Britain on any terms ... at Rugby League, fisticuffs or both.*" The article concluded, "*That the Australians will be formidable opponents in the Tests seems indisputable. That they have little to learn in the less praiseworthy tricks of 'headhunting,' obstruction and stealing the ball in the tackle is also beyond question.*" Kangaroo manager Jack Lynch was quoted as saying, "*I don't think it was an unduly rough game.*"

A downside to the Kangaroos' victory was the injury to Reg Gasnier who was to be sidelined for six weeks with a badly dislocated finger. The Kangaroos won the match 28-20. They gave a signal that they were prepared to be uncompromising when the going was tough and could also switch gears to play an open style of Rugby League to utilise their brilliant backline.

Over the next four weeks, the Kangaroos played another nine games before the first Test at Wembley. As the tour progressed, the Australians were becoming concerned about the reputation that was building around them for brawling rather than good football with *The SMH* reporting, *"The Kangaroos are trying to curb the more hot-headed players."* According to a Huddersfield forward, who played in the 6–5 loss to the Kangaroos in game 2, *"The Australians boxed rather than played football."*

The Australian War Cry

From 1908 to 1967, the Australian team performed a war cry before Tests played in England and France. It was developed after war cries had been performed on tours of England by the New Zealand All Blacks in 1905 and the New Zealand All Golds in 1907. The war cry was first performed in 1908 when the Kangaroos arrived at Tilbury Docks in England. It is believed that the war cry was derived from an Indigenous chant on Stradbroke Island, Queensland, Australia:

Wallee Mullalra Choomooroo Tingal
Nah! Nah! Nah! Nah!
Cannai, Barrang, Warrang, Warrang
Yallah, Yallah, Yallah, Yallah,
Ah! Jaleeba, Booga, Boorooloong
Yarnah meei, meei, meei
Meeyarra, Meeyarra, Jeeleeba, Cahwoon,
Cooeewah, Cooeewah, Wahh, Wooh.

Translated into English, it means:

We are a race of fighters, descended from the War Gods
Beware! Beware! Beware! Beware!
Where we fight there will be great bloodshed
Go! Go! Go! Go!
We are powerful, but merciful. Are you friends?
Good! Good!

THE NATURAL

The Kangaroo is dangerous when at bay.
Come on. Come on. Death.

Wally O'Connell, a player on the 1948 tour to England and France, said the war cry had made life easier for the poorly-paid players.

"It was pretty hard to get food and we didn't have much money so we would put on the war cry at nightclubs, and they'd respond by looking after us," he explained.

Johnny Raper enjoyed performing the war cry, which he did with his teammates on three Kangaroo tours of England and France. In a 2003 interview he said, "The English used to love it but the French even more. It was like performing on stage. It was very fearsome; you had to do the actions of an Aborigine. It livened you up, there's no doubt about it."

The war cry was last performed by the Kangaroos in December 1967 in France.

On September 18, the Australians suffered their first defeat of the tour against Yorkshire, going down 11–5 at Craven Park, Hull. The Kangaroos could have won this match if their goalkickers – Summons, Irvine and Richard – had been on target. Most were from positions close to the posts.

An *AAP* report appeared on September 20 which addressed rumours that were circling in Rugby League. "*The Kangaroos' managers, Messrs Jack Lynch and Arthur Sparks, have no intention of bringing in an English coach to help plan tactics during the side's tour of England. Nor do they intend to co-opt the services of former Australian international Arthur Clues for the present, Mr Sparks said today. Rumours buzzed in English circles, after Wednesday's defeat by Yorkshire, that the Kangaroos might call in Colin Hutton, who accompanied the last British team to Australia. The Australians view these rumours and press querying of Arthur Summons' ability to prepare the team for the Tests as propaganda aimed at their morale. As Mr Lynch said after the Hull defeat, the Kangaroos have realised they are playing football in England under English conditions.*"

This misinformation was clearly an attempt to destabilise the Kangaroos and put pressure on Arthur Summons.

Ken Thornett referred to the importance of Summons' leadership in his book

Tackling Rugby. *"He held us together over a long period and exhibited the finest attributes of team leadership."* Brian Hambly made the following observation, "Yeah, well Arthur didn't play much football, but he was a good motivator. He gives you a talk before the game on motivation and made you really enthusiastic. Yeah, he was pretty good, Arthur, he done [sic] a good job."

Johnny Gleeson re-joined his teammates and was able to train lightly for the first time since his release from hospital where fluid had to be drained from his spine.

In their next game, the Kangaroos defeated Leeds 13-10 at Headingley, in what Ian Heads described as, *"...basically a goalkicking shoot-out between Lewis Jones and Graeme Langlands who kicked five goals each."* Jones, uncharacteristically, missed a further eight shots at goal. It was Michael Cleary's long-range try that proved the difference between the teams. A crowd of 16,641 gave Ken Thornett a hero's welcome when he led his team out. Ken was visibly moved when he was presented with *"a silver tea service from the Leeds supporters' club in recognition of his selection as player of the year for Leeds in the 1962-63 season."*

Noel Kelly was selected at prop to play against Lancashire on September 25, his fifth game in 12 days. The team was Johns, Dimond, Rushworth, Langlands, M. Cleary; Harrison, Muir; Kelly, Walsh, Gallagher, Day, R. Thornett, Raper. The Kangaroos lost their second match against a county in seven days when at Central Park, Wigan, Lancashire beat them 13-11. Richard set up a try when in one motion, he knocked the ball on, regathered after it came off a Lancashire player and then flicked an inside pass to Peter Gallagher who sent Les Johns in for a try and a 5-3 lead to Australia. Once again, luck went against the Australians who scored two tries and missed a third in the last 20 minutes when Ken Irvine crossed the line just before fulltime after a 50-metre run, only for the try to be disallowed after he stepped into touch trying to avoid his opposite winger, John Stopford, the Great Britain international. In addition, Les Johns hit the post with one kick. Lancashire's forwards Jim Measures and Karalius played strongly and were in contention for Great Britain's first Test team to play at Wembley on October 16. Despite the loss, the Kangaroos' management were most impressed with the Australian display. *"Best and most improved display so far on the tour. Should have won,"* they wrote in their match report.

Richard had established himself as a mainstay of the Kangaroo forwards.

The next game was against the powerful St Helens, rated the best club in England and this match-up would provide a guide to Australia's chances in the first Test. Strong-running Dick Huddart was considered a danger man for the Kangaroos. Huddart had developed a good combination with St Helen's ball distributor John Tembey, while Ray French, his second-row partner, was a former English Rugby Union international. The Kangaroos chose a strong pack for this game. A newspaper report stated, *"Dick Thornett is playing so well he could overshadow Huddart in the loose."* A preview of the match read: **ILKLEY**, *Saturday Sept. 29 (AAP) – "Summons and his men have no illusions about the difficulty of their task, even though St. Helens will be without another major asset, Test halfback Murphy. Victory against St. Helens would give the Kangaroos the boost in morale they need to carry them to a Wembley Test win. The only Australian win over the famous Lancashire side in more than 30 years was the brilliant 15-2 triumph of the 1959 tour. They went on a week later to win the first Test."*

The Kangaroos were hoping history would repeat itself. And it did. The Kangaroos showed they were coming into form at the right time when they beat St Helens 8-2. *The Daily Express* commented, *"The Aussies' chances of shaking Great Britain increased 100 per cent with this new-look Kangaroo style against St Helens. For the first time this tour they introduced an ingredient frequently lacking in Aussie outfits — craft"* and *"Coupled with this was better cohesion and solid, sure tackling from the forwards and an all-round determination to open out at every opportunity."* The Kangaroos' pack more than held its own against the St Helens 'power' pack, with their star forward Dick Huddart tackled out of the game by the Australian forwards. This prompted the Australian managers to report, *"We feel they have acquired the necessary 'know how' to handle English forward play."* Huddart's biggest impact on the game was in the 15th minute when he fell across the outstretched legs of Kangaroo captain Arthur Summons, causing him to leave the field with a serious knee injury.

Barry Muir was sent off in the dying minutes of the game for taking a swing at the opposition halfback, Heaton. Peter Dimond crash-tackled the St Helen's 15-stone forward John Tembey, which according to reports from England, should have bounced him out of the front rower's union and first Test berth because *"In England, a front-rower knocked unconscious by a winger is regarded as too soft for Test football."* Peter Dimond remembers what happened next. "The crowd did not like seeing their hope felled and started pelting coins onto the field while I was copping my caution. They booed everything I did after that and kept pelting coins. If we could've gathered them up after the game, it would've been a nice bonus for us all."

As a result of his knee injury, Arthur Summons was unfit to play for a long period, which was a blow to Australia's chances in the Ashes series. His deputy, Ian Walsh, was elevated to the captaincy of the Kangaroos as they looked ahead to the tough assignments in the lead-up to the first Test.

The tour was not all training, strategising, playing and cold water. "Tiger" Black, who was travelling with the Kangaroos, reported in *The Rugby League News*, "*If anyone back home had not guessed, Mike Cleary is the life of the Kangaroo party. The first thing Mike did when the team settled in the 'Trouty' was to act as curator and select a cricket pitch. When it comes to cricket, Mike still retains his amateur status and no big signing-on fees are likely to be coming from the Lancashire League. Mike rounded up the Troutbeck electric mower and quickly cut a wicket and has organised a roller which is used when anyone needs an additional workout. The wicket is on a former tennis court, so the turf is quite level. I don't know whether they ever get Les Johns out but every time I look over that way, Johns has the bat and is slashing away. Added interest is given (to) the cricket by the close proximity of a glass hothouse, which so far has not gone off.*"

In addition to Richard and Michael Cleary, several of the Kangaroo tourists were highly skilled at other sports. Reg Gasnier (NSW junior representative) and Les Johns (prominent Sydney First Grader) were well-credentialled cricketers, and dual rugby international Kevin Ryan had been a Queensland heavyweight boxing champion who came close to qualifying for the 1960 Rome Olympics. For Kangaroo prop forward John Cleary, it was the sporting prowess of Richard and Ken that really stood out. "Dick was a big bloke of course, and he represented Australia in not only Rugby Union and Rugby League but also in Water Polo. But mate, the most exciting thing I ever saw with the two boys (Richard and Ken Thornett) was when they came to the Troutbeck Hotel in England which was in Yorkshire, of course, at Ilkley, and a bloke by the name of Fred Perry…he was 10 times (winner of 10 Majors including 8 Grand Slam tournaments and 2 Pro Slams) tennis player who was a world champion, also, table tennis player. So, we had a table tennis table in the sports room of the Troutbeck Hotel and… and of course

Fred was in his late-40s, his early-50s and still a great player, but Kenny and Dick took him to 21 both times. They just about took him to pieces. They were the greatest sportsmen I had ever seen."

Cleary added that Richard was just a phenomenal athlete, which extended to his prowess on the ski slopes of France. "We had an opportunity to go skiing when we were in France, and of course I elected to go to Lourdes because I'm a Catholic and all the Catholic boys went to Lourdes." Cleary continued, "Dick and Ken and a few of the others… went skiing. When they came back, I said, 'How'd you go?' and they said 'We had a bloody terrible time. Nobody could ski. The only bloke who skied and had never done it before was Dick. He just got straight up and skied.' Unbelievable. Unbelievable. Just (a) natural, natural bloody sportsman."

Johnny Gleeson was now back to full health and played his first tour game against Featherstone Rovers. Both teams scored three tries as the Kangaroos suffered their third loss 23–17. Featherstone's Don Fox, brother of Lions' international Neil, scored 17 points and their little stand-off, Ivor Lingard, was outstanding. Lingard's performance caught the attention of Ken Thornett who advised Jack Argent (president and founder of the Parramatta club) to sign him. Argent took Thornett's advice and Lingard joined Parramatta in 1964, bringing with him a unique tackling technique, which acclaimed journalist E. E. Christensen named "the Cumberland throw". According to *The SMH* report of October 4, the pleasing features for the Australians, *"…were the brilliant play in which Mike Cleary took his only real chance to score the first try and the immaculate catching of Johns at fullback."* Barry Rushworth made an impression when he handled three times before scoring a *"glorious"* try beside the posts.

The 'club notes' in the Featherstone Rovers match program stated, "*We extend a warm welcome to this 1963 side and look forward to an enjoyable game. Great interest is centred on this tour in that with Australian football going through a transitional period, many of these players are comparatively unknown and as an unknown quantity, they're capable of inflicting surprises and it may well turn out they will have a most successful tour.*" The Kangaroos continued to surprise and captivate the English crowds, and they would deliver a major surprise in the weeks ahead.

The game against Oldham was next. A press report of the game appeared on October 6. *"Australia defeated Oldham 12–4 with Johnny Raper, playing at five-eighth, the star."* The report continued, *"Dick Thornett combined better than second-row partner Ken Day but also showed a tendency to go too far himself."* Richard initiated an attacking play when Oldham's Smethurst, who had been niggling at Gasnier and Langlands all game, was crunched by two Australian forwards and *"The ball came loose and was thrown quickly to Dick Thornett, who sent his backs away with a right-wing overlap that seemed certain to bring a try. But as the referee turned to follow the play, he saw Langlands step in and hit Smethurst whose mouth was split by the blow."* Play was stopped and Langlands was sent off. Gasnier put the game beyond doubt with a try in the last minute of play. The match reports in the *Sunday Express, Sunday Mirror* and *Sunday Telegraph* pointed to lost opportunities through bad finishing by the Kangaroos. The Observer said, *"The match could hardly have given the Kangaroos confidence for the first Test. They moved the ball smartly but their finishing was bad and they left alarming gaps. Again, there were unseemly incidents, mostly the result of over-eager tackling and provocation from the crowd."* In a telling statistic, the referee awarded 20 penalties to Oldham and just 7 to the Kangaroos.

Only two changes were made for the next match against Leigh at Hilton Park. Michael Cleary replaced Peter Dimond and Brian Hambly came into the team for Ken Day. The team selected was considered a strong pointer to what might be the starting lineup for the first Test at Wembley: K. Thornett, Cleary, Langlands, Gasnier, Irvine, Harrison, Muir, Gallagher, Walsh, Quinn, R. Thornett, Hambly, Raper. Australia defeated Leigh comfortably, 33–7, before a crowd of 9,625.

The Kangaroos won the 7th of their 10 lead-up matches to the first Test with a 23–10 victory over a combined Hull/Hull Kingston Rovers XIII. However, the victory came at a cost with the fearsome Kevin "Kandos" Ryan ruled out for an extended period. "Kandos" was injured by one of his own when Noel Kelly fell across his legs, severely damaging the cartilage and ligaments in his knee.

The Australians found themselves in an England that was breaking the shackles of conservatism. The country was in the throes of a cultural revolution that was beginning to sweep through the Western world. The "Swinging Sixties" were really starting to swing in London with art, music and fashion flourishing. The view, at least in the Western world, was moving from monochrome to an explosion of vivid colours.

The Beatles were on their way to becoming the most influential pop/rock act of all time. "Beatlemania" was born when the "Fab Four" played the London Palladium on October 13, 1963, and some of the Kangaroos were there – Ken Thornett and his roommate Frank Stanton among them. Ken said, "One evening we went to the London Palladium to see *The Beatles* perform. We had great seats in the first two rows." Frank Stanton remembered the concert as a highlight and knew *The Beatles* were special "… although we didn't know how major they were until we got home."

Johnny Gleeson attended the concert and said it was the non-playing highlight of his tour. He went with his roommate Les Johns and Earl Harrison. They were wearing their Australian gear, so they were allowed to go around backstage and meet all the members of the "Fab Four". Johnny said, "The players actually sang a few verses of 'She Loves You' with John and Ringo." As a lifelong lover of music, Gleeson couldn't believe his good fortune. When the concert was on, they could hear John and Paul, but when each song stopped, "… the girls in the crowd screamed so loudly the Australians' ears were still ringing several hours later."

Daughters Sophie, Amanda and Liesl at the induction of their father into the Sport Australia Hall of Fame in 1999. The citation: Sport Australia Hall of Fame honours Dick Thornett as a Member for Excellent Performance in Rugby League, Rugby Union & Water Polo.

Richard was a law enforcer on and off the field. He is pictured here in the back row, far right.

Mine host at the Dolphin Hotel.

The Thornett Family (late 1940s): Harold, Marjorie;
(front L to R) John, Ken and Richard.

Richard loved his dogs. Here he is with Champ at the home of his parents, St Thomas Street, Bronte (late 1950s).

A man and his dog – Richard and Milo.

Before the Shute Shield grand final (Sydney, 1959). John captained Northern Suburbs; Ken and Richard represented Randwick. Randwick triumphed 16 – 0.

Richard, John and Ken – poised to take on the world.

The brothers and their mum, Marjorie (This is Your Life - John Thornett, ATN 7, 1978).

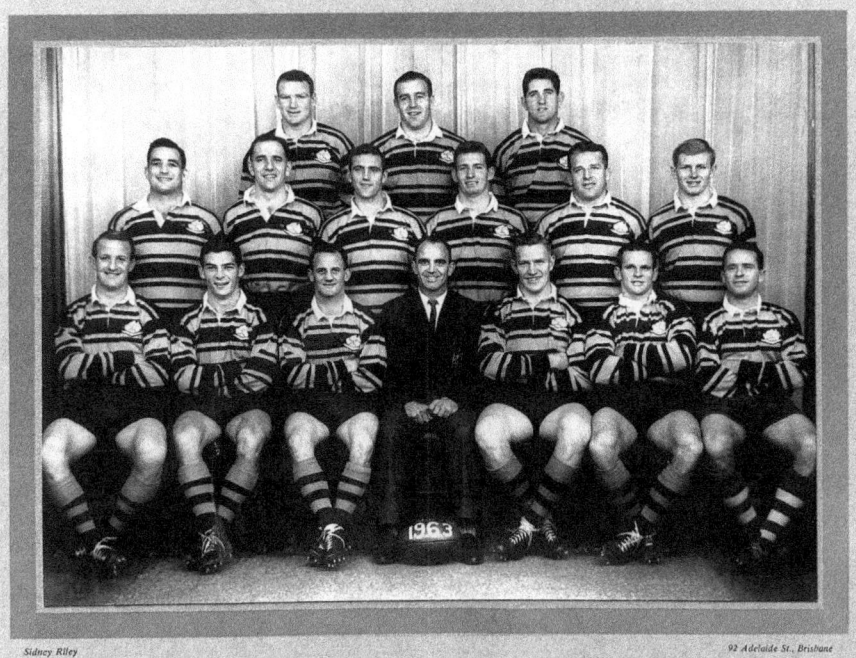

Richard becomes a triple international. Australia vs South Africa (1963).

The 1963/64 Kangaroo team. The first touring team to win the Ashes in 50 years.

Richard and Ken at the Kangaroos' first training session in England (1963).

2nd Test vs Great Britain, Swinton (1963). Richard is airborne between opposition forwards Len McIntyre and Cliff Watson as he crosses for Australia's ninth try.

On the road again. The 1963/64 Kangaroos spent many hours travelling by bus in the UK and France. Standing, L to R: Ken Irvine, Kevin Smyth, Paul Quinn, Peter Gallagher, Ken Day, Michael Cleary, Graham Wilson, Jimmy Lisle, John Cleary, Richard Thornett, Arthur Summons; In Front L to R: Frank Stanton, Les Johns, Ken Thornett, Barry Muir, Barry Rushworth, Brian Hambly, Earl Harrison.

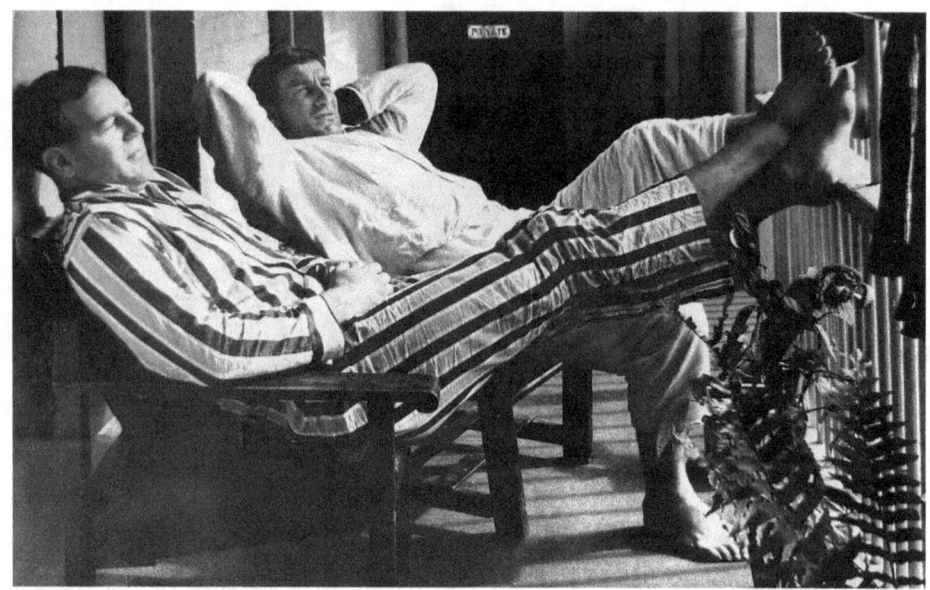

Laid back second row partners Richard Thornett and Mick Veivers before the 2nd Test against Great Britain, Brisbane (1966).

World Cup squad (1968.) Back row L to R: Graeme Langlands, Johnny Greaves, John Wittenberg, Denis Manteit, Elton Rasmussen, Ron Coote, Arthur Beetson. Lionel Williamson; Middle row L to R: Eric Simms, Tony Branson, Fred Jones, Alf Richards (Trainer), Johnny King, Brian Fitzsimmons, Billy Smith; Seated L to R: Harry Bath (coach), Brian James, Richard Thornett (Vice Captain), Johnny Raper (Captain), John Rhodes, Bobby Fulton, "Clancy" Kingston (Manager).

Winning smiles all around after Australia defeated France 20 - 2 to win the World Cup (1968). L to R: Johnny Raper, Ron Coote, Don Lane (entertainer), Billy Smith, Richard Thornett, Johnny Greaves, Eric Simms, Bobby Fulton.

"Australia's Costliest Footballer" (Sport Magazine - April, 1963).

Richard on the run against Eastern Suburbs with 'Bunny' Reilly in pursuit (1971). Note how he holds the ball in both hands, out in front, ready to pass, dummy or kick.

First Grade Premiers (1959).

A fearsome sight. Richard becomes a dual international, 1st Test, Wallabies vs Fiji, Brisbane (1961). Richard's favourite photo from his years in sport.

Goal kicking practice (1962).

Richard and John go through their paces behind the Brewongle Stand, Sydney Cricket Ground. They were Wallaby teammates (1961/1962).

Wallabies NZ Tour, 1962. Back row L to R: R.A.C. Evan, D.J. O'Neill, J.S. Spence, G.A. Chapman, B.J. Harland, J.S. Boyce, E.L.J. Heinrich; Third row L to R: K.P. Walshan, P.G. Johnson, C.P. Crittle, R.N. Thornett, R.J. Heming, P.G. Prosser, J.A. Douglas, J. Freedman; Seated L to R: A.A. Laurie, J.K.N. Lenehan (Vice Captain), J.A. McLean (Manager), J.E. Thornett (Captain), A.S. Roper (Assistant Manager), J.P.L. White, R.J.P. Marks; In Front L to R: K.V. McMullen, A.R. Town, B.J. Ellwood, P.F. Hawthorne, K.W. Catchpole.

Holding back the All Blacks to protect halfback Ken Catchpole (1962).

Primary School, 2nd Class. Richard is 5th from the left, back row.

Richard (third from left, front row) becomes an international when selected for the Australian Olympic Water Polo team (1960), pictured in Rockhampton before leaving for Rome.

Rome Olympics - Richard and Italian constabulary (1960).

Richard and teammate Vic McGrath check the temperature of the pool at the Rome Olympics (1960).

Richard Thornett, Olympian
- Piccadilly Circus, London (1960).

Richard in Water Polo cap and Combined High Schools representative blazer (1957).

CHAPTER FOURTEEN
The Ashes

'Tis not in mortals to command success, but we'll do more...we'll deserve it.
Joseph Addison

After 40 days on tour, the Kangaroos had played 10 games, produced some excellent football, suffered a number of serious injuries, including to their tour captain who could no longer lead them onto the field, and had travelled many miles by bus to and from games. They were now ready to play a Test on one of the biggest sporting stages in the world, Wembley.

On the day of the game, Wednesday October 16, *The Daily Mail* published the following headline: **Wembley Test May Be A Flop,** and it was claimed in the article that *"...only about 5,000 tickets had been sold in advance. Unless 20,000 people pay at the turnstiles, the experiment will have failed badly."* The Daily Mail also stated that *"Australia was unlikely to repeat their 1959 shock win in the first Test and as England were the (1960) World Cup holders, they should sweep the series."* The article concluded, *"In centre Neil Fox, who has scored 39 points in three Wembley Cup Final appearances and scrum-half Alex Murphy, they have two players who can win a match on their own. (The) Only comparable personality in the Kangaroos' team is centre Reg Gasnier."*

While the Wembley experiment might have failed to attract a large crowd (just over 13,000 people in a 90,000-seat venue) the Kangaroos sparkled under the lights of the historic stadium. Frank Stanton, a young utility back for the Kangaroos, watched the Test from the stands. Some 27 years later, Norman Tasker interviewed Stanton who reflected on the Wembley experience. *"The anticipation at the start of that tour was something else. Wembley is a grim place when there's only a small crowd, but just to be there (you) had a feeling that is hard to describe."* Stanton added, *"The game wasn't very well promoted, and we were all a bit lost in London. But it was still a great start to the tour, and a great experience. I have no negative memories of Wembley."*

The Australians had an opportunity to meet HRH Prince Philip before the Test. In the foreword to Ian Heads' book, *The Kangaroos*, Frank Stanton wrote, *"The Kangaroo tour experience encompasses many things. For young blokes, many of them from battling backgrounds, it is a life's experience never forgotten. I remember in 1963 shaking hands with the Duke of Edinburgh at Wembley. For a little boy from Frenchs Forest, that was something."*

The players all had to line up before the kick-off and were told that when HRH was approaching, they were just to hold their hand out – they weren't to take his hand or squeeze it. He would take their hand and shake it. Naturally, strict protocol was of paramount importance. Ian Walsh, who was leading Australia for the first time, recalled how he felt when introducing his players to the Prince. "I was so nervous, I forgot the names of men I had known and played with for years. He seemed to understand."

One Australian player, though, didn't adhere to the rules of the Royal Protocol. Australian five-eighth Johnny Gleeson recalled he was standing beside Richard in the lineup and when the Prince got to John, a voice said, "How's Liz, Phil?" The Australian managers thought Gleeson said it, and looked at him like they were going to shoot him. Gleeson blushed with embarrassment. When the Prince moved on to Les Johns, a voice asked an even more personal question about the Queen and all hell broke loose. In the aftermath, the Australian managers called all the players in and told them in no uncertain terms that they wanted to know who the culprit was. Richard owned up and said it was him.

The youngest Thornett brother was not the only one to breach Royal Protocol. The eldest Thornett brother did it too! John Thornett's first wife Di remembers receiving an invitation to an event on the Royal Yacht Britannia during a Royal Visit to Australia. "I opened the invitation before John came home; I was so excited. I don't know if you know John, very conservative, and he said, 'Don't tell anybody.' But, of course, I was busting. Anyway, we accepted, and it was just lovely. We got dressed up and had my hair done. We went on the boat – it was just mind-blowing really. It was just a thing that you can't explain. It was very proper.

Anyway, we're all lined up, and along came the Queen and as part of her itinerary, that day she'd been to Orange, to some factory where people were putting bits and pieces in radios. Then along came the Duke. He's a bit of a trickster, I must say. Beforehand, we were told that we weren't to (talk to the Royals unless spoken to). So, of course, after this long silence, John said (to Prince Philip), 'Have you had a hard day?' He just grimaced and laughed, and sort of that was it. I was sat next to (Australian) cricketer Doug Walters and opposite me was Basil 'Jika' Travers (Australian sportsman, English rugby international and Shore School Headmaster from 1959 to 1984). Anyhow, Doug Walters dropped his fork and (also) dropped an expletive (heard by most in the room). As Walters bent down to get it, of course all hell broke loose. The staff all ran to pick it up and took it away and gave him another one. What was meant to be quite the serious affair was turned on its head somewhat as the Australian casual style once again took little notice of protocol or expectation."

Under the headline **Six Forwards Share Honours with Gasnier,** AAP reported that the six Australian forwards *"backed up strongly and kept the ball flowing to their backs. Kelly and Hambly provided the fire, Dick Thornett the weight, pace and adroit handling, Ian Walsh the leadership and Peter Gallagher some great work in the tight defence. Behind them was the guiding hand of Johnny Raper, prompting, feeding and covering – the perfect link with his backs."*

Rain fell steadily and the wet playing conditions made ball handling difficult. For the first twenty minutes, the Kangaroos defended as if their lives depended on it as Great Britain forwards Vince Karalius and Jim Measures led relentless raids on the Australians' try line. The Kangaroos' defence held firm. In yet another raid on the Kangaroos' line, Measures put Karalius into open space before Ian Walsh pulled off a low covering tackle on him to stop what would have been a certain try. Walsh said it was the best tackle of his career. Ken Thornett recalled, "I remember Dave Bolton dislocating his shoulder early after a typically hard-driving tackle from Earl Harrison." Bolton left the field after 20 minutes of the first half and could not be replaced. Karalius shifted to five-eighth as the Lions continued with 12 men.

The Kangaroos' resolute defence and the departure of Bolton turned the game Australia's way. In his memoir, *Inside Rugby League,* Ian Walsh wrote, *"Our forwards really started to get the ball rolling with Dick Thornett running brilliantly."*

Richard played an integral part in the first try by the Kangaroos. The scores were locked 2–all when Raper found an opening in the Lions' defence and sent Richard Thornett on a 40-metre run before he was tackled close to Great Britain's line. Walsh also wrote, *"I sensed we were about to go in. I sent the ball straight out to Barry Muir. He threw it to Ken Thornett, who had loomed up from the rear. Ken was through that opening and over for a try before the Englishman realised where he was – a wonderful bit of football. Thus, he became the first fullback to score a try in an Anglo–Australian Test in England."*

Richard and Ken were performing at a level befitting the hallowed turf of Wembley. Another highlight of the first half was when Richard broke through the Lions' line before sending an inside ball to lock forward Johnny Raper, which initiated an 80-yard surge and a try scored by Gasnier. In front of the Duke of Edinburgh, Gasnier scored three tries to repeat his feat in the first Test of the 1959 tour. The final score was Australia 28 – Great Britain 2. The *AAP* report from London noted, *"Australia are clearly going to take the dickens of a lot of beating – by 12 men or 13, in any kind of weather."* The Times called the first Test *"a humiliating night for England."*

The journalist who penned the article headlined **Wembley May Be A Flop** should have turned in his journalist license. He was wrong with almost all of his predictions, including the Test being a commercial failure. The secretary of the English Rugby League, Bill Fallowfield, declared that the gate receipts and the television fee was *"roughly equal to that for a 30,000 crowd at a north of England ground."* He was correct, though, about Reg Gasnier. "Gaz" was a match-winner. At the official post-match celebration, Ian Walsh bumped into leading English commentator Eddie Waring who said to him, "Ian, we gave you a fair referee and a neutral ground in London for this first Test. From now on, you're on your own." Walsh now knew that the Kangaroos were going to find the going even tougher as they moved towards the second Test at Swinton in November.

In the next tour game, Ken Irvine captained Australia to a 3–0 win over Rochdale Hornets. Illegalities marred a game which did not rise to any level of excitement. Richard Thornett and Kevin Smyth worked well with their backs. In the 32nd minute, the Kangaroos were attacking just beyond the Rochdale 25 when Michael Cleary was held up. The *AAP* reported, *"Smyth, gave the ball right to Thornett, who slipped it to Barry Rushworth, the centre drawing the fullback to put*

Irvine over for the first try 10 yards from the right corner after 32 minutes. Les Johns missed the kick." Richard also stopped a dangerous Rochdale attack when he stopped five-eighth Levula's *"plunging run"* for the try line.

Kevin Ryan was ruled out of the rest of the English tour after undergoing a major operation on his knee ligaments and ripped cartilage, which were damaged in the game against the Hull/Hull Kingston Rovers XIII. This was a blow not only to Ryan but also the Kangaroos, as the injury toll among the forwards was mounting. On a positive note, Richard was playing well and according to a *"Special Correspondent's"* report, *"His form has vastly improved since arriving in England and (he) has established himself as the Kangaroos' top second rower."*

Australia did just enough to defeat Hunslet 17-13 at Parkside before a small crowd of 4,400. The Kangaroos were caned 22-5 in the penalties and Michael Cleary was sent off after an altercation with opposition player Griffiths. The Kangaroo team was: L. Johns, K. Irvine, B. Rushworth, R. Gasnier (Capt.), M. Cleary, E. Harrison, F. Stanton, K. Smyth, B. Hambly, K. Day, P. Quinn, G. Wilson, J. Cleary.

On October 26, the Kangaroos met Wakefield Trinity. It was their 14th game of the tour. A headline screamed **Roos win. Police quell wild brawl.** *AAP* reported, *"Late in the second half, six police were called to halt a wild brawl in which every player was involved. Australian hooker Ian Walsh and Wakefield's fiery captain, Derek 'Rocky' Turner, were lectured after the two-minute brawl."*

Richard was prominent in attack and defence. He set up a try when *"he timed his pass perfectly for Gasnier. The centre cleared away from Poynton and Fox on a 50-yard sprint to the post."* Richard then conceded two points when, after a report from the touch judge, he was *"penalised for a tackle on Holliday and Fox kicked a fine goal from near touch."* Arthur Summons tested his knee in this game but lasted only 30 minutes. The Kangaroos won 29-14 despite the referee who was taking every opportunity to stop Australia from playing their free-flowing game.

In an interesting side note, Wakefield lent its facilities and players for the English-produced feature film *This Sporting Life,* directed by Lindsay Anderson and starring Richard Harris. It was the story of a crude, violent Yorkshire coal miner who became a successful Rugby League player and Richard Harris received an Oscar nomination for Best Actor. One noted American movie guide pointed out, *"The squeamish will not like the games' scenes and with good reason! They* were filmed on Wakefield Trinity's Belle Vue ground and the 'extras' were members of the Wakefield senior team. They held nothing back as the director Lindsay Anderson strove for realism." Life imitated art when *"Anderson allegedly told Great Britain Test forward, Derek 'Rocky' Turner, 'I want you to hit Richard just like you would an opponent player in a normal game.'"* So, when Harris, in his role as a loose forward, broke from the next scrum, Turner hit him with a screamer of a stiff-arm tackle. Author Malcolm Andrews wrote, *"The actor was carried off the pitch unconscious and took longer to shake the cobwebs from his head than he took to sing his 1968 hit single MacArthur Park. Filming had to be postponed for 48 hours."* Harris survived one of "Rocky's" best hits since Turner's performances in Australia with the Lions in 1962. For that and his stunningly realistic performance in the film, Harris' Oscar nomination was well-deserved.

In the next tour match, which was against Cumberland, Les Johns played brilliantly, scoring two tries in the first half. For one of them he *"sliced into the attack, dummied to Barry Rushworth, then kept going for a breathtaking try."* The final score at Derwent Park, Workington was Australia 21 – Cumberland 0.

Richard sent a postcard home after the game against Cumberland:

Dear Mum, Dad, John and Champ,
Well, we are now in Keswick, the Lake District and it is really beautiful country only about 20 miles from the Scotch [sic] border. Had a good win against Cumberland and play Barrow tomorrow. We are confident of winning the 2nd Test next Sat. Listen to Tiger Black for the best description. Hope you are all well. Will try and write during the week.
    Love, Dick.

Richard scored a try in the unconvincing 18–5 win over second division team Barrow. There had been injury concerns over Ken Thornett and Peter Dimond in the lead-up to the game, but both came through the match unscathed. On November 4, *AAP* reported that this was the 13th win in 16 matches on tour and, *"...the ninth in succession – the longest winning sequence by a Kangaroo side since the War."*

The second Test at Swinton was a week away.

Going into the second Test on November 9, the 11th Kangaroos were in the same position as the 1959/60 tourists; they were seeking to win the Ashes in England for the first time since 1911/12. The Kangaroos took the field full of hope. However, the match did not begin well for Australia when Gasnier threw a pass which was intercepted by Neil Fox just inside the Australian half. Fox raced away with four Australians in pursuit and just as he was about to be rounded up, winger John Stopford loomed up in support, took Fox's pass and scored wide out. Fox failed with his attempted conversion.

From that point, Kangaroo forwards Richard Thornett, Paul Quinn, Noel Kelly, Ken Day and Ian Walsh dominated the Lions pack. Lock Johnny Raper then took control of the game. Richard said Raper was the best player he had seen and, in this game, "Chook" demonstrated the full range of his skills in what is believed to be the greatest individual performance by an Australian Test player. Raper shared this memory, "In the second half, I felt like I could run wherever I wanted to run" while Ian Walsh proclaimed, "His was the greatest game I have ever seen. Everything he tried came off." Ken Thornett commented, "John Raper, with his genius for switching play to unexpected points, had the Lions grasping at air."

Australia's backline contributed 44 points out of the 50 scored with the balance from Noel Kelly and Richard who scored a try apiece. Once again, the Lions were down to 12 men early when Frank Myler was forced off after 20 minutes and then to 11 men when Eric Ashton missed the entire second half. Both players suffered rib injuries from the hard-tackling Australians. Father Time had caught up with Vince Karalius, who did not improve on his performance in the first Test. Raper recalled, "Vince Karalius, the legendary 'Wild Bull' of football tried hard to rouse England's forwards, but we were not frightened of him this day. Years before, when I played for a Sydney Colts team against him, Karalius terrified me, but when I took the first pass and was tackled, all the fear went out of me." He added, "One of my big thrills now was picking Karalius up and dumping him." It was to be Karalius' last game for Great Britain.

Eddie Waring reported in the *Sunday Mirror*, "*What would've happened had Ashton and Myler not been injured? Obviously, it would've made a lot of difference to the final score. But that would've been all it could have done. The Aussies were magnificent.*" Ken Thornett offered the following opinion: "Great Britain simply had no answer when unexpectedly confronted by a team, equally skilled in the art of ball distribution, and who were speedier, younger, and possibly more experienced." Johnny Raper described Richard's ball distribution as "uncanny". Of Richard's performance, journalist Malcolm Brown wrote, *"At Swinton, fired by the antagonism of an opposing forward, he produced one of the greatest second-row performances of all time."*

The Kangaroos had won the Ashes 50–12. Coach Arthur Summons had prepared the Kangaroos extremely well for the first and second Tests and much of the credit for the success of the team was given to him. Raper said, "… the team were behind him to a man, and it gave every one of us a very warm feeling inside when we got him up on our shoulders as we came off the field and chaired him off." He expressed what this achievement meant to the Kangaroos in *The Johnny Raper Rugby League Book*. *"Arthur was not the only one among us who wept unashamedly."* During the Ashes series, Kangaroo Frank Stanton provided commentary alongside radio station 2KY's legendary caller Ernest "Tiger" Black and recalled the "…enormous pride…" he, Black and many others felt about the team's historic success.

The Kangaroos travelled to play Castleford at Wheldon Road four days after the second Test. Castleford won a see-sawing contest 13–12, the result determined by referee Davies who overruled the touch judges and awarded a goal to Castleford after the ball seemed to pass under the crossbar.

Injuries continued to plague the Kangaroos. During the morning training session the day after the loss to Castleford, Reg Gasnier, who injured his groin in the second Test, withdrew from the team to play Wigan. Front-rower Noel Kelly had his nose broken during the Swinton Test and required a further medical examination. Peter Gallagher ran surprisingly well given his injured knee and would replace Kelly if required. Barry Muir was in doubt, lock Kevin Smyth did not run at full pace but looked fit enough to play, and Johnny Raper did not train because of sore ribs but was standing by in case he was needed to play lock. These were just some of the Kangaroos who were the 'walking wounded' and the tour still had 8 weeks to go and 16 games to play! Noel Kelly, a three-time Kangaroo, made the following points about the rigours of a Kangaroo tour: "When you're playing 36 games, it might sound a lot that you have 26 players, but you're playing three games a week. I mean you're losing a couple of players all the time. There's blokes backin' up all the time."

Heavy fog delayed the match against Wigan, and it was switched to November

18. Noel Kelly was sent off early in the second half after punching a Wigan player. Richard and Ken played in this match, won 18–10 by the Kangaroos. Ian Heads wrote, *"Great goalkicking by Graeme Langlands and a superb display by Ken Thornett highlighted the win over Wigan."*

The Kangaroos were preparing to meet top English team Swinton on November 23 when "the shots that were heard around the world" ended the life of President John F. Kennedy in Dallas, Texas. This news affected the Kangaroos and Frank Stanton recalled – 59 years after that tragic event – the sombre nature of his teammates when they met for breakfast on game day. Before the kick-off, the two teams and the crowd stood silently in memory of the fallen President. Gowers and Langlands each kicked a penalty goal during this hard, unrelenting match. The Kangaroo forwards defended well but the team was disjointed and scrappy in attack. In one ruck, Richard was kicked by Swinton's Morgan and Langlands' penalty kick veered just to the side of the right post. The score was 2–2 at halftime.

In a dour second half, Richard, Brian Hambly, Reg Gasnier and Frank Stanton consistently made ground with the ball. But there was no change to the score and the game ended at 2–2. After the Swinton game, *AAP* observed, *"Their defence is perhaps the best that a touring side had ever produced."* It was a week of mixed emotions for Frank Stanton. The tragedy in Dallas was at one end of the spectrum while at the opposite end was the great joy – tinged with a longing for home – when he received the news that his second daughter was born. In 2023, Stanton observed just how much times have changed. "It is so different today, where players are allowed to travel home for the birth of their children." Frank Stanton's experience is an exemplar of the sacrifices players and their families made for the honour of representing Australia.

Heading into the third Test, the Kangaroos had conceded just 27 tries in 21 games, slightly more than half the previous lowest. They were also the highest-scoring Test side on record with 18 tries and 12 goals for a total of 78 points. The Kangaroo backs scored 65 of the 74 tries and Richard was the top try-scoring forward with four of the nine touchdowns.

The third Test at Headingley was played on November 30. There were threats of retribution from both sides in the lead-up to the Test. The Australians knew it would be difficult to win the Test when Eric "Sergeant Major" Clay was appointed referee. Clay was disliked in Australia due to his handling of the third Test in 1959, which the 10th Kangaroos and their fans believed cost them victory and the Ashes. The game was violent and was more a series of fights and 'getting-square' than Rugby League. Clay ordered the send-offs of Brian Hambly (17 minutes), Cliff Watson (46 minutes) and Barry Muir (56 minutes.) As for the football that was played between the pugilism, Australia started slowly and only superb covering by Raper and Richard prevented England scoring. Play was extremely rugged. Don Fox required ambulance attention after a crashing tackle by Richard. Then Hambly and Fox became involved in a scuffle at the scrum and Richard rushed to his aid as an all-in brawl was brewing. Referee Clay ordered Hambly from the field.

The Lions scored two converted tries in the first half to one by the Kangaroos. The Kangaroos' scoring movement came from a ruck, where Raper passed to Richard, who lobbed the ball over an English defender to Irvine. Irvine, with only yards to move, showed blistering speed to beat the English defence and score. Great Britain led 10–5 at halftime. The second half was a continuation of the violence witnessed in the first 40 minutes of the Test. The crowd was also becoming more involved in the game. At one point, Kangaroo halfback Barry Muir stood just inside the field of play and challenged spectators to come on the field and fight. As Muir stood shouting at the crowd, Graham Wilson, the Kangaroos' reserve forward, threw a bucket of water at several noisy spectators. Lions' prop Cliff Watson was sent off for kneeing Peter Dimond and Muir was dismissed for kicking his opposite number, Tommy Smales.

The Lions scored two more tries to triumph 16–5. Australia finished the game with 10 men after Ken Irvine was carried from the field. Australian captain Ian Walsh was critical of his team and wrote in his autobiography *Inside Rugby League*, "I was disgusted at the attitude of some Australian players who threw a punch every time they were tackled. Many of our boys blamed our defeat on Eric Clay. They said he was the greatest player Great Britain ever had. But I reckoned the 'Sergeant Major' was no worse than an Australian refereeing a Test in Sydney." Walsh might have been thinking about the third Test against the Lions in 1962 when he wrote those words. The reality was that Australia had abandoned their speed game, which had proved so successful in the first two Tests, for a war of attrition, which England withstood and then played enough Rugby League to win the game.

A Dimond in the Rough

Rugby League writer Tony Megahey recorded Noel Kelly's anecdote from the third Test, which was published in *Rugby League Week* as *A Dimond in the rough*. An extract from Megahey's article is reproduced here:

'Ned' Kelly was a character... a ruthlessly, tough international forward, but at the same time, one of the funniest men to ever lace on a football boot. Through the 1959, 1963 and 1967 tours, Kelly was involved in many uproarious situations, as well as the most brutal forward exchanges in Test history.

"I'd have to say a Test at Leeds (the third Test in 1963) produced one of the funniest situations I've ever seen in football. The 'Poms' picked a team of thugs to bash us, and we soon knew the referee wasn't going to be any help to us. They put the blue on, but when we retaliated the ref sent two of our blokes off. But all the 'Pommies' stayed on the field, no matter what they did."

Things were clearly going against the hot Kangaroo side, who had convincingly won the opening two Tests to clinch the series. Getting even became the theme for the rest of the afternoon.

"In the scrums, they were kicking the Christ out of me and the front-rowers. When I came off at halftime, I said I was #@%# sick to death of this. I said to Peter Dimond and a couple of others that it was open slather for them, but I wasn't going to cop this crap, anymore. #@%# him and the ref. In those days there was no dressing room. At halftime we just stood under the grandstand with a bit of a partition between us and them."

The antiquated facilities gave Dimond, a tough, uncompromising winger, an opening too good to resist.

"Big Cliff Watson was standing away from the other 'Pommies'. He was leaning against a corner, chewing gum, and looking cocky at the way things were going,' Kelly grinned. "We were first out, and our players had to pass right alongside where Watson was standing. Well, you wouldn't believe what happened next. When Dimond filed past, he just hung one on Watson. Poleaxed him with a beauty, and then kept going as though nothing had happened. One second big Cliffy was grinning like a Cheshire Cat, and the next he was flat on his back with his eyes rolling like a poker machine."

Kelly said the 'Poms' had no idea what had happened.

"I reckon they thought a brick dropped on Cliffy's head from the stand," he laughed.

As the Englishmen filed back on to the ground, Watson, one of Britain's toughest ever forwards, was dazed, and things were beginning to look a little rosier for the beleaguered Aussies.

"Poor old Cliffy was lurching around like a drunken sailor. Then, as we waited for the restart, Dimond sidled up to me, and said, 'That's one back.' I just burst out laughing, I couldn't help it."

When Watson recovered, he was an angry giant. There was one thing on his mind, and that was squaring up. When he found out it was Dimond who flattened him, that was it.

"He bolted straight across field and belted him," said Kelly. "The ref couldn't do anything but send Watson off. He marched off, really spitting chips – he knew we had a loan of him. Later that night, when both teams were together for the after-match reception, I ran into Cliffy, and we had a drink. I said how unlucky I thought he was, and what a terrible thing to do to a bloke who wasn't even on the field of play. You should've seen the look on Cliffy's face when I said that."

Australian manager Jack Lynch let his feelings of disappointment get the better of him when he was called on to speak at the official post-Test function. "I thought Great Britain's team played better football today – all 14 of them. I thought it was a frightful exhibition of refereeing." Lynch added, "He's known as the Sergeant Major, but after today he should be promoted to Brigadier."

According to Ken Thornett, "Criticism of the referee by Mr J Lynch elicited a strong response from British critics."

No matter how disappointed the Australians were in their performance during the third Test, their sense of mischief and fun remained intact. Peter Dimond tells the story of enjoying a night out with Barry Muir just before the team embarked on the French leg of the tour. Somehow, they came into possession of 'penny bungers' (firecrackers) and returned to the Troutbeck Hotel in the early hours. They decided to go from room to room lighting the bungers to set off a series of explosions which roused their sleeping teammates. Dimond explained what happened next in his autobiography *Playing with Legends*. "I took off, but Muir wasn't smart enough or was laughing too much, and he gets nabbed by Hambly and (Richard) Thornett outside their room and they promptly run a cold bath and plonk him in, clothes and all. I'm thinking, 'Beauty, I got away with it,' and present myself for breakfast the next morning. Not a word was said, so I go back to the room pretty pleased with myself and open the door. Hambly and Thornett had been out on the moors behind the pub and gathered up two sheep which they had then deposited in my room. So, here's these bloody sheep bleating away and jumping and shitting everywhere. The more I chased them the more they left reminders. I suspect Cleary was involved in some way. It would be just like him."

During their ten weeks in England, the Kangaroos made memories and friendships to last a lifetime. They also added a new chapter to the legendary achievements of Australians in sport. The Kangaroos won sixteen, drew one and lost five out of the twenty-two matches in England.

In a *Special Kangaroos' edition* of *Rugby League Week*, writer David Page expressed the following: *"The Kangaroos' brilliance failed to win the hearts of the English crowds, who had very little experience at losing, and were far from gracious."* More than a quarter of a century later, Kangaroo utility back Jimmy Lisle recalled, "We were given a bitter reception, wherever we went. It was on a par with playing in front of a Queensland crowd. They were certainly pleased to see the back of us."

Richard played superbly in all three Tests against Great Britain, and with Johnny Raper was ranked at the top of an outstanding group of Australian forwards. He had recently turned 23 and was now one of the best Rugby League forwards in the world. Peter Dimond appreciated Richard's ball skills, writing in his autobiography, *"I will always remember Dick for his ball distribution and blindside play. Dick had what I call beautiful hands and to explain that, he could move the ball quickly and accurately, also hold back the pass and time it perfectly, and pass either way."*

When asked about Richard's performance during the 1963/64 tour, Barry Rushworth offered, "He was a wonderful footballer; a wonderful Rugby League player. And he was also such a gentleman off the field. He didn't play up at all. And he was a great mate of mine. Dick and Johnny Raper were close together in performance (on tour)."

Ian Walsh was interviewed in 1976 and reflected on Richard's contribution to his team. "We were running hot in England and after about the fifth game, we started to fall into a pattern of forward play that proved very successful. We were tending to use brute strength, like we did at home, but Roy Francis, who coached Norths here for a while, came along with a great deal of help on English forward play. Then we woke up to the fact that Dick Thornett was an outstanding ball player. I always say Australian fans never saw the best of Dick. He was great under English conditions."

Ken also played very well in all three Tests, confirming his position as Australia's premier fullback. He enhanced his reputation further through some memorable performances in the 'minor' games.

It is appropriate to reflect on the quests for the "Holy Grails" that the three Thornett brothers pursued in 1963. With the Ashes victory, Richard and Ken had achieved their objective. John, too, had achieved great things against the Springboks in South Africa where the Wallabies drew the Test series 2-2. The brothers had reached incredible heights in world sport and were key players in the renaissance of both rugby codes.

In June 1959, *Sport Magazine* published an article by Alan Hulls about the Thornett brothers who were playing Rugby Union at that time. Hulls included a reference to their father Harold. *"Mr Thornett may yet see his three sons play together. It would not be highly improbable for three Thornetts to be listed on the program as playing for Australia."* Although his sons did not play together for Australia, Harold Rowe Thornett must have been immensely proud of his boys.

After England, in late 1963 the Kangaroo tourists embarked on the French leg of their tour where they would play three Tests in the 14 games scheduled.

CHAPTER FIFTEEN
France

On a number of occasions when we would visit a town, there would be a reception for us and the mayor would greet us. They always gave us a gift and it was almost always wine. So, the wine got stored down the back of the bus, and when we felt there was an occasion for a party, out came the wine. We had quite a few good evenings on the French leg.
Peter Dimond

PARIS, Dec. 4 (AAP): "The Kangaroo managers will be anxiously awaiting news from England this evening. Noel Kelly's case will be dealt with by a special meeting of the English Rugby League Disciplinary Committee. They have to fix the meeting for tomorrow because the rules specify that a player must be dealt with within 16 days of being sent off. Kelly was dismissed in the Wigan match on November 18. He is chosen to play against Paris-Celtic on Thursday afternoon."

Kelly was handed a one-match suspension. He missed the game against Paris-Celtic at Stade Pershing on December 5 but was available for the first Test. Richard had a hand in two of his team's tries against Paris-Celtic. The Kangaroos were leading 8–0 after 26 minutes when he combined with Smyth and Lisle for Michael Cleary to cross the stripe for a try. Then, as halftime approached, "The Kangaroos ended the first half with another fine try, Dick Thornett running from the dummy-half and Smyth linking with Gleeson" for another touchdown. Australia defeated Paris-Celtic 30–2.

France scored two tries to one in the first Test, defeating Australia 8–5 before 8,000 spectators at Stade Municipal, Bordeaux. The Australians were starved of possession as the French hooker Jean Graciet won a two-to-one share of the ball from scrums, which to some degree nullified the brilliance of the Australian backline. The Australian managers, Lynch and Sparks, claimed the referee was *"...not exactly impartial."* The managers also said, *"We had no chance in the scrums and heavy penalties against us. We allowed ourselves to be ruffled."* According to the *AAP* match report printed in the SMH: **BORDEAUX**, December 9 — *"Two Test defeats within eight days have been a salutary lesson for the Kangaroos. Yesterday's unexpected crash in the first Test against France has shaken the team far more than the loss of the third Test in England. The tour of France, regarded by some of the players as a holiday before their return to Australia, has suddenly taken on a very different light. The Kangaroos realise now that this French tour must be taken very seriously."*

Injuries continued to mount for the Kangaroos during a spiteful game at Bayonne on December 12. Ian Walsh broke his arm in the 18–5 victory over Basque-Bearnaise team, which included eight former Rugby League or Rugby Union internationals. Players on both sides showed resentment of tackles and after one clash, which threatened to become a brawl, the referee lectured both packs. Kangaroo five-eighth Jim Lisle was sent off in the 38th minute. In an extraordinary move, Antoine Blain, the secretary-general of the French League, gathered both teams around him at halftime. Blain spoke in English and then French, telling the players to calm down. He said, "The public does not like these brutalities. You have come here to play football and not to fight each other. Play the three yards on the play the ball and behave yourself." Blain convinced captains Summons and Lacaze to shake hands, which according to the local paper, *Sud Ouest, "...was the turning point of the match."*

The playing strength of the Kangaroo squad was reduced to 24 with Walsh ruled out of the tour and minus Kevin Ryan who returned to Australia. In addition, some of the injured Kangaroos were not recovering as well as expected. Among them were Ken Day, Barry Muir, Peter Dimond, Ken Thornett and Les Johns. The French leg of the tour was now looking very arduous, and the Kangaroos sadly missed the services of their masseur, Bill Hunter, who died tragically in the moment of their triumph after the second Test against England.

The Kangaroos beat South West France 41–11 on a partially frozen field at Villeneuve-sur-Lot, the first town in France to embrace the new rugby code in 1934, and scored nine tries to one in a convincing performance. Richard scored a try set up by Johnny Gleeson and then featured in what *AAP* (December 15) reported as, *"a brilliant try in which Dick Thornett handled twice with Gallagher, Irvine, Rushworth and Cleary handling before Summons drew the fullback and sent Cleary over."*

Wild brawls marked the match in which the Kangaroos beat a Pyrenees team 14-10 in Saint-Gaudens. The violence came into the game in the second half, in which Barry Muir was ordered off the field after he put his hand on the referee. Tough winger Peter Dimond was knocked out and at one stage most of the players were involved in a brawl. The Australians had difficulty with the referee who appeared to have no idea of the advantage rule and who repeatedly allowed the local players to stand offside. Richard played on after he ran into opposition second-rower Barthes and suffered what appeared to be a rib injury. It was confirmed later to be a cracked sternum and it put him out for the next two weeks, including the second Test.

The second Test was played at Toulouse. The press reported, *"Thornett's late withdrawal did nothing for Australia's chances."* Back-row forward Kevin Smyth came into the starting team. The Australians played magnificently to beat France 21-9. When Ken Thornett scored a try, he achieved the remarkable record of touchdowns against New Zealand, South Africa, Great Britain and France in Australia's Test campaigns of 1963. The handling and backing-up of the entire team in the sweeping attacks set the French crowd of 10,000 cheering. However, referee Martung was none too kind to Australia, awarding the home team 18 penalties to 2.

Brian Hambly became the seventh member of the touring party to captain the Kangaroos. The next tour match against Rouergue Province at Albi was won by the Kangaroos 13-2. *AAP* (December 26) reported, *"The Australians carried their resentment at having to play on Christmas Day onto the field, and the fly kicks of the French players stirred smouldering tempers into flames before halftime. Kangaroo halfback Frank Stanton kept the match on the boil when he turned himself into a one-man punitive expedition."*

At this stage of the tour, many of the Kangaroos were looking homeward. For Frank Stanton, "Christmas Day was a fairly forlorn experience, spent in the town of Toulouse Lautrec's birth – Albi. We played a match that day, a fiery affair, which completely lacked the spirit of goodwill. The previous night, Christmas

Eve, I accompanied a homesick Johnny Raper to midnight mass. We had a match called off because of the snow (Lyon) and played another in a near-snow storm (Roanne)." Stanton told the authors of this book that the outbreak of homesickness among the Kangaroo tourists bordered on an epidemic.

CARCASSONNE *(France), Dec. 30 (AAP) — "One man short, but aided by a neutral referee, the Kangaroos yesterday defeated an Aude Province side 16-12. Referee Georges Jameau, who would have charge of the final Test in Paris, came off the field to boos and insults from an excited crowd. He had penalised the home team in the final seconds of a thrilling match to leave the Kangaroos deserved victors."*

The Kangaroos, many of them carrying injuries and in various stages of homesickness, saw in the New Year with an 11–5 loss against Catalans at the Stade Gilbert Brutus in Perpignan. Johnny Raper broke his thumb and did not play again on tour. Co-manager Jack Lynch said he would recommend that the Board of Control give serious consideration to cutting the length of future tours. *"Now I really understand what it means to make a five months' tour,"* he said. *"Christmas is a bad time to be away. It doesn't help morale. Like other people, Rugby League players want to be with their loved ones then."*

The Kangaroos recorded their highest score of the tour when they beat Marseilles-Montpellier 51–11 before 889 spectators at Marseilles on January 4, 1964. Despite the easy win, the game produced more injuries for the team, now reduced to barely covering a starting lineup for the matches ahead. Jim Lisle damaged a hamstring and Graeme Langlands injured a stomach muscle. Richard played for the first time since injuring his sternum and shared the forward honours with Smyth, Kelly and Quinn.

Twenty-four hours later, the Kangaroos played an "exhibition" match in Avignon, defeating a combined Provence side 35–4. During the game, centre Graeme Langlands scored two tries and four goals to take his tally on tour to 207 points. Peter Dimond crossed the stripe three times. Gallagher, John Cleary and Richard Thornett opened the way for a Langlands thrust which gave Noel Kelly the next try. Kelly was ordered off four minutes from fulltime. He refused to go but after the usual two-minute argument, in which Summons and Stanton played leading parts, the referee allowed Kelly to remain.

Injuries had hit the 11th Kangaroos hard. The third Test against France was twelve days away and according to *AAP Reuters*, the team's leaders were very concerned that there were only 17 'reasonably fit' players who could take the field if selected. Richard was under consideration for the third Test although on January 6. *AAP* reported that he was *"...still very conscious of the injury to his breastbone which put him out of the second Test."*

The Walking Wounded

LYON, *January 9 (AAP)* — *"The Kangaroos delayed their training this morning to allow the ground to recover from overnight frost. The temperature was still below freezing point this morning. With a long injury list, the tourists are not anxious to incur more trouble through strains and pulled muscles on frozen grounds, with the final Test little more than a week away. The Kangaroos play France "B" on Saturday. Selection of the teams to play France "B" and Roanne at Roanne on Sunday has been delayed as late as possible. Today's training will be an illness trial for several players including Earl Harrison, Les Johns, Mike Cleary, Graham Wilson, Brian Hambly, Paul Quinn and Ken Thornett. The whole party has benefited from a three-day holiday from football, including training. It was hoped to give the probable Test team a run together either in Saturday's game or at Roanne. But the selectors do not want to overwork the key Test men, some of whom will have to play both matches. Graham Wilson, who looks certain to be a second rower in the Test, will probably have to hook in one of the two weekend games."*

ROANNE, *January 12 (AAP)* — *"The Kangaroos beat the Roanne XIII 38 points to 2. Playing in a snow storm on a slippery ground, they threw the ball about to score 10 tries, with Irvine, Dimond and Muir each getting two. The stars of the game were Ken Thornett, whose strong running worried the Roanne's defensive line, and hardman Brian Hambly, who kicked four goals after an injured Langlands left the field."*

In the penultimate game of the tour, the Kangaroos beat a French "Colts" team 19–12 at Pilages. Ken Day starred at lock, Les Johns was in the centres and Jimmy Lisle played much of the game with a pronounced 'hobble' at fullback. Graham Wilson, who had given Trojan service to the Kangaroos during the tour of France, was the hooker. The wingers – Irvine and Cleary – scored two tries each. Richard and prop Paul Quinn played in the match even though they were not fit. Richard's sternum injury was still worrying him. He was selected in the squad for the third Test but did not play.

The newspaper headline said it all: **Kangaroos Win French Series, To Rate Best in the World. PARIS,** *Jan. 19 (AAP) — "The Kangaroos yesterday became undisputed Rugby League champions of the world. They followed their unprecedented Ashes win over England by winning the final Test of the series against France with a 16–8 decision at the Parc des Princes. Thus, in one year they have beaten New Zealand, South Africa, England and France — the only other countries to play the game."*

The Kangaroos fielded a patched-up side and were missing six players who played in the third Test against Great Britain – Richard, Johnny Raper, Graeme Langlands, Earl Harrison, Ian Walsh and Paul Quinn. The Australians produced dazzling football at times with Ken Thornett and Reg Gasnier in scintillating form. The Kangaroos scored four tries – the first by 21-year-old Test debutant Barry Rushworth, who handled twice before he scored in the 16th minute. Muir and Irvine crossed for tries before Ken Day scored the final try of the tour. The French captain, Jean Barthe, said later, *"The best side won today – there is no doubt of that."*

It is said that 'all good things must come to an end' and the 11th Kangaroos wound up their adventure having completed victorious campaigns in England and France. They could rightly claim to be the best team in the world.

Antoine Blain summed up the quality of the 1963/64 Kangaroos this way: *"Most national teams have three or four exceptional players backed by less gifted teammates. Every 10 or 20 years, a national team appears composed of football's elite. This is the case with these Kangaroos. Their collective speed is bewildering. This is a team without a single weakness. It is full of destructive power."*

John Cleary reflected on his Kangaroo tour experience. "It was a fantastic tour, mate. It was just one of the best groups of blokes you would ever meet."

The Kangaroos arrived in Sydney after several flight delays and were whisked away to a small reception where they reconnected with their loved ones. From there, the team travelled into the city where Lord Mayor Harry Jensen received them. At the end of the civic formalities, the Kangaroos were paraded in open cars via George Street and Martin Place to the N.S.W. Rugby League's headquarters in Phillip Street.

FRANCE

Barry Rushworth and Graeme Langlands, who roomed together during the tour, were in one of the cars in the motorcade. Rushworth recalls, "I used to play a bit of hockey and had a hockey stick with me which was autographed by all of the Kangaroos." He noticed that Langlands seemed to be increasingly uneasy as the motorcade progressed. "Graeme said to me, 'This is going to look stupid if somebody takes a photo of us. Me and you sitting on the back of this car, and you nursing a hockey stick.' He said 'We've been away on the road. Kangaroos. Rugby League. And you've got a hockey stick over your shoulders.'" Rushworth said, "I've got the hockey stick on the wall, with my jumper and with a blazer and kept everything (from the 1963/64 Kangaroos tour)."

Frank Stanton described the ticker-tape parade as "very special and something that is not done today."

The authors of this book asked Frank Stanton if it is possible to compare one era of Kangaroo tourists to another to determine which team was the best. His only comment was, "Suffice to say that the players in 1963 were skilful and unlike today, most players had day jobs." Stanton added that they did not have the benefit of the holistic training and sports medicine regimes that evolved much later.

Richard was finally home, and it was time to start pre-season training with Parramatta. In front of him was at least 8 months of weekly grind and tough competition games. For Richard (and Ken), the 1963 domestic season plus the Kangaroo tour and the 1964 season would be equivalent to playing three seasons in two years.

Richard said, "We arrived back to a civic reception in Sydney and a motor cavalcade through the streets after a 36-match tour over a period of about 22 weeks. After such a long tour, it was lovely to get home to Sydney again and see all my old friends. We only had a couple of weeks off to relax before we started club training again."

CHAPTER SIXTEEN
1964 – The Eels Come of Age

It was Einstein who made the real trouble. He announced in 1905 that there was no such thing as absolute rest. After that, there never was.
Stephen Leacock

There was very little time off or any off-season at all to speak of for the Kangaroo tourists. The last game for them was the third Test against the French in Paris on January 18 and the Kangaroos stepped off the plane on January 22, 1964. It meant they had roughly five weeks until their first pre-season game, which for Richard was the March 1 fixture against Newtown – an 11–9 victory at Cumberland Oval. And this isn't even considering pre-season training beforehand…

After going so close in 1963, and on the back of the 'four-year plan' mentioned in Chapter 9 which targeted the 1964 season as the year for a tilt at the premiership, the Parramatta faithful looked ahead with great anticipation. Brother Ken Thornett was back for the whole season and coach Ken Kearney was now in his third year at the helm, well-entrenched with both playing style and player management. Ken was returning permanently from his Leeds commitments and along with successful 1963/64 Kangaroo tourists Brian Hambly, Barry Rushworth (who had signed a five-year contract) and Richard Thornett, they had the nucleus of an extremely talented and wiser team.

Of course, Ron Lynch would have made five Parramatta tourists in the Kangaroos had he not injured himself in the Possibles vs Probables Kangaroos trial match on the selection day. Just as it is inconceivable these days for club sides to play matches so close together, such as Parramatta playing the touring South Africans between their last 1963 preliminary game and their semi-final, so too was

1964 - THE EELS COME OF AGE

Lynch a victim of a crazy playing schedule that ultimately cost him an experience of a lifetime.

The Parramatta backline that joined Ken in 1964 included Derek Hallas and Ivor Lingard, as well as wingers Ken Foord and Mike Jackson. And there was Billy Rayner, Bobby Bugden and Noel Dolton; it was a mouth-watering lineup bristling with talent and experience, and if you believed coach Kearney, they weren't short on confidence either. He predicted that Parramatta were ready to take the title, comparing his three-year coaching timeframe at St George, which led to a premiership, to his current similar stint that he crowed would yield the same result for his new team.

The 1964 season started 'on song' with a 25-4 win over Canterbury at Cumberland Oval, five tries to nil, which saw two Rugby League legends up against one another as coaches – Kearney vs Churchill. The very next week though, the lights of reality descended as Balmain cut Parramatta down to size, 8-12 at the Sydney Cricket Ground in front of over 26,000 spectators, with Kearney's opposite being Harry Bath. Ever-accurate Keith Barnes kicked six goals to Parramatta's one (by Brian Hambly) along with tries to Richard Thornett and Bobby Bugden.

It was a rugged battle, with *The Sun-Herald*'s Tom Goodman calling it a match that *"was disfigured by many 'tough' incidents."* Richard was good enough in a losing side to pick up a point in *The Sun-Herald's* "Best and Fairest" award. Goodman wrote, *"... after a series of Parramatta assaults, under which Balmain looked like cracking, big second-rower Dick Thornett, up in the 'dummy' half position for a ruck, found the defence missing and strode 20 yards to the posts."*

It seemed that the loss was just what was needed, as is often the case when the ability doesn't always align with expectation or self-perception. From this point, Parramatta won twelve consecutive matches in front of some huge crowds (four times over 20,000 people), rocketing to the top of the table and hurtling towards a minor premiership. In the Norths game on May 2, *The Sun-Herald*'s Tom Goodman reported that Ken Kearney called Ken Thornett *"an amazing player"* while *"Norths' forwards, though they fought on, with Warner and Cane best, lacked the cleverness of Lynch and Dick Thornett."* Jack Argent and Ken Kearney were watching their plans and predictions coming to fruition before their eyes. What could go wrong?

With four preliminary games to go until the finals, Parramatta had only lost the single game, almost four months earlier in April. Richard was playing extremely well in a dominant, bruising pack, although St George were looking ominously dangerous. Despite some commentary that the Saints were getting old and leg-weary, they were once again a threat although Parramatta had defeated them in their one game thus far.

On August 1, Parramatta were beaten by South Sydney, 6–2 in a try-less match at the SCG in front of over 24,000 people. They managed to hold onto their premiership lead, for the time being at least, but those old, leg-weary men in the red-and-white were breathing fire down their necks.

The lead only lasted another week when Parramatta lost at Pratten Park to the struggling Wests who would eventually finish 7th. Both Thornetts would come in for special mention in Tom Goodman's August 2 *Sun-Herald* article, but their efforts weren't enough. It was hardly the preparation leading into the battle of the season the next week – second-placed Parramatta against new leaders, St George. The less said about that game, the better, with St George flexing their muscles in a powerhouse 36–0 drubbing.

Parramatta did win its final game of the preliminary rounds against Newtown, 22–2, finishing two points adrift of minor premiers, St George, the highest position in their history to date. Three years earlier, they had finished dead-last, as they did the five consecutive years before that.

Because of their second placing at the end of the competition proper, Parramatta was given two bites of the 'cherry' to book a place in the 1964 grand final. Fans and followers of the game were fairly confident that if they missed the first chance against St George (and given recent results, that was a distinct possibility), they would slide through on the second. St George had been flexing their muscles as the games before the playoffs wound down, and their points differential was impressive. Parramatta was going in the opposite direction, and so confidence in the blue and golds was beginning to falter. Additionally, in *The SMH* the day before the game, Tom Goodman reported that *"Kangaroo second-rower Dick Thornett retired from training at Cumberland Oval last night and had heat treatment for his injured knee. He said he was still 'confident' of being able to play for Parramatta against St George in the Rugby League second semi-final at the SCG tomorrow. He is still on the team list… On top of Parramatta's injury worries*

1964 - THE EELS COME OF AGE

last night (there were others), their training operations were impeded through the centre of the arena having been roped off for preparation of a cricket match. Dick Thornett had developed fluid on the knee as a result of a knock in the State Cup final at Newcastle last Saturday. He exercised and did some jogtrotting before joining coach Ken Kearney's team squad last night. After 30 minutes, Thornett retired to the dressing room. He said, 'My knee is still a bit sore, but another day could make all the difference.'" It didn't, and Richard succumbed to injury, and worse still, had to watch the match from the sideline. It wasn't pretty.

In the same newspaper, on the same page, Jim Webster wrote that *"Two of the finest front-row forwards in Australia will be rival captains in the second Rugby Union semi-final tomorrow at the Sports Ground. They are John Thornett (Northern Suburbs) and John Freedman (Drummoyne)."* Ken was next door at the SCG playing for Parramatta but if Richard had been fit, he and Ken would have been a Richard Thornett field-goal's distance from John, playing a semi-final next door at the same time, in two different codes.

Two weeks later, John would go on to lead Norths to grand final victory against Sydney University (his old club) 27-13, with his two Rugby League brothers cheering him on from the stands, with Parramatta having been eliminated. Five years earlier, on the same ground, they were rivals, this time; teammates, at least in spirit.

St George won the major semi-final 42-0 at the SCG in front of 33,000 people on September 5. If doubts about Parramatta's chances hadn't been creeping in before this game, they were literally storming through the door afterwards. It was one win apiece between the two preliminary finalists, Balmain and Parramatta, heading into the September 12 fixture, but the Tigers won the day, thanks to Keith Barnes' five goals from five attempts (Richard Thornett kicked two) as they put Parramatta to sleep, 16-7, two tries to one. Tom Goodman's September 13 *Sun-Herald* article suggested Richard's knee was still not up to a full performance, *"Dick Thornett lasted the game, despite his doubtful knee. Dick made strong relieving runs in the early play, but he faded in the second half."* The two St George stalwarts in the coaches' boxes, Kearney and Bath, had both done an excellent job in preparing their teams for the season. St George went on to win the premiership the next week, 11-6 (their ninth premiership in a row). As it turned out, Harry Bath would come back into Richard's life soon enough, in a more than interesting way.

Parramatta had finished the season on a disappointing note, having promised so much and starting so well. Richard finished with five tries and six goals for the season. After having won 13 of their first 14 matches, they lost five of the next six, but no one could deny St George the premiership based on such a strong showing, consistently, throughout the season.

From a representative perspective, Parramatta did well, and Richard in particular. In the City vs Country matches at the Sydney Cricket Ground on May 16, Richard was joined by his brother Ken, Bob Bugden, Brian Hambly and Billy Rayner for Sydney Firsts which contained ten members of the recent Kangaroos' Great Britain/France tour, while Barry Rushworth and Ron Lynch were selected in the Sydney Seconds.

In the interstate series of 1964, stretching from May 30 to June 27 and consisting of four games (two in NSW – both at the SCG and two in Queensland – one at the Brisbane Exhibition Ground and one at Lang Park), NSW won all four. Richard played in three and scored a try in two of them, an impressive display coming off the back of the big tour and leading into the Test Series against the French. Reporting on June 28 in *The Sun-Herald* on the last game of the series, Tom Goodman wrote, after earlier reporting that coach Eddie Burns was very unhappy with their performance early in the game, that *"Dick Thornett handled twice in neat combination with Raper and Lynch in getting NSW in front 14–11... Four minutes later, Raper sent Dick Thornett over for a fine try."*

Queensland writer, former Kangaroo Jack Reardon, put forward an idea that Queensland should be allowed to call on their former players who were playing with Sydney clubs. It sounded very much like a concept that bore fruit in 1980.

Reminiscing in 2006, champion lock Ron Coote remembered how it had been at Souths in 1964. "We trained for one hour, two nights a week (Tuesdays and Thursdays). Afterwards, for some of the boys, it would be over to the club for half a dozen schooners. There was no weight training, no emphasis on diet. One of the few words of 'expert' advice was to 'dry out' before games – that is, drink no water on the day of the match!"

France, known as "The Chanticleers" ("proud and fierce roosters who dominate the barnyard"), arrived in Australia to play a three-Test series less than five months after their last Test against the Kangaroos in Paris. Australia won the first Test well, in fact they won all three well, proving themselves a fierce, functioning

1964 - THE EELS COME OF AGE

and fluid machine, so clinical were they in disposing of their opponents and showing the world how far they had come since the start of the 1963/64 tour. Ken Day was the only Queenslander in the side, while there were just the two non-tourists from a few months ago – St George's Billy Smith and forward Ron Crowe from West Wyalong.

For the first time in 40 years, reserve players were allowed but the option wasn't taken by captain Ian Walsh, who broke his arm but refused to leave the field in the first Test. Australian backs scored all four tries in the 20-6 win on June 13 at the Sydney Cricket Ground. The second Test, set for Lang Park in Brisbane, didn't take place for three weeks after the first and Tom Goodman, in his June 28 *SMH* column, wrote that there were **"Shocks in Test side"** as Ken Thornett and Graeme Langlands were dropped for Les Johns and Jimmy Lisle respectively. Reg Gasnier was selected as captain/coach of the side, a now long-deceased appointment.

Interestingly, an Australian selection team played a match against North Queensland under lights in Townsville the week before the second French Test, with Australia winning as expected, 32-2. It may not have been the best idea as it was later reported that some players lost up to 5 pounds in weight in the heat.

In the second Test in Brisbane, Reg Gasnier celebrated his appointment as Australian captain/coach for the remainder of the Test series by scoring a hat-trick of tries in the 27-2 victory; France was yet to cross the try line in 160 minutes of Test football. Australia led only 2-0 at halftime but Gasnier's tries, scored in quick succession, put the match beyond doubt. Two of Gasnier's tries were set up by Queensland five-eighth Johnny Gleeson who, on debut, combined brilliantly with St George halfback sensation, Billy Smith.

A Test-hardened Australian team thrashed France in the third Test in Sydney, 35-9. Ken Thornett returned to fullback (and scored a try) ahead of Graeme Langlands, with Kangaroo forwards Graham Wilson and Paul Quinn substituting for the injured Ken Day and Ron Crowe. The match was dominated by winger Ken Irvine, who scored two tries and kicked seven goals for a personal total of 20 points. Australia led 23-4 at halftime and France did not score their first try of the series until 14 minutes from fulltime. Champion lock Johnny Raper was awarded the inaugural 'Harry Sunderland Medal' for the best Australian player in the Test series.

THE NATURAL

It was a somewhat satisfying way for Richard to see off his 1964 season – an unbelievable two-year introduction to the game of Rugby League and a meteoric ascent through the ranks; two-time premiership finalist, City and NSW representative and Kangaroo tourist. Only four years ago, Richard was in a Rome pool as an Olympian before representing the Wallabies for two years. He had, at this point in his career, played against, both within Australia and abroad, five nations, not to mention the many he faced in the water at the Rome Olympics.

CHAPTER SEVENTEEN
1965 – The Brothers Thornett Shine

He was the sort of player that you wanted in your side. He wasn't an easy guy to get to know, but once you got to know him and he respected you, then it was a great bond of friendship with him.
   Peter "Zorba" Peters (Ex-Parramatta forward)

By 1965, Parramatta had established themselves as a real force in the Sydney Rugby League competition, and while they were yet to compete in a grand final, this was the fourth successive year that they were semi-finalists or finalists. Journalist Peter Frilingos was credited with naming Parramatta "The Eels" after the district's Indigenous name was translated as "The place where eels dwell." Ken Thornett was appointed captain/coach of the side which finished the competition rounds in third place.

Parramatta met South Sydney in the minor semi-final, losing 17–2, after Souths led 7–2 at halftime, in front of a crowd of nearly 55,000. It didn't stop there for the Rabbitohs as they marched all the way from fourth position (accounting for Wests and Norths) to the grand final, falling agonisingly short against the mighty St George machine, 8–12. The match was played in front of a record-breaking crowd of over 78,000, a record that stood for 44 years. It was the Dragons' tenth successive grand final win.

Before the season began, *The SMH* reported on January 29 that Rugby Union Test forward Ted Heinrich would be signing a four-year contract to play for Parramatta. Ted played union with Richard at Randwick and they toured with one another to South Africa and New Zealand with the Wallabies. They made their Rugby Union debuts together in the first Test against Fiji in Brisbane in 1961 and remained life-long friends for over 50 years.

The season provided many highlights for Richard, and indeed Ken. *The SMH* reported on May 2 that the previous day, Richard *"...had his best game this season with Hambly, Lynch and the rest of the pack sorely testing South's defences. Ken Thornett figured in more damaging runs than any player on the field."* The same publication said on May 16, after Parramatta defeated Canterbury 19-11 in what was described as an upset, *"The Parramatta forwards staged an improved showing, with Dick Thornett outstanding."*

In the May 22 City Firsts fixture against Country Firsts, *The SMH* the next day reported that Richard's performance was *"not inspired"* in their 32-2 victory. Nevertheless, in the same newspaper on May 30, former Test halfback Keith Holman wrote that in the first interstate game of the year against Queensland which NSW won 31-7, *"The improved showing of second-rower Thornett had much to do with the display of the NSW forwards... In his best game of the season, the big fellow did a lot of tackling, and running wide and giving clean long passes... he joined Raper in getting the wingers, especially Irvine, moving."*

Tom Goodman, writing in *The SMH* on May 31, reported that the Kangaroo team to tour New Zealand was wracked with injuries and withdrawals. He wrote that selections had been *"complicated by the shock announcement yesterday by Kangaroo second-rower Dick Thornett that through 'business reasons' he would not be available for the tour. Thornett, who is a partner with his brother Ken in a trucking business, said yesterday that arrangements made for a relief driver during the three weeks of the tour had fallen through."*

Later in the season, on June 7, in Parramatta's 19-11 win over Manly, *The SMH* reported that *"Former Test second-row forward Dick Thornett spearheaded the thrilling second-half rally for Parramatta. Thornett was masterly around the rucks, frequently cutting the defence to pieces with his smart running and great feeding of the ball to his supports. He combined well with his brother, Ken, to score a try 18 minutes from the finish, when he used his weight and speed to brush off two would-be tacklers."*

A week later, Richard's parents faced a dilemma. *The SMH* set it up nicely on June 14. *"The footballing Thornett brothers of Bronte have set their parents a problem. Should they go to the Sports Ground today and see their eldest son John lead the NSW Rugby Union team against the Springboks – or to the Cricket Ground where Ken and Dick play for Parramatta in the 'Match of the Day' against Balmain?*

Mr H. R. Thornett last night admitted giving the question a lot of thought. 'I will probably see the Springbok match and my wife will go to the league,' he said."

Parramatta won the rugged encounter 12-7 in what *The SMH's* Tom Goodman headlined **Many Players Hurt in Grim League Match.** Richard gave the last pass for the winning try while wearing stitches above his eye from an earlier clash. Richard's brother John was even more fortunate next door, defeating the Springboks 12-3 in an outstanding display.

By the end of June, the press were certainly starting to get excited about Parramatta's 1965 chances. In a June 25 *SMH* piece headlined **Parramatta Big League Threat**, Alan Clarkson spoke of Richard: *"Dick Thornett is another who is just starting to get himself into top condition. Thornett started the season slowly but over the past few matches his form has improved tremendously, and this has helped lift his club's display."*

On July 3, with four minutes left, Richard scored the winning try that started back in their own quarter to help Parramatta defeat Norths by a point, 17-16. A week later, he scored twice in their bruising 10-18 loss to premiership leaders, St George. In their August 7 hard-earned 14-10 win over Manly, Alan Clarkson wrote in his *SMH* article the next day, *"Star player was the great second-row forward, Dick Thornett, who repeatedly bamboozled the Manly forwards with his ball distribution and runs from the rucks."* Clarkson spoke on another occasion about Richard's *"...brainwork around the rucks..."*, further proof of Richard's superior physical presence, his silky skills and Rugby League intelligence combining as one to give him the edge over his rivals.

Heading into the final round, Ken Thornett, on 20 points, led younger brother Richard by two points in the *Sun-Herald*'s "Best and Fairest" award, with £400 up for grabs. In the other code, brother John was running third in the *Sun-Herald's* Rugby Union version of the award. Ultimately, Ken prevailed, winning the prestigious award with Richard in second place, while the mercurial Ken Catchpole won the Rugby Union equivalent. Amazingly, seven years earlier while playing for Randwick with Richard who was fresh out of high school, Ken Thornett won *The Sun-Herald* Rugby Union award as well – a remarkable achievement. The fact that the three brothers were vying for such significant awards says so much about their unique skill sets. Playing at the same time, they were setting the Sydney Rugby League and union scenes alight with their prodigious talents.

CHAPTER EIGHTEEN
1966 – The Ashes in Australia

To a place in the past we've been cast out of
Now we're back in the fight,
We're back on the train, yeah
Oh, back on the chain gang.
The Pretenders (Back on the Chain Gang)

1966 saw Richard and Maureen Thornett welcome their first-born, Liesl.

1966 also saw Great Britain arrive in Australia to play three Tests for the Ashes. While not a particularly formidable side, at least on paper, Great Britain were still regarded as competitive with their usual toughness.

On June 3, Alan Clarkson's *SMH* article stated that *"Talented second-row forward Dick Thornett will be striving tomorrow to regain his place in the top Sydney Rugby League team. Thornett, keen to regain his top form, will captain (the) Sydney Seconds team against Country at the SCG. Thornett was a regular member of the Australian Test side in recent years, but this year his form slipped and he lost his place in the Firsts team. Tomorrow, he will be trying his hardest to force his way into the Sydney team to play England at the SCG tomorrow week. This match is a stepping stone to the NSW sides and then possibly the Test team. Thornett, with his gifted ball distribution and his great speed for such a big man, is needed for the Test series against England."*

It didn't help Richard's cause when Country Seconds won the match 16–6 against their more-fancied rivals, although *"... he did a tremendous amount of tackling, he cover defended well and rarely went to ground with the ball."* Nonetheless, he must have impressed enough for he was chosen in the Sydney team to face Great Britain on June 11 in a superb pack that also featured Raper, Beetson, Ryan, Walsh and Hambly. Sydney went down to a late converted try, 14–15, after being up 14–3 four minutes into the second half. Tom Goodman's *Sun-Herald* article on June 12 said that *"Thirteen minutes before halftime, second-rower Dick Thornett, who did more running in this game than he had done in weeks, added a try."*

A week later, Richard injured his leg in NSW's bruising win over Great Britain, 18–13, with winger Ken Irvine scoring three tries. The injury kept him out of the July 5 NSW vs Queensland game in Brisbane, along with seven other players, five of them forwards.

Keith Barnes, who was chosen at fullback for Australia, said: "We lost the first Test against Great Britain (17–13). There was never very much difference between the two teams, I didn't think. There wasn't much in it in the first Test." Richard missed selection for this Test, which was played at the SCG on June 25 in front of nearly 58,000 people. The Australian side included five debutants, prompting Australian captain/coach Ian Walsh to plead with selectors to provide him with greater experience to counter the Lions in the next Test.

Walsh got his wish when a whole new pack arrived around him for the Lang Park clash, including Richard, Noel Kelly, Mick Veivers and Ron Lynch, although Walsh's request, from a personal perspective, almost backfired, with lock John Raper mooted as his possible replacement. Raper, perhaps fortuitously for Walsh, was ruled out with a broken thumb. There was widespread speculation Walsh would have been a victim of the pack reshuffle if Raper had been fit. Ken Thornett had dislocated his shoulder against Canterbury on May 29, which ruled him out of any hope of selection.

Australia won the second Test in another close, dour and try-less contest, 6–4 on July 16. Australia, desperate to stay in the series race, muscled up to the Brits with their returning veteran hardmen in what turned into a slugfest, with British forward Bill Ramsay sent off in what was a spiteful match. Keith Barnes got Australia home minutes from the end to keep Australia's Ashes hopes alive. There was as much controversy off the field as there was on it, with spectators also showing off their pugilistic skills. One match report stated, *"For periods of an ugly afternoon, fighting on the terraces at Lang Park commanded as much attention as the action on the field. In a rare occurrence, spectators were allowed on the arena in an overflow crowd, and early on there was a sensational incident when an elderly spectator invaded the field and punched English fullback Arthur Keegan."*

Writing in *The SMH* on July 17, Clive Churchill said that the *"...second Test was the toughest I have seen. In my opinion, the better team lost. All Test matches are hard, no-quarter affairs, but today's surpassed anything I have seen. I played in 13 Tests against England and have seen a lot more. But nothing could match the ferocity, and at times the savagery, of today's clash between these two great rivals."* On the same page Tom Goodman reported that Richard had *"...sent the home side's left winger Johnny King sprinting for the corner...but...he was stopped a few yards from the line."* Later, he wrote that Richard, *"...and Mick Veivers were staunch performers."*

Keith Barnes remembers, after sharing a room with Richard and playing in the Brisbane Test, that "He was a great ball player. He brought a different style to the game, I thought. He was more of a running, ball-playing second rower. He created a lot of chances for his support players. I thought distribution was a major plus in his game." When asked to compare the styles of Richard and Arthur Beetson, Barnes said: "Beetson was the best player in that position that I've ever seen, he was a great player. I think he (Richard Thornett) was just a pace behind Beetson. Instead of downgrading Dick, I'm upgrading Artie."

Back in clubland, because Test duty had ruled out Richard and Ron Lynch, and Ted Heinrich was injured, Ken Thornett played lock in Parramatta's victory over Newtown, 17–10.

During his interview for this book, Keith Barnes said, "I got injured in that (second) Test and missed the next one." Barnes was replaced by Les Johns whom he said was "a very great player". Les was a true contemporary of Richard's, having moved from Newcastle to Sydney in 1963 until retiring a year shy of Richard in 1971. The battles he fought for the Kangaroo fullback position during that time with Richard's brother, Ken, as well as greats Keith Barnes and Graeme Langlands, were epic, yet Richard and Les' friendship remained throughout.

Noel "Ned" Kelly, who was one of the Australian front-row forwards in the third Test, followed his typical game-day routine. It was Saturday and kick-off was 3:00 p.m. "Ned" went to work at a butcher shop owned by Mick Wood at Military Road, Mosman. He worked in the shop from 5:30 am until 1:00 p.m., changed out of his work clothes, was picked up at the door by Mick Wood's son, Chris, and driven to the SCG where he went to the dressing room to lie down until near kick-off! It most certainly was a different time.

Played in front of over 63,000 people at the SCG on July 23, Australia scored five tries (including three to Ken Irvine) in a 19–14 victory over Great Britain, with Richard coming off the bench in this game for Arthur Beetson, who had recovered from a knee injury. Beetson had a tremendous first half but was replaced by Richard for the second. The popular view is that Beetson ran out of steam, but he had suffered a recurrence of the shoulder injury which put him out of contention for the earlier Tests. Fiery British prop Cliff Watson seemed on a mission to stamp his physical presence on the game but went too far in the 46th minute when he was sent off for allegedly kicking Australia's Peter Dimond. Two minutes from the end, an all-in brawl broke out, with Alan Clarkson reporting in July 24's *SMH* that *"Punches were thrown as the players milled about and one big English forward aimed several kicks at Australian players"* while Richard had several stitches inserted over a gashed eye. Spectators were *"camping outside the gates for up to 16 hours before they opened at 10 a.m."* and *"Thirty spectators collapsed in the third Test crush...Three had to be taken to hospital for treatment."* Interestingly, Richard was initially not selected in the third Test 15, but the Australian Rugby League refused to accept the team until he was added – quite a bizarre intervention.

Because of injury (a broken toe) and representative duties, Richard played fewer games for Parramatta in the domestic season, one where they finished out of the finals in 7th position. Alan Clarkson reported in *The SMH* on April 3 that *"Players brawled after the final bell in a sensational climax to the South Sydney and Parramatta Rugby League match at Cumberland Oval yesterday. Punches were thrown and referee Keith Holman and his linesmen tried to separate the players as police struggled to hold back children who had hurdled the fence. Prime target seemed to be Souths second-rower, John Sattler, who had earned Dick Thornett's ire early with a questionable tackle."*

At the end of the year, both Richard and Ron Lynch expressed their desires to stay with the club, extending their contracts a further five years as reported on November 9. Nonetheless, eight days later, things did not seem so certain, when *The SMH* reported that *"'The Thornett Brothers will be playing for us next season,' Parramatta Rugby League secretary Mr Spencer O'Neill said last night. Mr O'Neill was commenting on reports that fullback Ken Thornett wanted to leave Parramatta and that second-row forward Dick Thornett has not yet signed another contract with the club. On Tuesday night, Ken Thornett was beaten by Brian Hambly in a close vote for the position as Parramatta coach for next season. 'I have no doubt that both Thornetts will play for us next season,' Mr O'Neill said. 'Ken undoubtedly is disappointed at missing the coaching position but he would not be inclined to sulk about it. He has two years of his contract to go with us. Dick has finished his four-year contract and a new contract has been sent to us by his solicitor.'* Later in the same article, Hambly *"revealed that he almost withdrew his application for the coaching job. 'When I applied, Ken Thornett had not applied,' he said. 'When he did I thought about withdrawing because I did not want to tread on anyone's toes. I decided to leave it in and was surprised when I was chosen.'"*

By December, things were still cloudy, with Alan Clarkson reporting in *The SMH* on December 15: *"Parramatta Rugby League fullback Ken Thornett will apply for a transfer. Thornett, upset with his treatment by the club, decided this after conferring with his solicitor yesterday. He will seek a meeting with the club's retention committee as soon as possible. Thornett, captain/coach for the past two years, was beaten for the position for next season by Brian Hambly. He wants to play with Easts. Top forwards, second-rower Dick Thornett and lock Ron Lynch, have not yet signed new contracts with Parramatta."*

It was going to be an awkward time ahead with the four Test stars fighting it out for their playing futures. The dressing room was sure to be an interesting place to be if new captain/coach, Hambly, was to be instructing his former captain/coach, Ken Thornett (and his brother), on how to play the game. Ken was obviously upset with the club's decision to go down this path, particularly when it involved a teammate replacing him for this senior role, and it must have affected his younger brother as well.

CHAPTER NINETEEN
1967 – A Difficult Season

Victory has a hundred fathers and defeat is an orphan.
  John F. Kennedy

Richard's second daughter, Amanda, entered the world in 1967.

On the other side of the world, on February 11 at Stade Colombes in Paris, France, big brother John Thornett played his last rugby Test match for Australia. Fittingly, he was captain. John announced his retirement at the conclusion of the four-month tour of Britain, Ireland and France, ending the very special career for one of the greatest Wallaby captains and players of all time.

Brian Hambly took the reins of Parramatta at a time when the new rules formulated by the NSWRFL challenged even the most experienced coaches. He was also replacing Parramatta's favourite son, the "Mayor" Ken Thornett, who was surprised that Hambly put his hand up to coach the team. This situation led to friction between Ken, Parramatta officials and almost certainly, Hambly.

During an interview in 2008, Hambly recalled what transpired. "When Parramatta officials fronted me – I don't know whether Ken knows this – they wanted me to be coach and I didn't want to stand against Ken because we'd been away together and you don't sort of do them [sic] sort of things, I don't think. And they 'ummed' and 'aahed' and they wanted me to be coach and I said, well, I wouldn't stand against Ken. But in the long and short of it all, they said he's not standing, he hasn't stood, he hasn't put an application in, so about a week before, I put an application in. Well, the next minute Ken's come in late with his application. There were a few other nominees, but I got the job and well, I thought we had the forwards to do a lot of good things and by the time I was coach they changed the rules from the open tackle to four tackles. So, you were restricted with your forwards. You had to kick the ball back and tackle; there wasn't much playing time. Oh, and blokes were kicking the ball, and it was just --- it's not about me but we lost a few games by a couple of points and the next minute they had the knife into me, so I retired and just finished off there as a coach. I've got no regrets; I wasn't going to play second grade, I've been up there, and I said I'll just retire. They went and put Bob O'Reilly on, and I said it's okay, but I just won't play."

Troubled by a chronic knee injury, Brian Hambly retired from playing before the end of the season, although he continued to coach the team. He played his last game against Souths on June 18, 1967. Interestingly, not long after, Richard hit top form.

Other than Brian Hambly replacing Ken Thornett as the captain/coach at Parramatta, there were other changes taking place in the game as 1967 arrived. New clubs Penrith and Cronulla joined the competition. In addition, the controversial four-tackle rule was introduced, which had both its fans and critics. Although Parramatta's fortunes on the field were mixed, it did see the emergence of future stars Bob O'Reilly, Ron Graham and John McMartin.

Richard's form was up and down throughout the season. He played well in the pre-season but in the first round against Balmain, Tom Goodman reported, *"Second-rower Dick Thornett failed to reach anywhere near the standard he had set in the pre-season match with St George."*

Parramatta struggled for consistency in the first six rounds of the premiership. As did Richard, and he was dropped to reserve grade after the Eels lost to Newtown 10–15. In the lead-up to the round 7 match against Manly, the headline **Parramatta selectors again 'drop' Thornett** was above an article stating *"Parramatta Rugby League selectors last night refused to reinstate Kangaroo second-rower Dick Thornett to fill a vacancy in First Grade. The chance came when lock forward Wayne Brown was forced out with an ankle injury. The selectors moved Ron Lynch from second row to lock and chose Barry Leaney in the second row. Thornett had been one of four players dropped last Tuesday night from the team to play Manly-Warringah at Cumberland Oval on Sunday."* It seemed that Richard was on the outer at Parramatta, and he wore the unaccustomed number 23 on his back in at least two matches – against Balmain and Souths.

In *The SMH* on June 4, 1967, it was reported that the Test series against New Zealand was one where one of the second-row positions for the Kangaroos was up for grabs. By that time, Richard was back in First Grade. In a preview of Parramatta's match against Penrith, Alan Clarkson wrote, *"Former Test second rower, Dick Thornett comes back into the selection picture today in a spot that is obviously wide open in the Test side. Thornett played well last week (coming off the bench against North Sydney) but needs a sustained effort to prompt the selectors to give him more than a passing thought."*

Richard was overlooked for the home series against the Kiwis. The second rowers selected ahead of him were Dennis Tutty, Allan Thomson, Ron Lynch and Geoff Connell.

The SMH on June 26, 1967, reported that *"Parramatta's form in their 9-8 loss to Wests (it was 9-7) was punctuated with poor defence and lack of teamwork, which plagued them throughout 1967."* Two days later, the same publication wrote that *"Richard had his best game of the season to date when after four successive defeats, Parramatta defeated Balmain 11-6 at Redfern Oval. Parramatta played a superior brand of football and overcame a heavy penalty count against it."* Leading journalist Alan Clarkson reported *"Spearheading Parramatta yesterday was former Test second-row forward, Dick Thornett. Thornett gave one of the most polished displays seen in Sydney this season, with his running from the rucks, great distribution of the ball and his defence. He almost broke the hearts of out-of-form Balmain by landing two long-range field goals in three minutes of the second half to set up the match-winning lead. Thornett's first field goal was from 40 yards out and lifted Parramatta to a 9-4 lead. Three minutes later, the ball was fired back to him and with a mighty right-foot kick he sent the ball high over the crossbar to make it 11-4. But Thornett's biggest drop kick was to come. From a 25-yard drop-out, he put the ball into touch about 8 yards from Balmain's line, a kick of almost 70 yards."* Ferris Ashton gave three 'best-and-fairest' points to Richard - his first for the season - for a brilliant all-round performance.

The headline in *The SMH* on July 3, 1967, blared **Thornett in Classy Display**. Judge Alf O'Connor awarded Richard three points in *The Sun Herald*'s "Best and Fairest" award for his performance in Parramatta's 15-10 win over Cronulla-Sutherland. Cronulla led 7-2 at halftime and had the best of the penalties, 14-5. Parramatta were led superbly by Richard who with Peter Linde and Bob O'Reilly was *"... brilliant in defence and attack."* The match report singled out Richard's outstanding ball distribution and stated that he played a *"blinder".*

In *The SMH* on July 8, 1967, under the headline **Tour Candidates on View in R.L. Round**, Tom Goodman wrote that the selectors were now keen to assess Richard's candidacy for the Kangaroo Tour as he was *"...now back to something like top form"*. **Dick Thornett Hits Top Form** was the headline nine days later in *The SMH*. It was another man-of-match performance by Richard as judged by Frank Johnson. Parramatta comprehensively defeated Newtown 32–7 at Cumberland Oval and Richard was a threat whenever he handled the ball; his judicious kicks kept Parramatta on the attack. Richard's personal contribution to the scoreline came from two tries and two field goals.

Parramatta played Manly in round 18 on July 23 at Brookvale Oval and the next day, a report appeared under the dramatic headline: **Day in Hospital; head injuries**

The SMH, 24 July 1967

"Manly-Warringah Rugby League team's Kangaroo second-row forward Ken Day is in Manly District Hospital with head injuries, sustained at Brookvale Oval yesterday.

Day has concussion, a fractured cheekbone and a fractured nose.

His condition last night was reported as satisfactory. Day sustained the injuries when tackled by a Parramatta forward after 28 minutes' play.

The former Queensland player is in his third season with Manly.

He is a highly popular player and Manly paid a heavy price for its 27–9 win over Parramatta, whose defence was poor.

After Day had been taken from the field and replaced by David Knox, referee Barry spoke to Parramatta second-rower Dick Thornett.

Ron Lynch described the incident. "We played Manly one day and I saw 'Moby', he and Ken Day were having a bit of a run-in, but Ken Day made a break and next thing 'Moby' come from out of the clouds and wiped him right out. They took him off the field and I saw a photo of him in the paper (the) next day. You couldn't recognise the bloke. So, 'Moby' finished well in front in that incident. And he was a big man, Ken Day, too. I don't know, but I heard they had a bit of a row on tour once...'63 Kangas [sic], yeah. So, I heard they had a bit of a dust-up over that and I think that was why they were niggling one another at the game."

The SMH reported on July 30, 1967, that *"Richard played a strong game in Parramatta's 16–24 loss to St George at Cumberland Oval."* Alan Clarkson wrote, *"Of the Kangaroo candidates, Parramatta's Ron Lynch and Dick Thornett kept*

1967 - A DIFFICULT SEASON

themselves right in the picture and Saints' Graeme Langlands had an immaculate match." The SMH on August 10, 1967, highlighted that *"Against North Sydney, Richard demonstrated his kicking prowess yet again with a 45-yard drop goal which contributed to the 11–0 lead Parramatta took to sheds at halftime. The plague of inconsistency affected Parramatta in the second half and Norths scored 15 points to 3 to win the match by a point."*

Disappointingly for its fans, Parramatta finished the season in 9th position. Richard had a quiet year, scoring three tries but, amazingly, six field goals.

He was selected in the Sydney side to play Country on September 3 at the Sports Ground, with Country getting over their City rivals 16–12. The game was used as a Kangaroo selection trial for those not involved in the Canterbury, St George, Easts and Souths semi-finals. The importance of this game was evidenced by the attendance of all five national selectors. In the Sydney side were 20-year-old Bob Fulton (captain/coach), Billy Bradstreet, Richard Thornett, Mick Veivers and Arthur Beetson. Peter Dimond was the reserve back. The Country team included John Cootes, Tony Branson, Terry Pannowitz, Allan Thomson, Ron Costello and Alan Buman.

Representatively, this was as far as Richard achieved in an incongruous time sandwiched between an Ashes Series the year before and a World Cup the year after.

The big news in 1967 had nothing to do with the Kangaroos or Parramatta. It concerned the St George juggernaut of 1956–66 which was not so invincible in 1967. It was thought that the four-tackle rule would adversely affect St George's chances of extending their record to 12 premierships in a row. However, according to Ian Walsh, it was less the four-tackle rule and more *"...we were getting on in years, playing strength was not as good as before, and there was behind-the-scenes bickering that affected our team spirit. That was the year we lost our way."* Although the Dragons were minor premiers, their form leading up to the play-offs was patchy. They were not the convincing, confident team of years gone by and they lost to South Sydney in the major semi-final. It was Canterbury, led by former Dragon Kevin "Kandos" Ryan, that delivered the knock-out blow to St George when they won the preliminary final 12–11. Canterbury went on to play South Sydney in the grand final only to go down 10–12. It was the end of one reign and the beginning of another.

Richard did not have a great season. His form throughout was patchy. However, he was still held in high regard by the great Rugby League writers Tom Goodman and Alan Clarkson who had faith in his ability to represent Australia with distinction.

In *The SMH* on September 7, 1967, Goodman included Richard among his 26 players for the 1967/68 Kangaroo tour. He justified Richard's inclusion over Canterbury-Bankstown's George Taylforth because he felt Richard would find his best form during the tour of England and France. Similarly, in *The SMH* on September 12, 1967, journalist Alan Clarkson also included Richard in his team. Like Tom Goodman, Clarkson chose Richard not for his current form but rather what he could produce if selected to tour. Clarkson wrote, *"Thornett has vast experience and on tour, with regular matches, could become a vital part of the Australian forward lineup."*

The Kangaroo team was chosen after the grand final between South Sydney and Canterbury. Richard missed selection. The second rowers were Elton Rasmussen, Allan Thomson, Kevin Goldspink and Ron Lynch. Richard was down on form and the selectors were not willing to gamble by selecting him to tour in the hope/expectation that he would find his best with the Kangaroos.

The Kangaroos had an underwhelming tour of Great Britain and France in 1967/68. They won the Lions' Series 2–1 but went down to the French 2–0, after drawing the first Test. The Australian team, as was the custom, were accommodated in Ilkley, about 25 km west of Leeds. There were concerns about off-field behaviour, which cast a shadow over their football. The isolated location, chosen for financial and player-management purposes, failed to prevent one player, wearing a bowler hat and nothing else, from striding through the streets of Ilkley. The hotel was really showing its age by now, and for subsequent tours, the Australian Rugby League made the long overdue decision to house the players in accommodation more fitting for an elite sporting team.

At home, Richard was left to reflect on his season. He was 27 years of age and in a period of four years, he had slipped from Australia's number one second rower, to at best, number five. He was now being spoken of as a "former international".

There were challenges for Richard to meet for sure, but perhaps there was some fight left in the 'old dog' yet.

CHAPTER TWENTY
1968 – The World Cup Australia/NZ

Do not go gentle into that good night,
Old age should burn and rave at close of day;
Rage, rage against the dying of the light.

Though wise men at their end know dark is right,
Because their words had forked no lightning they
Do not go gentle into that good night.

Good men, the last wave by, crying how bright
Their frail deeds might have danced in a green bay,
Rage, rage against the dying of the light.

Wild men who caught and sang the sun in flight,
And learn, too late, they grieved it on its way,
Do not go gentle into that good night.

Grave men, near death, who see with blinding sight
Blind eyes could blaze like meteors and be gay,
Rage, rage against the dying of the light.

And you, my father, there on the sad height,
Curse, bless, me now with your fierce tears, I pray.
Do not go gentle into that good night.
Rage, rage against the dying of the light.

Dylan Thomas (***Do Not Go Gentle Into That Good Night***)

Under a newspaper headline **The Big Show is Ready to Roll**, Rugby League pundits expressed their beliefs that the 1968 season would be remembered for St George's big-spending in an attempt to recapture the premiership owned for 11 seasons prior to 1967, players vying for World Cup selection, the World Cup competition, new incentive payments introduced by some clubs to promote more exciting play, and new training methods influenced by the routines employed by football teams in North America.

Parramatta promoted Ian Johnston from reserve grade coach to take control of the Firsts. In 1949, Johnston became the first player from the club to represent Australia. Richard was appointed captain in preference to Kangaroo Ron Lynch. Notable recruits were Peter Peters, a 20-year-old goalkicking second rower from Goulburn who the club hoped would eventually fill the big boots of Brian Hambly, and Keith Campbell, a promising 17-year-old lock forward and first rate goalkicker from Wentworthville. Peter "Zorba" Peters recalled, "I didn't know much about the coach, Ian Johnston, but it was an era of Parramatta where the senior players had a big influence over the club and it was Dick, Ronny Lynch, those sort of players that were current internationals at the time, that held sway and they virtually guided the side throughout the season. I was in awe of 'Moby' Dick and 'Thirsty' Lynch. And if they'd told me to run through a brick wall, I would have."

Parramatta was one of the clubs that decided to offer incentive payments to its players to motivate the team to play the brand of football that proved so successful in the 1963–1965 seasons.

The incentive payments seemed to have an immediate effect and Parramatta performed strongly in the Wills pre-season competition. Their first game was against St George who had spent like millionaires during the off-season in the hope of re-establishing their supremacy in the NSWRFL competition. On debut were ex-Wallaby Phil Hawthorne, current Kangaroo five-eighth Tony Branson and giant Fijian Apisai Toga fresh from a sensational stint with Rochdale Hornets in England. Also on debut was Test prop John Wittenberg who was playing his first game for 17 months after sitting out the 1967 season because the Queensland Rugby League (QRL) enforced *punitive transfer fee rules which prevented him from signing with St George in Sydney*. Parramatta more than matched the star-studded Saints, scoring a surprising 12–9 win, after gaining the ascendancy during a three-minute period of the first half when Arch Brown and then Paul Gibson crossed for tries. Richard played strongly as Parramatta held on to their lead. *The SMH's* well-respected journalist, Alan Clarkson, wrote, *"Dick Thornett proved he could be right back in representative calculations with a strong match which featured a lot of solid defensive work."* Clarkson noted, *"Weighing under 16 stone for the first time in seven years, Thornett showed he retains the skill at getting movements going."*

In their next game, Parramatta recorded a 17-16 win over premiers South Sydney at Cumberland Oval, in what Alan Clarkson described as a *"fiery"* contest. Parramatta scored three tries to two. Richard's name was added to the scoresheet when he raced through to touchdown after five-eighth Fred Pickup kicked over the top of the Souths players.

Tom Goodman observed that the game against South Sydney was *"extraordinarily good"* and a *"fiery contest"* played in extreme heat – a day for Noel Coward's *Mad Dogs and Englishmen*. Goodman was impressed by the comeback by Souths, who at one point were hopelessly placed but rallied in the second half through some excellent football. The legendary scribe wrote, *"Equally impressive was the way Parramatta, rocking on their feet, recovered under the drive of Dick and Ken Thornett, and hurled the enemy back."*

Parramatta won their next two games against Easts (12-9) and Newtown (18-15) to qualify for the semi-finals of the pre-season competition against Penrith. In a low-scoring game contested on a heavy ground, Richard tried to get his team moving and cracks occasionally appeared in the Penrith defence with a match report noting *"especially when the Parramatta forwards ran onto Dick Thornett's passes, but generally the team's efforts lacked polish and drive."* Penrith led 7-0 at halftime after an exhilarating 90 metre try by their powerful winger Bob Landers, who also kicked two goals. Landers kicked a penalty 15 minutes into the second half and Peter Peters, Parramatta's new second rower from Goulburn, kicked two goals. The score was 9-4 just before fulltime. In a last-ditch attempt to pull the game out of the fire for Parramatta, Richard hoisted an up-and-under, which bounced and evaded everyone until a tangle of players landed on the ball. Richard was adamant he had scored, but referee Jack Bradley ruled that Penrith's Maurie Raper had forced the ball.

Richard and his Eels had made a good start to the season and except for the game against Penrith, Parramatta was playing a brand of football that could take them a long way in the competition.

They were to meet Balmain in the opening round of the NSWRFL premiership. Richard was troubled by a hand injury and an x-ray revealed a break just above the knuckles, which meant he was in doubt for the game. However, he passed a fitness test and played in the game which according to Tom Goodman, Balmain *"stole"* from Parramatta 17-16 when Len *Killeen "kicked a thrilling (and controversial) last second goal"* – a match-winning effort worthy of coach "Golden Boots," Keith Barnes himself. This game was the premiership debut of Peter Peters. *"The first game I played, I gave away a penalty in a late tackle and the touch judge, for some reason, marched it 20 metres up the field. And Len Killeen, the great goalkicker from South Africa, kicked the goal and we got beaten by 1 point, 17-16. I cost my new team a victory in my first game for the club, which wasn't a very good start."*

Continuing their good early season form, Parramatta bounced back from their unlucky loss to Balmain and defeated Western Suburbs on April 7 at Lidcombe Oval, 10-8, in what was described as a *"fast, exciting"* game. From the outset, Wests hooker Ken Stonestreet won a major share of the ball (26-10) from the scrums, allowing his team to launch many attacking raids in Parramatta's half of the field, but the Eels' defence held firm with Richard scoring a try, converted by Peter Peters, for Parramatta to lead 5-3 at halftime. Bob O'Reilly and Ken Thornett led the way in the second half and Arch Brown ensured a Parramatta victory when he scored a 45-metre try after deft interchange of passes by Fred Pickup, Barry Rushworth and Bob O'Reilly.

Peter "Zorba" Peters was a qualified journalist who joined *The Sun* newspaper when he signed with Parramatta. He later shared the following anecdote from the Wests game. *"I remember we were playing at Lidcombe Oval I think it was. Well, playing Wests anyway. And, I remember I had an issue with Noel Kelly. I tackled a Wests player high... I remember waiting to be cautioned by the referee who happened to be the former West great halfback Keith Holman, and Holman said, 'Parramatta number ten, wait there,' while he checked on the injured player, and Noel Kelly sauntered up to me and said 'Hey.' And I said, 'Yeah.' He said, 'I've got a story for you.' I said, 'Yeah, oh, that's nice of you. What about?' And he said, 'About your funeral arrangements,' and of course, I was shaken....I was a young player in a very early game in my career in the competition. Dick saw it. He was always looking out for the younger players. Dick came up to me and said, 'Look, whatever you do, don't turn your back. Keep him in front of you at all times.' And I got through till about a minute from the end of the game and I felt this tap on my shoulder when I was jogging to a scrum. And I turned my head, and as I turned, I thought, 'You idiot.' And I woke up in the dressing room. Stupid me to even run foul of a guy that was one of the boxing champions in Ipswich in Queensland before he came to Sydney to play. Kelly and I became great mates. I mean he lived on the northern beaches, and he had a butcher shop at Collaroy Plateau. And I actually went there to get the family meat at his butcher shop."*

Parramatta won seven of its first ten matches. On April 25, Parramatta defeated Penrith 21-6 at Cumberland Oval, avenging their loss in the pre-season semi-final. The Parramatta forwards played as a pack, often exchanging short passes and switching the point of attack which kept Penrith on the back foot. Still, the game was close at 9-6 to Parramatta until midway through the second half when Ken Thornett scored a marvellous try running off Richard, who *The SMH* reported *"...had shaped up for a field goal on the Penrith 25, but changed his mind and slipped a pass to his brother who left the defence standing."*

Richard was rated a certainty for selection in the City Firsts team to play Country Firsts. The feeling of some journalists was that the selection of the two City teams were critical decisions for the Kangaroos with *The SMH* reporting on May 4, *"Wrong selections and thoughtless appraisal of a player's worth could be disastrous in future selections. Like it or not, Sydney is the hub of Rugby League in Australia. It has the best players, and these players will form the basis from which the World Cup squad will evolve. Mistakes tomorrow night could give the edge to Country and Queensland selectors later, to force in players of lesser ability."*

The selectors chose a very strong City Firsts side which included Richard and Arthur Beetson in the second row of a huge and skilful forward pack. In front of 18,155 spectators, City ran over the top of Country to the tune of 34 to 14. However, Australia's chances of winning the World Cup were dealt a blow when Country's Ron Costello smashed City fullback Les Johns in the face with his elbow and forearm as Johns was racing after a kick through. Rod Humphries of *The SMH* reported that Johns, who suffered *"two nose fractures and two cheek fractures, plus possible torn ligaments in the neck and concussion, will not be able to train for two weeks."* A specialist said it was likely that Johns would miss the entire World Cup.

THE NATURAL

In round 9 on May 19, Parramatta's forwards dominated in their team's hard-fought 13–7 victory over Eastern Suburbs. The match report under the headline of **Forwards Called the Tune** noted, *"Dick Thornett and Ron Lynch made many crashing 30-to-40-yard bursts through the lighter Easts pack. Dick Thornett was the star of the game. His long, low, raking kicks continually put Parramatta on the attack."*

In April, Ken Thornett announced he was unavailable to play for Australia in the World Cup. With an eye to life after football, Ken had purchased a property at Binnaway. He said, *"There's no way I could be available. I have too much work on my property to even contemplate playing representative football."*

Richard's performances for Parramatta demonstrated he was in peak form for the representative season. He was selected for the NSW team to play Queensland in May.

The SMH's Alan Clarkson covered the interstate game on May 18 at the SCG. He wrote, *"Spearheaded by second-rower Dick Thornett, who had a great game, the NSW forwards completely overran the Queenslanders."* NSW carved up Queensland to win 30–7. Clarkson reported that Richard scored a try and was involved in setting up three others, noting *"His cleverness in getting the ball to his supports makes him dangerous every time he handles,"* and that on this performance, *"He must be one of the best second-rowers in the world."* Clarkson, who covered the 1967/68 Kangaroo tour, said he *"did not see better"* during that campaign in England and France. It seemed that Richard had recaptured the form that previously made him the best player in his position in Australia.

Wednesday, June 26, 1968. In what was regarded as their best performance since World War II, Queensland defeated NSW 15–8 at the Brisbane Exhibition Ground. Ten minutes into the second half, Richard was sent off for the first time in his career for kicking Geoff Connell. Under the headline of **Thornett off as Queensland beat NSW**, *The SMH* reported, *"Spectators disagreed with referee Henry Albert's decision."* A few minutes earlier, Richard ran 45 yards to score a try, converted by Graeme Langlands for an 8–6 lead to NSW. Langlands and captain Billy Smith tried valiantly to win the game for NSW but to no avail. The next day, Richard was exonerated by the Queensland Rugby League Judiciary Committee.

Richard was well on his way to his 28th birthday and although his mobility was hampered due to a knee that troubled him, he was still one of the finest all-round players in the game. He could hit hard in defence and his ability with the ball was on a par with Arthur Beetson and Johnny Raper. Peter Peters said, *"When you're talking about Beetson, and Malcolm Reilly, and Dick Thornett, they were players that could handle the tough stuff but had the skills to give them that advantage over the average forward."*

Bob "The Bear" O'Reilly on Richard Thornett

"I thought he was the best footballer I ever saw and still think he is the best footballer that I have ever come across. I'd say to Mick Cronin, I do not talk to him a lot about it, but we always gather all the ratings they have on these players and we would say this bloke was the best player, and you would tend to go and vote for Johnny Raper and all vote for Reg Gasnier and all vote for these blokes, and I said to Cronin one day, 'I played with him for 5 or 6 seasons, this is Dick.' I just went through some of the things he did in the football game. I said he was 6 feet 2 and he was 16-and-a-half stone. I said he could run, he was powerful, but he did not train, he did not do a lot of weights, but at one stage, he held the record for tries scored for Parramatta there in one single game. I think he was one of the players that held that until a couple of years ago. I remember playing a game at Redfern Oval against South Sydney and not only did he have a good game, but he ended up kicking two field goals from 60 metres out or something like that. We would say, 'Where did this all come from?' At one stage he was kicker at the line on penalties, he was a kicker in general play, and I think he even goalkicked for us at certain stages in the game. He was cruel when he wanted to be. I have seen him put a few blokes to sleep; some pretty rugged characters too. Malcolm Reilly took about 4 or 5 minutes to wake up one day at the (Sydney) Cricket Ground. I remember that one. He was to me.... he had everything. If he had the work ethic of Johnny Raper, we might have had the greatest footballer the world has ever seen, ever, I think, but I still say he was. Pound-for-pound, he just had more skills than any player I ever played with or against."

(From an interview with the authors, 2008)

According to Peter Peters, *"I felt like a midget packing into the second row with* him. *I mean, he wasn't called 'Moby' Dick for nothing. He was a giant of a man. He had huge legs. He was fast for a big man. He could be brutal if he wanted to be and when he was on his game, he was.... he was almost impossible to stop, but he had silky skills as well."*

Richard continued with his excellent form, which augured well for Australia's chances in the World Cup.

The 1968 World Cup was hosted by Australia and New Zealand. Australia had hosted the World Cup once before in 1957, when led by the great Newtown centre, Dick Poole, the team won all three of its round-robin games and succeeded Great Britain as world champions without having to play a final. However, the 1968 World Cup would see a round-robin series and the winner would be decided in a final between the two top teams.

Richard's good form was rewarded when he was selected as the Australian vice-captain, under Johnny Raper. The 19-man World Cup squad included future NRL Immortals Raper, Graeme Langlands, Arthur Beetson, Ron Coote and Bob Fulton. The squad was rounded out by 1967/68 Kangaroos Johnny King, Elton Rasmussen, Johnny Greaves, Dennis Manteit, Billy Smith and Tony Branson, experienced internationals John Wittenberg and Brian Fitzsimmons, and debutants Eric Simms, Fred Jones, Brian James, Johnny Rhodes and Lionel Williamson. The coach was Harry Bath.

Unfortunately, the horrific injuries Les Johns suffered during the City vs Country match forced him to miss the World Cup.

The draw for the World Cup was:

Saturday, May 25: Australia v Great Britain at the SCG
    New Zealand v France in Auckland.
Saturday, June 1: Australia v New Zealand in Brisbane;
Sunday, June 2: Great Britain v France in Auckland.
Saturday, June 8: Australia v France in Brisbane;
    New Zealand v Great Britain at the SCG
Monday, June 10: Final at the SCG.

A crowd of 62,256 saw Australia defeat Great Britain 25–10 in a thrilling round-robin match at the SCG. The Lions made a good fist of things in the first 40 minutes, and Australia only led 10-7 at the break. For Great Britain, their halves Roger Millward and Tommy Bishop were in scintillating form and it was unfortunate that their teammates could not capitalise on their brilliant play. The Lions gave away 18 penalties and Australian fullback Eric Simms, who was on debut, obliged by landing eight goals from nine attempts. Simms also played well in the open. Although coach Harry Bath was pleased with the result, he had concerns about performances by some of his players. *The SMH* reported: *"Those who played well, in addition to Simms, of course, were centre Greaves, halfback Smith, lock, Raper, prop Wittenberg and second-rowers Coote and Thornett."*

When interviewed for this book, John Rhodes looked back. "Yeah, it was a terrific era; some great footballers in those days, including Dick. I enjoyed the camaraderie (with everyone). It was just a privilege to play with them." Rhodes well remembers a moment in that World Cup round-robin match against Great Britain. "I remember one time we were playing against Great Britain at the Sydney Cricket Ground and there was a kick through. Eric Simms caught it and he passed (to) me and I ran about 40, 50 metres, and backing me up on the inside was Dick. I thought, '*Gee, how did he get there?*'"

In Auckland, tough-tackling France defeated New Zealand 15-10 before a crowd of 18,000, at Carlaw Park. The Kiwis played with a man short for most of the match after second-rower Brian Lee was sent off after 11 minutes. The French team surprised the Kiwis with their aggression and pace around the ruck and out wide.

Australia was expected to play Great Britain in the World Cup Final. However, in an astonishing upset, France eliminated any chance Great Britain had of an appearance in the Final by defeating them 7-2 on a mud heap in Auckland.

Australia then defeated New Zealand 31-12 on June 1 at Lang Park, Brisbane, in front of 23,608 spectators. The Australians were down 4-7 at halftime but then scored 20 points in 11 minutes to have the match 'in the bag'. This was Richard's first and only international against the Kiwis. In the lead-up to the match, John Rhodes remembers a moment when Richard lost his temper, but it wasn't on the football field: "When we came home from training one time before playing New Zealand in Brisbane, Dick had put his New South Wales and Parramatta jerseys out to dry where we were staying at the Colmslie Hotel. Somebody came in and pinched them, and I remember him going off about it. He wasn't very happy. He came back from training to bring them inside and (they were gone). He was furious."

Australia and France had already qualified for the World Cup Final when they met in Brisbane on June 8 for a round-robin match. So, in an almost farcical situation, France rested several of their best players, and the game was little more than a training run for the Australians, who scored seven tries to nil as they cantered to a 37–4 win. Australian forward Arthur Beetson and France's winger Jean Ledru were sent off, but they were free to play in the Final as they did not have to front the International Rugby League Board until after the scheduled SCG clash.

With the exception of Ken Kearney, Richard did not respond well to being coached because he believed that once players made First Grade or higher honours, they should be capable of making the right decisions on the field, without being told what decisions they should make.

One of the coaches Richard did not gel with was Harry Bath, his coach during the World Cup. He said, "See, Harry Bath, really, he didn't have to do anything; he was just a disciplinarian and a trainer in my eyes."

In a storied playing career, Harry "The Old Fox" Bath had been a tough, skilful and at times, brutal forward. In this sense, he was similar to Richard. Bath was graded with Brisbane Souths at 16. He represented Queensland in 1945 before transferring to Balmain in Sydney where he was a member of the 1946 and 1947 premiership teams. A serious injury ruled him out from playing for Australia in 1946 and he represented NSW in 1947. He went to England, joined Barrow (briefly) in late 1947 and then Warrington, who, in 1954, he led to an 8–4 Challenge Cup victory at Odsal Stadium in front of 102,575 fans (a world record Rugby League crowd at that time). He was a brilliant goalkicker, landing 700-plus goals. Bath also represented Other Nationalities on 12 occasions. Returning to Australia, he joined St George, winning premierships with them from 1957 to 1959. He was sent off in the 1959 grand final, which was his last game.

Bath pursued a coaching career with Balmain in 1961 and first coached Australia in the 1962 Ashes series against Great Britain. He was a strict disciplinarian who favoured 'locking down' his players during international competition. Michael Cleary, who played on the wing for Australia in the first Test of that series, remembers Bath's attempts to keep the players in camp. "We weren't allowed out. We stayed at the Pacific Hotel, in Manly. And he said, 'Give us your car keys. Yeah, no one's going out.' Bugger that! So, I snuck out there. And he finished up just personally tying a rope around our wrists and walking up to Manly Oval (to train)!" Cleary recalls the players singing Sam Cooke's *Working on a Chain Gang* as they walked along.

Bath said the Australian players blamed him for the first Test loss to the Lions in 1962. He is quoted in Alan Clarkson's article headlined **Little Dictator Report; Bath Will Request Interview with RL Board.** *"I have been made out to be a little dictator and I want to clear myself of these charges."* Bath submitted his report to the Board and was then given more control of the team when his position was upgraded to manager/coach for the second Test. Reg Gasnier, who captained Australia in the first Test, denied there were any issues between the coach and his team. According to Gasnier, *"...coach Harry Bath had put on restrictions which could be expected for a team in training for a Test."* Australia lost the first Test 31-12, the next one 17-10, and the series 2-1.

In the 1968 World Cup Final, coach Harry Bath selected Richard in the starting lineup to partner Ron Coote in the second row. Richard's recollection of that game was one of embarrassment. "I played in the Final which was against France. Harry Bath, he took me off at halftime. I don't know why, because a lot of my friends that were watching the game said, 'You were good in the first half, why did he take you off?'"

Richard had played strongly in the first half. An example: in the 38th minute, he combined nicely with Arthur Beetson and running freely, he sent winger Lionel Williamson in for the first of his two tries. *"A damaged ankle"* was the official reason given for replacing Richard at halftime. His roommate, Elton Rasmussen, took the field in Richard's place.

The Australian team had been away from their loved ones for a long period during the 1968 World Cup campaign and Richard was keen to see his wife Maureen when the team returned to Sydney after defeating New Zealand in Brisbane in their round-robin match. 40 years later, Richard suspected that Harry Bath replaced him in the Final as a punishment, "...we came back from Brisbane to play in the Final, and on the Wednesday, he (Bath) said, 'You are all to be in bed by ten o'clock' or something like that."

THE NATURAL

Maureen Thornett recalled, "There was no contact allowed. We hadn't seen each other for two weeks. I was feeling lonely and distressed." Richard said, "...so I went to meet her for a coffee in Kings Cross somewhere... I jumped the back fence, and I was only gone a couple of hours having a coffee and he (Harry Bath) checked the rooms and (when I returned) Elton Rasmussen said, 'Well, he'd (Bath) had been in.' So, he couldn't change the team then, but I reckon that's the reason why (I was replaced in the Final), because I went against his decision."

John Rhodes has a similar recollection to Richard and Michael Cleary of coach, Harry Bath: "He (Bath) had this silly thing where you had to be in bed at 10 o'clock and you couldn't be with your wife the night before a game. He really stood by that. I can remember Barry Muir ….. (a) young fella came up to Barry and said, 'Well listen, what do I do tonight? Do I stay off the grog? Or what time do you want me to (go to) bed?' He (Muir) said, 'You're an adult.' You just did what you normally do. Harry was a stickler for (going) early to bed and all this sort of thing, but (some players) didn't. Johnny Raper, for argument's sake, he used to always have a late night before a game. (Nonetheless), he was a good coach. He had a bloody good bunch of blokes around him too. A coach in those days (could) just gather the players and say, 'Look, just do what you've got to do.'"

Australia led 7-0 at halftime in the Final, and won a tough, hard game 20-2. It was the last time captain Johnny Raper would represent Australia. It was also the last time Richard Thornett would don the green and gold.

The photos taken during the presentation of the World Cup show Richard in his Australian blazer and uniform standing behind Bath and Johnny Raper. He looks to be removed from that moment of triumph. Bath's possibly premeditated decision to replace Richard Thornett that day tarnished what should have been a proud, joyful moment for Richard, his family and friends.

When questioned, John Rhodes provided his take on Richard's replacing: "I don't think it was because of the way he was playing. I don't think he was replaced for form, just to give him a rest, he was playing too well." It was an interesting perspective given Richard wasn't usually the player replaced at halftime in games.

While Richard was on World Cup duty, Ron Lynch captained Parramatta to an 18-14 win over South Sydney followed by an 11-11 draw with St George.

Richard was back on duty with Parramatta for the round 15 match with top-of-the-table Manly.

1968 - THE WORLD CUP AUSTRALIA/NZ

The Rugby League News reported on the game played July 7, won by Parramatta 11-7. *"Parramatta look to their international second-row pair, Dick Thornett and Ron Lynch, playing an important dual role in the team's bid to maintain a forward position. Thornett is in fine form, and his 50-yard drop-kicked goal against Manly last Sunday was a gem. Perhaps even more satisfying to Parramatta followers was the return to something like 'form' of Ron Lynch."*

Of Richard's mentorship and 'bonding' sessions, Peter Peters said, "I think his influence on young players was paramount. I mean a young Bob O'Reilly was in that side during some games in 1968 and Thornett took him under his wing, as he did myself. He was a great support for me. Him and Ronny Lynch were....well, I looked up to them, and I wanted to be just like them; going to the pub after training sessions at the old Royal Exhibition in Parramatta, not far from Cumberland Oval and where the Leagues Club is today. It was the place to go to for the players after training and I was only young. I was only just out of my teen years and I wasn't a great drinker, but I certainly made myself go to the after-training sessions and after a couple of sessions where they would drink 18 schooners, I would be looking for my car to go to sleep in, but then drive back to Goulburn after even a couple of schooners. But I couldn't believe what they could drink and then turn up for training the next night. They didn't call Ronny Lynch 'Thirsty' for nothing. And you got to remember that they all had jobs. Dick was a publican at North Sydney. A lot of the players drove brewery trucks, which were a good way to make money in those days. Lots of players from lots of clubs found their way into the breweries and were driving brewery trucks which they owned and leased out to the breweries."

Richard's good friend and teammate, Ron Lynch, recalled the ritualistic trips home after those bonding sessions. "He was living over at North Sydney. He had a big Rambler, a Nash Rambler, and I was living at Rydalmere at the time, and we used to leave the pub and take off together. There was no breathalyser in those days and he used to have a cigar – I don't know what the cigar was, just to get rid of the breath on the way home, I think – but he'd follow me, because we used to both go along Victoria Road at that stage and he'd follow me along there and every now and then I'd see the big cigar, the big red thing come on, and I think the cigar was only for the breath freshener. Yeah, so I don't know how many times he followed me home like that, big 'Moby'."

Bob "The Bear" O'Reilly added his thoughts about the influence Richard had on him. "I did not have anything to do with him till about '66, '67 when I came to Parramatta. He made a tremendous impression on me. I think the first thing that came to me was that I suppose I had a lot of confidence in myself too and the style of football I played, that Dick was sort of my role model, and I developed my football on him and how he played the game. I think he sort of took me under his wing in '66, '67 and he probably saw something there and we became very friendly. I think it was a real honor that (at) certain stages in my early career in '67, '68, I was invited to his home or if he lived in the hotel, upstairs, where we would have dinner and he would invite maybe Peter Johnson, the Rugby Union guy. I remember Mick O'Gorman was one of his friends and we would have dinner. I would be there, I would be 18, 19, 20 – sitting there. Maureen would be there, and I remember some of the women. You would keep in your place and not open your mouth too much but would listen and have a good time and have a couple of drinks and then you would see him again at training the following night. So, I really became a friend. He was a great friend to me."

Lionel Williamson was a recipient of Richard's generosity of spirit when he joined the Australian team from Queensland for the 1968 World Cup. Williamson told the authors of this book: "I liked talking to Dick," (or 'Moby' Dick as Lionel would sometimes call him). "He was a very nice bloke. I was new on the scene, and I found him very welcoming and always great to have a chat to……(he) made you feel at home and made you feel welcome."

Parramatta were in 6th place going into round 16 of the 1968 season against Penrith and slipped to 8th position after losing a close game 12–14. On July 21, Richard showcased his try-scoring ability in the 48–9 victory over the 1967 grand finalists Canterbury at Cumberland Oval. He scored four tries, equalling Mitch Wallace's club record. John Rhodes played that day: "I can recall (Dick) when he was playing with Parramatta. They thrashed us one day up at Parramatta and Dick scored four tries, all four of them under the posts." Two of Richard's tries were scored in a space of four minutes midway through the first half. After 28 minutes, Parramatta led 14–2 and were in control of the game when Canterbury's lock Ron Raper was sent from the field after a head-high tackle. At 32 minutes, referee Don McDonald also dismissed Canterbury centre John Greaves for foul language. Things didn't improve when Ross Kidd had to leave the field with a rib injury at

17 minutes of the second half, and with 13 men against 10, Parramatta went on to score a feast of tries. Richard's second-row partner that day was Peter "Zorba" Peters who kicked nine goals. He recalls, "I remember Dick just ran riot that day, scored four tries. They couldn't handle him. He just buried them in that game. He was a great ball player. He was also a tremendous runner of the football. And if he came through on the burst, he was awfully hard to stop. And he had a step and a change of direction for a big man as well. I mean, for a lot of years that was the pinnacle of my career, kicking nine goals in a game in the New South Wales Rugby League was very special and I think it was a record that was the most points – 18 – scored by any player in one game in that year for Parramatta and I think it was a record for the club until that great goalkicker Mick Cronin broke it and it was a privilege to hold that for however long I did."

Parramatta moved back up to 6th spot on the ladder after their big win over Canterbury. They then lost to North Sydney 2–22 but won 21–14 against Newtown to remain in 6th position.

Their round 20 game – August 11 – was against Eastern Suburbs who by then were leading the competition. In what was a similar pattern to their clash in round 9, the big Parramatta forwards controlled the game with Bob O'Reilly's clever ball distribution and the running game of Richard and Peter Peters providing a treat for spectators. Parramatta scored its three tries – one each to Richard, Peters and Paul Gibson (a future NSW parliamentarian) – in the first half to lead 11–2. Richard landed a 40-metre drop goal for good measure as his team ran out winners 13–9. Richard and Peters, who had developed into a formidable second-row combination, contributed 10 of the 13 points scored by Parramatta.

The Parramatta Rugby League 'nursery' was now feeding quality young players to the three grades. Seven players in the game against Easts were ex-local juniors – forwards Bob O'Reilly, Keith Campbell, John McMartin and Barry Leaney, and backs Barry Norden, Dave Irvine and Joe Turski. During the season, O'Reilly (at 19 years of age) and Campbell (17) were beginning to show the benefits of playing alongside Richard and 'Thirsty' Lynch.

Parramatta played consistently well in the first half of the 1968 season, exceeding the expectations of even its most devoted fans, and by round 10 they were leading the competition. However, a draw with St George (11–11) and close losses to Balmain (17–16), Penrith (14–12) and Cronulla (10–7) were costly as they finished just outside of the top four and missed the semi-finals. Peter Peters commented, "Well, we finished 6th in a 12-team competition, two wins out of the finals. Our average crowd was 14,000. The best in the competition was the Bulldogs with 15,000. So, it was a big improvement, I think, on expectations. And I think they were a side that was on the rise, rather than one of the red-hot favourites."

In yet another significant milestone for the Thornett family, Richard and Ken celebrated 100 games with Parramatta. Ken's last game for Parramatta was August 25, an 8–0 win against St George. "Zorba" Peters played that day and recalls, "… well it was a great era, the 60s. I mean I remember in that year we played St George in the final game and they made the semis. We beat them eight to nil. No tries in the game. I kicked two goals and a field goal to score six points and Arch Brown kicked a goal. In that St George side were players like Johnny Raper, Graeme Langlands, Dick Huddart, Billy Smith, Elton Rasmussen, John Wittenberg, Tony Branson – every one of them, an international, Barry Beath an international, Johnny King an international. So, the players from that great era were still there."

At fulltime, and as a gesture of great respect, Ken Thornett's 1963/64 Kangaroo teammates Graeme Langlands and Johnny Raper chaired him from the field.

Ken settled with his family on a farm at Binnaway where he enjoyed some success as the captain/coach of Coonabarabran. Another great fullback, Keith Barnes, also retired. And so it was that "The Mayor" and "Golden Boots," two of the greatest fullbacks in the history of Australian Rugby League, exited after storied careers that made them household names both at home and overseas.

Peter Peters had signed a one-year contract with Parramatta and left the Eels at the end of 1968. Here, for the first time, he explains why he switched clubs. "I got a buzz on the intercom from my editor, and he called me to his office. And sitting in his office was his best friend, Ken Arthurson. I thought, *'Oh, okay.'* And my boss, Jack Teer, who was the editor of *The Sun* and (a) great man, said to me, 'Son, what grade are you as a journalist?' And I said, 'I'm D grade.' And he said, 'How would you like to become an A-grade journalist?' And I said, 'I would love it.' 'Well,' he said, 'You can be an A-grade tomorrow.' I said, 'Oh, yeah. How?' He said, 'Well, switching from Parramatta to Manly.' And I said, 'Oh'. And then Ken Arthurson said, 'Look I'll drive you around the area tomorrow and you tell me if you want to come.' So, the next day when we got to Balgowlah, I said, 'You can go back now. We'll get back to your office and I'll sign the contract."

"Zorba" joined Manly and alongside his great friend from childhood, Bob Fulton, enjoyed premiership success when the Sea Eagles defeated Tommy Bishop's Cronulla-Sutherland 10–7 in the infamous 1973 grand final. After his playing days, "Zorba" and Greg Hartley joined forces on radio where they were popular, knowledgeable and often outspoken commentators on Rugby League.

With the retirement of his brother Ken, Richard was the last of the Thornetts – John had retired at the end of the 1966/67 Wallaby tour of England, Ireland and France – left to carry the torch that was ignited during their formative years at Bronte. It was the beginning of the end of an extraordinary period of sporting achievements by the three siblings who had made their friends and family proud, inspired teammates and thrilled legions of fans across the world.

CHAPTER TWENTY-ONE
1969 – Injury-Plagued

Never saw him have an angry word, to be honest he would roll with the punches, if anything went wrong, he shrugged his shoulders and said, 'It is on again next week!'
Bob O'Reilly

In 1969, Richard's youngest daughter, Sophie was born.

Parramatta finished 6th again in 1969, winning as many as they lost – 11. For the first time in many years, Parramatta had no representative in the annual City v Country fixtures. However, Richard played well enough to represent NSW against Queensland at Lang Park on May 17. His season was cut short when he sustained a severe shoulder injury, claiming it was "the worst I ever had," although he still managed to play 19 games for four tries and eight field goals!

Parramatta had a poor pre-season competition followed by a win and two losses in the first three games of the premiership. Richard was troubled by a knee injury that restricted his abilities on the field. *The SMH's* Rod Humphries was scathing of Parramatta's early season form, writing on April 16 that *"Parramatta, which turned in a disgraceful performance last week (a 22–6 loss to Canterbury) is unchanged for the match against Newtown. Officials freely admit there would be changes but for lack of talent in reserve grade. Captain Dick Thornett, who has a knee injury, told club officials yesterday he would be fit to play."*

Nonetheless, the next day, Richard admitted that he did not think he would play in the home match against Newtown the next week. His knee injury was still worrying him, and he decided to see a specialist if it didn't improve. It didn't, and he was replaced by the experienced Mike Jones for the game the following week as well, against Western Suburbs at Lidcombe Oval.

1969 – INJURY-PLAGUED

Things looked brighter on May 4 when Col Pearce's article in *The SMH* suggested that Richard was back in contention for representative honours, including him in the second row of the Sydney Firsts team he wanted to see selected. He was subsequently selected in the Seconds and Rod Humphries, writing in *The SMH* on May 6, stated, *"Sydney Seconds' second-rower Dick Thornett adopted a wait and see attitude on the knee injury, which forced him to play so badly against South Sydney last Sunday."* Three days later, he reported that Richard had delayed his fitness trial until that morning to give himself every chance of being fit in a bid to play against St George at Cumberland Oval. *"'My knee hasn't improved as much as I would like but I still have a chance of playing,' Thornett said."*

If fit, Richard was prepared to challenge the New South Wales Rugby League's rule, which at the time barred him from playing against the Dragons because he was ruled unfit for the Sydney Seconds team. He was eventually passed fit to play for Parramatta, however the NSW Rugby League refused him permission to take the field.

The representative scene was a mess, and the lack of selection clarity worsened as reputations were put to the sword in the City/Country clashes. Alan Clarkson, in *The SMH* on May 11, headlined his article – **Herculean tasks faces state R.L. selectors.** Clarkson wrote, *"The New South Wales Rugby League selectors tonight face a Herculean task in sorting out a team for Queensland after yesterday's reputation-shattering game at the SCG. The Country teams burst the bubble about the invincibility of Sydney's players. Sydney Firsts, expected to be the backbone of the Australian team to tour New Zealand, scrambled home 27–20, and the star-studded Sydney Seconds, facing a team of 'kids' was trounced 24–18."*

In the same publication, Rod Humphries reported on the Seconds' match under the by-line – **Country tarnishes some big reputations**, writing, *"One of the main problems was around the scrum base, where the World Cup combination of only last year – Johnny Raper, Billy Smith, and Bob Fulton – played second fiddle to the country boys... You could put forward many reasons (or excuses) for the star-studded Sydney team's defeat. The players had only two training sessions together and therefore had no combination; players like to play for themselves in these games, rather than for the team... Nobody could dispute that the Sydney selectors did not choose, with one or two exceptions, the form players in the Sydney competition.*

Maybe, just maybe, the footballers we have running around the paddocks of Sydney First Grade football each week are not as good as we think they are. Yesterday's matches certainly gave me, and probably many of the 33,572 people in the crowd, more food for thought on the present standard of Sydney football coming on top of the many sloppy competition matches where players have failed in basic fundamentals. It certainly makes you think."

Also in the same publication, Col Pearce wrote, *"Even though the City Slickers won 27–20 against the Country Rugby League side yesterday, they weren't as slick as everybody thought they were going to be. The Sydney forwards were a failure yesterday, and as a unit were outplayed by their Country counterparts, but the main weakness of the Sydney pack was the lack of a strategist to set the pattern of play. Bobby McCarthy, Ron Coote and John Spencer need this type of player to utilise their speed. Instead, none of them had a good game yesterday. This job was possibly given to John Sattler, but he was not the man for it. Bob Moses, who had a good game in the Seconds, could be the man, but I still prefer Dick Thornett if he is fit."*

Richard was eventually selected for NSW, however, there was still concern over his fitness. When John McDonald was ruled out of the NSW team, the NSWRFL executive committee agreed he could play for Manly-Warringah against Penrith if passed fit. This was a peculiar ruling given the executive's decision which barred Richard from playing for his club after he was ruled unfit for Sydney Seconds a few days before.

Alan Clarkson, in *The SMH* on May 18, headlined his article **32-13 Runaway in Brisbane.** He went on to say that *"Second-rower Dick Thornett showed he's urgently in need of match play."*

The Australian team to tour New Zealand provided major shocks with the selection of Queenslanders Dennis Manteit and Ian Robson, and the omission of halfback Billy Smith. Alan Clarkson wrote on Monday, May 19 in *The SMH*, *"Of last year's successful World Cup team, who were available for selection, 10 missed out. They are Smith, Rasmussen, Eric Simms, Brian James, Bobby Fulton, Johnny Raper, Johnny King, Tony Branson, Dick Thornett, and Fred Jones. The omission of Dick Thornett was not unexpected. But the team will certainly miss his skill in getting movements started around the rucks."* Ultimately, a knee injury and variable form cost him a place in the squad.

Meanwhile, Balmain was leading the competition when 9th-placed Parramatta met them at Leichhardt Oval on May 25. Unfortunately for Parramatta, it was an error by Richard right on fulltime that cost his team the game. A match report explained what occurred. *"With the scores locked at 15-all, Thornett threw a pass to his skipper, Ron Lynch, who was clearly standing offside. The helpless Lynch, along with every other person at Leichhardt Oval, knew that it was purely a formality for referee Don McDonald to award a penalty to the Tigers, 30 yards out and right in front of the posts. Len Killeen, who had been off target for most of the day, made no mistake this time and the Balmain supporters' cheers drowned out the fulltime siren. In a game of fluctuating fortunes, Parramatta appeared to have had the better of it for most of the 80 minutes."* Balmain 17-15 over Parramatta.

The Eels needed to beat Newtown to keep their semi-final hopes alive and they did just that in a thrilling game that ended 11-10 in their favour. Five minutes from fulltime, Richard, now captaining the Eels, was given the ball in the clear and he coolly snapped a towering field goal from 30 yards out to win the game. Lionel Williamson, who was in his first season with Newtown, watched Richard's performance from out wide on the field. In his interview for this book Williamson said: "I was on the wing. I didn't ever contact with him directly. Never contacted him face-to-face. But he was a big, strong man. He made a lot of breaks and he was very good with the ball in his hands. He was always trying to unload and create. He was a great, great creator, but a big, strong man... he made inroads in the game... Very good on his feet... and he was thinking all the time."

Parramatta were now on 16 competition points and just outside of the top four.

Kevin Ryan Collides with Richard Thornett – Lionel Williamson's Point of View

Lionel Williamson is a legend at the Newtown Jets although he could easily have been one at Canterbury-Bankstown. Williamson came to Sydney in 1969 ready to play in the NSWRFL premiership. In 2024, he said in an interview for this book: "I was trying to join Canterbury. I was training with them, and they wanted me but (there was) a balls-up over a transfer fee."

Williamson would attend Canterbury's matches while he waited for the clearance to play with them. On Sunday, April 13, 1969, he was at Belmore Oval for the third-round match between Canterbury, led by Kevin Ryan, and

Parramatta, led by Richard Thornett. When asked if he could share an anecdote about Richard, Lionel said: "Yeah. There's one story I got about big 'Moby' Dick."

He then drew on his memory of an incident involving Richard and "Kandos" Ryan during the match at Belmore almost fifty-five years ago. He said: "Kevin Ryan come [sic] down the blind side and Dick moved across and just hung his arm out to try and stop him and got him right under the chin and lifted him off the bloody ground and on his back. I was sitting right there on the sideline, and it happened in front of me, and I looked, and I said, this is going to be a big brawl here. Before the referee could blow the whistle, he (Ryan) just hit the ground and bounced back up and to his feet. Dick was basically right in front of him; face-to-face. The referee, it may have been Holman (it was Arthur Neville), just said, 'Play the ball!'"

Perhaps the reason "Kandos" Ryan did not take matters further was due to the great respect he had for Richard, or he knew that Richard would stand his ground, even against a former champion boxer. We may never know.

When the transfer fee fell through, Lionel Williamson joined Newtown and played under his World Cup coach Harry Bath. Of Bath's coaching, Williamson said: "Well, I liked Harry insofar as I played in England and he was coaching, very much off the English style. And I clicked with it and that's why I ended up at Newtown, because Bathy went to Newtown."

Against Western Suburbs at Cumberland Oval on July 13, Parramatta was dominant throughout the contest and *The SMH* match report stated that Richard was outstanding. Richard's Kangaroo teammate, Noel Kelly, had an unfortunate afternoon that saw him cautioned twice for rough play before referee Don McDonald had enough and sent Kelly from the field five minutes before fulltime. Parramatta were 6th on the competition ladder and were pressing hard for a place in the semi-finals.

Parramatta had won four matches in a row leading into their SCG clash against St George, with their semi-final aspirations on the line. The occasion and the brilliance of the 'old firm' – Graeme Langlands and Billy Smith – was too much for Parramatta who were overwhelmed 32–7 by *"power, speed and precision"* as St George *"bundled them out of the semi-final scramble,"* wrote Alan Clarkson, in *The*

1969 - INJURY-PLAGUED

SMH on July 27 under the headline **Premiership-winning form from St George**.

The eventual 1969 premiers, Balmain, ended Parramatta's faint semi-final hopes with a 16–11 win at Cumberland Oval. Balmain were under-strength because of injuries but still had enough 'tiger in their tank' to achieve a hard-fought victory. Parramatta squandered their chances to score points and could not complete their plays. To compound matters, their goalkicker Arch Brown had an off day. Richard contributed another field goal. Journalist Rod Humphries concluded his press report with, *"Although Parramatta played it hard and tough and pushed Balmain the full distance, the Tigers deserved the two competition points."* Parramatta finished just outside of the final four (equal with Wests on 22 points), but 6th when considering for and against.

Former leading referee Col Pearce reported on an interesting interaction that took place during the match against Balmain, which spoke to Richard's leadership style, and his willingness to challenge both the rules and his coach. Pearce wrote, *"Should a captain, a non-playing coach, or the rule book be the first authority on the replacement of a player? The question arose at Cumberland Oval last Sunday when Parramatta captain Dick Thornett overruled 'the book' as well as coach, Ian Johnston. Parramatta hooker John McMartin was injured and receiving attention outside the sideline when a replacement sent out by coach Johnston reported to the touch judge. When the ball was out of play, the replacement entered the field of play, and was promptly sent off by Thornett. The replacement retired to outside the touchline but was ordered back by the coach. Again, he took the field when the ball was out of play, but again he was sent off by Thornett. Eventually, McMartin returned to the field. Disregarding the lack of cooperation between coach and captain, the important point was with McMartin, (whether) having been replaced, could return to the field. The rule is very clear, and states (that the) replacement must be sanctioned by the referee or touch judge and can only be affected when the ball is out of play. Another ruling says that any player who has been replaced is not permitted to take any further part in the match. Had Balmain lost, the League may have been obliged to uphold a protest over this breach."*

It was Ian Johnston's final season as the First Grade coach of Parramatta. Ron Lynch was subsequently appointed to the post.

The New Zealand Rugby League (NZRL) website contains an interesting article on *Ray Cranch, The Oldest Surviving Kiwi* that mentions Richard appearing as a guest player for Auckland in 1969. It read, "*When the great Australian forward Dick Thornett appeared for Auckland as a guest player in a match against New Zealand in 1969 to mark the NZRL's Diamond Jubilee, his boots were ruined after he left them in the Carlaw Park boiler room to dry. Requiring size 13 boots, Thornett was in a jam until Cranch, who worked in the footwear industry, came to the rescue with a new pair.*" Johnny Raper and Phil Hawthorne played alongside Richard who crossed for a try as Auckland defeated New Zealand at Carlaw Park in front of 12,000 fans.

In a 2006 promotion, a panel of experts appointed by the NRL picked the "Team of the 1960s". It was: Les Johns, Ken Irvine, Reg Gasnier, Graeme Langlands, Johnny King, Bob Fulton, Billy Smith, Arthur Beetson, Ian Walsh, Noel Kelly, Ron Coote, Dick Thornett and Johnny Raper. The list included six of the 14 National Rugby League Hall of Fame Immortals. And, of course, the great Dick Thornett.

CHAPTER TWENTY-TWO
1970 – Annus Horribilis

Tomorrow is the most important thing in life. Comes into us at midnight very clean. It's perfect when it arrives and it puts itself in our hands. It hopes we've learned something from yesterday.
John Wayne

The "Swinging '60s" had ended and if Woodstock (1969) was a touchstone that defined the era of counterculture, then the break-up of *The Beatles* and the deaths of Jimi Hendrix, Janis Joplin (1970) and Jim Morrison (1971) marked a reset of the cultural zeitgeist for the decade ahead.

Australia was in transition, too. 1970 heralded a decade of great debate and social change. Community members who had been marginalised – women, First Nations people and peace activists – sought to be heard. The debate about Australia's involvement in Vietnam escalated as opponents of the War took to the streets across the nation. Australia's troops began withdrawing from Vietnam in 1970.

In Rugby League, the NSWRFL made a significant rule change after the previous season's 'stop/start' and 'lay down' grand final between South Sydney and Balmain. Under the new rule, if a player went down injured, the ball would be given to a teammate who would play it. A doctor would still assess the injured player on the field, but the play would continue without a stoppage.

This season was Richard's *annus horribilis*. He continued to be plagued by the severe shoulder injury he suffered in 1969, which delayed his return to the field.

Richard's first game of the season was on April 25 in the loss against Newtown (18–12) and he played in the next seven games, with Parramatta victorious in just two of them – against the premiers Balmain (17–12) and the second-round win against Western Suburbs (19–15).

On May 24, Parramatta met St George at Cumberland Oval. One of the spectators was a boy aged 10 who would become a dual-code First Grade player for the Parramatta Two Blues and Gordon Highlanders (Rugby Union) and the Parramatta Eels, South Sydney Rabbitohs, Manly Sea Eagles and Sydney Roosters (Rugby League). He would also become a Rugby Union Wallaby and NSW State-of-Origin representative in Rugby League. The *Classic Wallaby* website describes him as *"..a drop-goal sharpshooter who could kick equally well with both feet."* His name? Tony Melrose. More than half a century on, Melrose remembers – vividly – one moment of magic. "Dick Thornett kicked this field goal from just the other side of halfway. There was like 30 seconds on the clock to halftime. They were playing Saints and someone took a long drop-out and Thornett's caught it, literally 50….55 metres out. He knew what the time on the clock was and just turned around and kicked this field goal, ten metres in from the sideline near the entrance to the grandstand. So, maybe he wanted a quick shower – a quick halftime shower. I don't know who the referee was; whether it was Col Pearce or Bruyeres… it was someone like that. And he (the referee) sort of looked at him. I think he was in amazement. And it was like, 'Well, that'll do me. Halftime!' I just remember watching him do it and I thought, *'He's a second rower, for Christ's sake!'* Like, that's unexpected. I knew he was talented. Yeah, one of the best field goals I've ever seen. Just the nonchalance of the way he did it. It was like #%?# it! Let's kick a field goal."

Richard's sense of position and timing was impeccable – as always. He was also an inspiration to fans of any age.

Although losing six of the first eight games of the 1970 season, Parramatta was competitive. The team just could not find a way to win.

Unfortunately for Richard (and Parramatta), his season also ended after just those eight games when he was struck down by a life-threatening bout of hepatitis and blood clots, which led to a long confinement in hospital.

It was also an Ashes year. "Thirsty" Lynch was in top form and selected at lock forward for the first Test against the Lions to be played in Brisbane. In what became known as the "Battle of Brisbane III", *The Courier Mail*'s journalist, Jack Reardon, said the Lang Park Test had started with *"…spiteful, bruising manhandling by both sets of forwards, obviously trying to soften each other up."* In front of a crowd of 42,807, Australia won the Test 37–15 although, *"Maybe Britain finished in front of the softening up, because there were plenty of bruised and bleeding Australians."* Reardon continued, *"There were plenty of stiff arms, punches and head tackles, and some sly kicking. The clash of the 'engine rooms' eventually erupted into a brawl. It was a nasty situation, with players running from all quarters, following a shin-kicking duel between Morgan and Dave Chisnall. In the skirmish, Morgan was felled by Watson."* Cliff Watson, who was no stranger to controversial moments when he played against Australia, introduced the "Liverpool kiss" to his opposition prop Jim Morgan, spreading Morgan's nose across his face. However, on this occasion, Watson was not the provocateur. Watson remembered the incident clearly. "Actually, Jimmy tried to put the head(butt) on me. So, I thought I'll turn around and show him how it's correctly done, which I did. Consequently, he had a funny nose." Ron Lynch suffered a depressed fracture of the cheekbone in the 28th minute of the first half and was replaced by Queenslander Col Weiss.

The Lions won the next two Tests to recapture the Ashes they had lost in 1963.

Meanwhile, Lynch underwent a difficult operation to repair his fractured cheekbone and there were concerns that he might miss the rest of the season.

Richard's long-term illness, and the injury to Ron Lynch which put him out of action for many weeks, did not help Parramatta's cause. Not even the recruitment of four talented 1970 Country representatives could make up for the loss of Richard and "Thirsty" Lynch. Parramatta signed five-eighth Graham Lye from Wollongong (who played for NSW against the Lions and then was the reserve back for the third Test), prop and goalkicker Dennis Mount from Warialda, winger/centre Terry Scurfield from Parkes (who scored all three tries for Western Division against the touring British Lions) and fullback Laurie Wakefield, also from Parkes, who represented NSW against Queensland.

Reminiscent of its pre-1962 premiership performances, Parramatta won 4 and lost 18 games in the 1970 season, scoring 240 points and conceding 484 to finish last.

Tony Melrose grew up in Baulkham Hills, northwest of Sydney, where "Rugby League was the order of the day. Although I played rugby all my life as a kid for local club teams, not schools, all the schools played league. And so, you played a bit of League, which was obviously in the papers and hence you had to follow

Parramatta." Melrose felt like many long-suffering fans who followed the Eels in the late '60s through to the mid-'70s. "I just got really frustrated with them. They had so many good players, some international players and you think, 'Well what's going on here?' They used to sort of run middle of the table to bottom of the table and they'd beat the good sides like Saints and Souths and perform well, and they would get beat by the teams they should beat." Melrose went on to play First Grade for the Eels in 1980 and 1981, at the start of their "golden era", On August 30, 1981, he was Mick Cronin's centre partner in the last ever game at Cumberland Oval; a rousing 20–all draw against Manly in front of a crowd of 18,849. Melrose scored a try and, yes, he kicked a field goal.

The emergence of a young second-row forward was one of the few highlights in an otherwise dismal season. Denis Fitzgerald (20) made his First Grade debut against a rugged Wests team that featured hard man John Elford in its forward lineup. Fitzgerald and Elford had the distinction of appearing on the cover of the first issue of *Rugby League Week*. The image showed Elford spearing Fitzgerald into the Lidcombe Oval turf. Fitzgerald survived his 'baptism of fire' and went on to be a fine player for Parramatta, representing NSW and Australia with distinction before becoming the CEO of Parramatta and presiding over its golden era during the 1980s.

The brightest light of Parramatta's season was the form of Bob O'Reilly, who played for NSW in the 17–all draw against Great Britain. At the end of the season, he was selected to represent Australia in the World Cup. It was a big year for on-field 'battles' between the Kangaroos and the Lions. In the World Cup Final, O'Reilly and John O'Neill more than matched the Englishmen in the rugged exchanges around the rucks, which helped Australia win the match 12–7. The brutal nature of the "Battle of Headingley" made the "Battle of Brisbane III" look relatively tame in comparison. The match was broadcast live on television and afterwards, there was an outcry from the UK public about the brutal, physical and often violent pictures they had viewed in the comfort of their sitting rooms. According to Rugby League World Cup historian, Tony Collins, some people called for Rugby League to be banned in schools.

It is ironic that Father John Cootes, a man of God and an advocate for anti-violence, played at both Brisbane and Headingley. Cootes, it seemed, was the only player who did not strike, headbutt, knee, kick or stomp on an opponent during the 1970 World Cup Final. When speaking about the game, he explained, "Luckily I was treated (by the opposition) with great deference. They realised the restrictions I was playing under. If I'd lost my temper on the field, or been involved in some of the punch-ups, that would have been my last game of football." The only Lions player to test Cootes' resolve was Cliff Watson. "Watson thumped me one time," Cootes said, and the next time Watson took the ball up "...he disappeared under a swarm of Australians" who reminded him that Father Cootes was to be respected.

For the trivia buffs, the 1970 World Cup that was presented to Australian captain Ron Coote was not the one Johnny Raper held up when Australia was victorious in 1968. The Australians had taken that World Cup trophy to England in 1970 and put it on display in the Midland Hotel in Bradford where they were staying. It was stolen. Twenty years later, it was found in a tip near Bradford.

Ron Lynch did not coach Parramatta again.

It was time for another legendary hooker from St George to take control of the team's destiny, while Richard resumed fitness training during the off-season in preparation for the 1971 premiership. Given the season that just was, it would prove to be a season of highs few would ever have imagined.

CHAPTER TWENTY-THREE
1971 – Farewell Eels

It is not the critic who counts; not the man who points out how the strong man stumbles, or where the doer of deeds could have done them better. The credit belongs to the man who is actually in the arena, whose face is marred by dust and sweat and blood; who strives valiantly; who errs, who comes short again and again, because there is no effort without error and shortcoming; but who does actually strive to do the deeds; who knows great enthusiasms, the great devotions; who spends himself in a worthy cause; who at the best knows in the end the triumph of high achievement, and who at the worst, if he fails, at least fails while daring greatly, so that his place shall never be with those cold and timid souls who neither know victory nor defeat.
Theodore Roosevelt

There was good news in January, 1971, when *The Rugby League News* reported that Richard was *"doing his share of heavy training recently and is beginning to look like his old self again."* Sadly though, a few weeks later, tragedy struck for Richard and wife Maureen when their infant son died two weeks after being born. His name was Richard. The mountains Richard Thornett faced were sometimes more fearsome and frightening off the field than on it. We will see how much so, later in our journey.

As the 1971 season approached, Parramatta fans were excited at the prospect of a good year. The team had a new coach, Ian Walsh, and Richard was healthy again, resuming his spot in the team alongside captain Ron Lynch who also had a wretched year in 1970. Meanwhile, "The Mayor of Parramatta" returned from captain/coaching Coonabarabran for one final season in the big time. Their young forwards were expected to strongly support Richard and Lynch. Prop Bob O'Reilly (22) had returned to

Parramatta as one of the 1970 World Cup heroes. Front-rower Denis Fitzgerald (21) and lock Keith Campbell (20) were also maturing into fine players who seemed destined for higher honours.

Richard Thornett: the 'X' Factor?

In Writing this book, we often wrestled with the question, "Was it a coincidence that teams seemed to improve upon Richard's arrival?" The Paddington Central Junior Technical School's 1955 school magazine Tricolour contained a football report. It detailed that by season's end, the 1st team "... was undefeated, scoring 276 points to 4, Bondi being the only side to score against us." Richard was a standout player in the team. In 1956 and '57, he starred in Randwick Boys' High School's very successful First XV and a mere two years after finishing school, in 1959, he played in Randwick's First Grade side that won its first premiership in 11 years. At the same time, he was playing Water Polo for Bronte's First Grade team that won its first ever premiership in the 1958/9 season. The next year, Richard was starring in the now competitive Australian Olympic Water Polo team and in the next two years after that, he was part of a resurgent (if not winning) Wallabies' outfit against the Springboks and All Blacks. In 1963, after switching to Rugby League, Richard toured with the virtually unstoppable Kangaroo side, a side that in the previous year had lost four from five games against Great Britain and New Zealand. This evidence certainly provides food for thought when pondering our question.

In 1970, the absence of Richard (and Ron Lynch) for most of the season seemed to have had a dramatic impact on the Eels. They finished with the wooden spoon after having finished the 1969 season in 6th place. Richard's return to the side in 1971 coincided with a dramatic reversal of fortune and success, with the team storming back into form and the semi-finals. In 1972, after Richard had left his beloved Eels, they finished with another wooden spoon.

On March 11, Rod Humphries wrote in his *SMH* article, *"Parramatta Rugby League selectors last night chose second-rower Dick Thornett as captain of the team to play Western Suburbs at Cumberland Oval next Sunday afternoon. Thornett* takes over from Graham Lye who is under suspension. The selection of Thornett follows the refusal to accept the position by the former captain, Ron Lynch, who was overlooked by the selectors last week when they chose Lye."

In a surprising article some three weeks later, Humphries, reported, *"Rugby League international Ron Lynch was carpeted over his poor form, then voted captain by the players in an incident-packed night at Parramatta training last night. The Parramatta selectors called out Lynch and World Cup forward Bob O'Reilly at training for an explanation on their poor form and warned them to improve or be dropped. Soon after, the players met in the centre of Cumberland Oval and asked that Lynch be reinstated as captain. The vote was accepted by the selectors, who earlier had named Graham Lye as captain. Five-eighth, Lye, who displaced Lynch as captain during the pre-season competition, said he sincerely wanted Lynch to take back the job for the team's sake."*

In a May 24 *SMH* article, Richard was observed to still be in sparkling form as Parramatta defeated Eastern Suburbs 16–8. Humphries wrote, *"Dick Thornett had one of his most constructive games for some time. It was Thornett who threw a long pass to the centres for the first try."*

Richard Thornett Stood Up for his Teammates

In its first appearance at the SCG for many years, Parramatta performed like a 'deer caught in the headlights' against Manly on June 14 before a crowd of 34,859. Parramatta's highly rated forward pack was outplayed by Manly's six who were brilliantly led by Malcolm Reilly. Reilly took control of the match early with a series of deft kicks which continually turned the Parramatta forwards around and four of his kicks – two grubbers and two over the top – set up tries for Manly to go for oranges with a 16–4 lead. Parramatta lost Ron Lynch with an ankle injury at halftime, replaced by the free-running John Vincent. In the second half, Richard and Bob O'Reilly demonstrated the form that their fans expected. Richard and Vincent scored tries as Parramatta rallied to reduce Manly's lead to 21–14 before John "Cracker" McDonald scored twice for Manly who triumphed 31–14.

Malcolm Reilly – like Richard – could mix his game, often demonstrating outstanding ball-handling skills one minute and brutal defence the next.

On one occasion, Reilly targeted the slight-of-frame Parramatta halfback John Wilson. Parramatta's Denis Fitzgerald was in the front row that day and was a witness to what transpired. "I remember Malcolm Reilly was one of the best players, the toughest of players that played. He came out from England, played with Manly for quite a few years, and we were playing against him in 1971 when we did have a good team and made the semis. Reilly got John Wilson, who was halfback-cum-five-eighth for Parramatta at the time. He was my vintage. But anyway, Reilly got him with a head-high (tackle) and that was very common back in the '60s and 70s."

Richard, as we have learned previously from Colin Meads, Kevin Ryan and others, was a hard but fair player. We also know he looked after his teammates on the field and knew that Reilly's tackle on Wilson demanded retribution. Fitzgerald recalls, "Dick said, 'Just leave a bit of a gap for Reilly when he takes the ball up next time.' So he (Reilly) took it up. Reilly came streaming through and Dick just got him with the best stiff arm of all time. It gave me confidence and I thought Reilly wouldn't be hitting too many little Parramatta players (again), or hopefully even the bigger players like myself. Reilly went off, which was most unusual for him at the time." The Canberra Times reported, "Reilly, after causing Parramatta nightmares, suffered concussion in a heavy tackle and left the field 12 minutes from fulltime."

In a June 21 *SMH* article by Humphries, Les Johns was praised for virtually beating Parramatta 14–13 single-handedly at Cumberland Oval. The match was marred by shocking violence against referee Laurie Bruyeres, who was struck on the ear by a Parramatta spectator as he was leaving the playing field after the match. Even in defeat, it was reported that *"...the Thornett brothers, Dick and Ken, tried everything they knew to whip Parramatta past the post but the players around them just could not lift their game."* In fact, coach Walsh went as far as to say that *"When Dick Thornett 'fires' the team 'fires.'"*

Richard continued to battle knee problems, but his tenacity and resilience triumphed over the hurdles he faced. In *The SMH* on August 23, Alan Clarkson praised Bob O'Reilly as being *"...the brains behind two of Parramatta's three tries against Western Suburbs that cemented their spot in the semi-finals."* He went on to describe the rest of the pack playing *"superbly with Dick Thornett producing his best game for some time."*

Parramatta's qualification for the semi-finals was a tremendous climb out of the pits of despair that crippled the club the year before. Spirits were high among players and supporters alike, as a young, upcoming playing brigade was well supported by the return or appointment of such experienced campaigners as Walsh, Lynch, Ken and Richard Thornett. Crowds returned, up nearly 150,000 from the year before, as the Eels rumbled ominously towards a big finish. Bob O'Reilly said of Ian Walsh, who drove the team hard, *"Ian Walsh called a spade a spade. There were no beg your pardons with him."*

In *The Rugby League News* of August 1, 1971, the headline read **Parramatta's Great Year – Whatever Happens.**

"Whatever happens from now on, this season will be accepted in the Parramatta camp as one of the club's best ever, what with team performances and representative selections. The First Grade team has a fairly tight hold on fourth place in the semi-final list. That's a dramatic rise for a side which was a miserable last in 1970. It reflects great credit on First Grade coach Ian Walsh and on the club administration; it also shows the players in a good light, especially as many of them, including First Graders, were lacking solid experience.

This speaks well for the immediate future, though it is recognised that some of the long-service players in the top team would be difficult to replace... Lynch, the skipper, and the Thornett brothers have had much influence on Parramatta's success this year, their experience supplementing the great football 'know-how' of Ian Walsh."

Bob O'Reilly remembers, "I think we got rolled; we had to go to extra time in the semi-final, we got beaten that game and St George ended up making the grand final and gave Souths a run for their money. When the season was over, we all went on a trip away, all as happy as Larry. Dick could have played for Australia had he not have been hurt and when we came back, they let him go. Walsh decided we could do without him."

Even amid such a successful season, Collis and Whiticker wrote in their book *100 Years of Rugby League* that *"Parramatta's return to the semi-finals ended unhappily, both on and off the field. After finishing last in 1970, the Eels made a welcome return to form under the coaching of former Test great Ian Walsh and the*

1971 - FAREWELL EELS

return of club legend Ken Thornett from country football. From 'The Mayor's' first match, the 38-14 thrashing of Canterbury, Parramatta looked like a semi-final team but Walsh, it appears, has had his detractors at the club. With Parramatta vying for a semi-final place, Walsh publicly stated that he had lost confidence in his ability as a coach after one of the Eels' star players turned up to training drunk. When Walsh tried to drop the player, he was overruled by the club committee, which he complained to Rugby League Week is 'too benevolent' towards the players.

Even though Walsh was named 1971 "Coach of the Year", he would find 1972 more of a challenge.

On December 13, 1971, the full bench of the High Court of Australia confirmed the NSW Equity Court's ruling that the NSW Rugby League's transfer system was an unreasonable restraint of trade. *"The decision is a vindication of the stance maintained by Balmain lock, Dennis Tutty. In May 1968, the former Test local applied to his club to be placed on open transfer but the Tigers refused... Tutty sat out the 1969 and 1970 seasons but returned to the field while the League appealed the Equity Court decision and (he) was judged to be Balmain's best player. This decision has not only left Tutty free to finally join Penrith, it has (also) opened the floodgates in regard to player movement between clubs. Souths lost three internationals, John O'Neill and Ray Branighan had joined Manly while Ron Coote has left for Easts, the Roosters have signed Dick Thornett and John Armstrong. Long-serving Parramatta captain Ron Lynch, who played his 194th game for the club last year, has signed with the Panthers and will lead the club in 1972."*

Alan Clarkson, in *The SMH* on October 13, 1971, headlined his article **Parramatta offer reduced terms**. Richard and Ron Lynch were coming off contract and Parramatta decided to offer both men reduced playing fees for 1972. Parramatta secretary Spencer O'Neill said, *"A one-year playing contract will be offered to both players next Friday night. Whether they accept the terms or not is entirely up to the players themselves."* The club was looking to ensure the future of its young star players at the club and had re-signed Keith Campbell. The remuneration committee were considering offers to Bob O'Reilly, Ron Graham and others. Alan Clarkson, in *The SMH* on December 3, 1971, wrote that Parramatta had secured the services of several of their young players and re-signed Gary Pethybridge, John McMartin, Peter Langmack and Denis Fitzgerald. The club was also confident that Bob O'Reilly would sign on again. Clarkson continued,

"The only regular First Graders who have not signed are Dick Thornett and Ron Lynch who are dissatisfied with the club."

It is worth noting John McMartin's reflections, who said that he was taught the right attitudes and the right way to play the game by both Richard and Lynch when he arrived at Parramatta. "They teach you how to play tough, how to handle pain. They played tough but they were fair. There was no way you could ever be a lair in their company."

Good friend and long-time playing partner at club and representative level, Ron Lynch, remembers Richard fondly. "Wonderful ball handler and tackler; when he tackled, whoever he tackled knew all about it. He had a good technique about him. Very good scrummager. I think that came from the union side of it; he was very strong in the scrum. Wonderful bloke to play with. I suppose he would have been about 16-and-a-half stone then and quite quick too. I saw him one day we played Balmain in a deferred match at Redfern Oval. Someone threw him the ball and he went for a drop kick and he kicked a field goal and I don't think they've found the ball yet. I think it's around Cleveland Street somewhere still. It went over the posts and kept going. He could do anything. He was a very gifted footballer."

When asked about his memories of Parramatta, Richard was emotional in response; well, as emotional as Richard could be. "Well, I thoroughly enjoyed it. Met a lot of good people and Parramatta was probably the real deal, like a country team in a way because a lot of them were from the bush, but the blokes were all knock-about, good dinky-di Aussies and I think that was probably the best part of it; that we did develop quite a good camaraderie amongst the players out there. There was always a race to get to the pub first to see who'd buy the first round of drinks. 'Lynchy' would call the training off early a lot of times."

Richard saw his time at Parramatta as being more than just being a player in a football team; it was more like being part of a family. To say goodbye to this after nine years would have been heartbreaking.

He even found himself in the middle of a political sandstorm in 1971, perhaps not surprising given the gravitas he held in the local community at the time. He was part of a newly formed North Sydney citizens' group which contested four of North Sydney's five wards under the slogan *"We care"*. In a September 6 *SMH* article by Gavin Souter, it was reported that *"Mr Thornett, who is running against*

Mrs Baker in Victoria ward, believes in 'balanced development'. He thinks that North Sydney could do with more development of the Park Regis type, and that North Sydney Council has not been sufficiently businesslike. 'Everything seems to get blocked,' he said. 'It takes ages for any development to get through council.'"

CHAPTER TWENTY-FOUR
1972 – The Roosters

Don't let life discourage you; everyone who got where he is had to begin where he was.

Richard L. Evans

To set the context, 1972 was a tumultuous year, not just for Richard but for Parramatta and Rugby League in general. Ron Lynch and Richard's contracts were coming to an end in 1971 and Parramatta insisted on a transfer fee if Richard and Ron were thinking of going to another Sydney club. Then, the Dennis Tutty situation emerged in relation to restraint of trade. Balmain wouldn't release Tutty to allow him to go to Penrith, so he took the issue to court and won. The win meant that both Richard and Ron were now free agents, and Parramatta, who had called their bluff, rang to see if both would reconsider their decisions to leave. Even though they re-thought their predicament, they had given their word to Easts and Penrith respectively, and they intended to honour it.

Bob O'Reilly said that he arrived at training to hear that the club had let Ron and Richard go. Ken had retired and Barry Rushworth had left to go back to the country. After clawing their way back from wooden spooners to semi-finalists in 1971, 1972 looked ominous for the Eels, and so it proved to be. Without pointing fingers, by season's end, for a myriad of reasons, Parramatta once again found themselves dwelling in the cellar of the competition.

O'Reilly was concerned at the time that the club had lost some experienced players who were still playing very good football, and he feels that it was one of the

1972 - THE ROOSTERS

big mistakes that the club has made over the years. He went on to say, "Walsh felt he could do without Lynch and Richard and go with the younger team. We lost respect with the other clubs who now saw us as an easy touch. We didn't have these two old warriors out there with us and they always did command a lot of respect."

This led to dissension within the club with Walsh. Denis Fitzgerald put some of the drama down to the fact Walsh wasn't used to losing, having played and coached at St George during their dominant era. Walsh was writing in *Rugby League Week* and submitting articles that were critical of the team. The players would hear about the changes to the team and criticisms via the publication before they'd hear it from their own coach and this led to Walsh eventually 'losing the dressing room'. Bob O'Reilly said later that he was just happy that the '72 season came to an end. "Walsh's plan for 1972 went by the wayside when at the end of '71 he decided that he would chop players that I thought should have played for at least another year."

So, to the season itself. Richard left Parramatta at the end of 1971 and joined Eastern Suburbs on a two-year contract. He stayed for one. 1972 was Richard's final year in the game he had served so well. His decision to leave Parramatta ran almost parallel with fellow Rugby League international and former team-mate and opponent, Michael Cleary, who left South Sydney the year before after disagreements with his club bosses. He, like Richard, went to Eastern Suburbs, lasting a single year as well before retiring as Richard was walking in the door. It was a sad Parramatta career conclusion for two club legends, with Ron "Thirsty" Lynch also leaving for Penrith but lasting one year longer at the foot of the mountains than Richard did at Easts.

The SMH on January 23 reported, "*The incredible off-season buying spree by Sydney Rugby League clubs has developed into a dollar war between the lush Leagues clubs. In the splurge that has gone on since the High Court ruled the League's transfer and retention system invalid, 31 'name' players have changed clubs. Heading the buying spree are Eastern Suburbs and Manly-Warringah. Certainly, the unprecedented movement of players supports the feeling of the High Court that the former transfer and retention system operated as a 'restraint of trade'. Under the old system, it is doubtful whether half the players would have switched clubs because the transfer fees would have been prohibitive.*"

THE NATURAL

On Sunday, April 16, Richard lined up in First Grade against his old club (and directly opposite his old teammate, Denis Fitzgerald) in what would have been an emotional afternoon for him. In a barnstorming performance, Richard was tremendous as Easts triumphed 50–12. Richard played in the top side nine times during the season and the Roosters lost only one of those games, and there was a 2–all draw with St George.

Arthur Beetson was under suspension for the Parramatta game, and it was reported that he would slot straight back into First Grade. The question was, who would make way for him? In Rod Humphries' *SMH* article on April 18, he wrote that *"Eastern Suburbs will choose their team this afternoon, and the big question surrounds the forwards, where Arthur Beetson resumes after two weeks' suspension. It is almost certain that he will go straight back to First Grade, and the tip last night was that ex-international Dick Thornett might be relegated. The thinking is that the forwards would be overloaded with ball-distributor-type forwards if Beetson and Thornett were in together."* This sentiment, in relation to similar ball-playing forwards, was certainly a theory bandied about to explain coach Don Furner's selection decisions during the 1972 season.

Injuries in the front row pushed Richard up into the position against St George on May 27. It was a position he preferred not to play, to put it mildly. Nonetheless, in Alan Clarkson's *SMH* article on May 26, it was reported that *"Furner had no doubt last night that Thornett, an experienced second rower but an inexperienced prop, would do well. Furner has spent some time in the last two training sessions in packing scrums against Thornett. 'Dick is the type of footballer who will do well no matter where you play him,' Furner said. 'I packed down against him and it's been a long, long time since I have struck a man as strong as he is. He will adjust to the change of position without the slightest worry.'"* This prediction did indeed prove to be correct.

Richard was still displaying his old prodigious form in the July 15 match against Canterbury, a victory for Easts, 22–15. *The SMH* the next day wrote that *"Two minutes into the second half, Easts prop, Dick Thornett, who had shown remarkable speed to score his team's first try with a 45-yard run, cut through to send Bill Mullins in for the second touchdown."*

Even though Alan Clarkson said in his *SMH* article on January 15 that *"Thornett… should be a great acquisition to Easts' forward strength,"* he managed

1972 - THE ROOSTERS

only a handful of First Grade games, overlooked for Greg Bandiera as Arthur Beetson's second-row partner in the grand final against Manly, which Easts lost 19–14. He failed to win a spot on the bench as well, Easts preferring the services of Laurie Freier for the big game. It was the first time in 24 years that a NSWRFL First Grade grand final didn't have a Souths or St George team competing.

Looking back, Richard recalled, "I went to Easts and I don't laugh about it but Parramatta were wooden spooners in '72. That's after 'Lynchy' had gone and I'd gone to Easts. Yeah, but I think Walshy just thought that 'Lynchy' and I had too much to say in the training routine and he didn't like it. So, he told the hierarchy at Parramatta, Spencer O'Neill, that he didn't want us. My world was still with Parramatta; Easts I never liked. Even though I was born there (in the Eastern Suburbs). I played against Parramatta at the Sports Ground and I got the points for the day (on April 16) and Easts beat Parramatta… that in some way was a bit of satisfaction for Parramatta getting rid of me. Don Furner wouldn't play me when Beetson was in the side because he thought the two of us were too slow in coming back in defence. But that's how they got beaten in the grand final because they only had one ball player, they only had Beetson. And if you go through the rest of the Easts players, there was Jim Morgan who was not a ball player. Laurie Freier, Greg Bandiera, Ron Coote. Well, Ron Coote, he's a runner, the rest of them are tacklers. Kevin Junee and 'Monkey' Mayes were the two halves. I mean we had six internationals in second grade."

Kevin Junee remembers his year at Easts with Richard. "It's just wonderful that I get a chance to talk to you because my association with Dick was fantastic and there was a novelty attached to that, with five internationals and probably a couple of dual internationals playing second grade together, one because of injury, two because of the silly issues, the coach of First Grade didn't like you or whatever it might have been. And at one stage there, I think, I haven't checked the program at the time, but I'm fairly certain we looked around (at reserve grade training), and there was Dick, myself, I thought there was Johnny Brass, there might have been Mark Harris and somebody else. I'm guessing, but all I know was there was about five. We looked at each other and there were five internationals or thereabouts."

Michael Cleary would recall, "Well, we used to say over there (at Easts), 'Don't play well or you'll get dropped to First Grade.'"

THE NATURAL

Don Furner OAM – Coach of Eastern Suburbs (1970–72)

The citation for Don Furner's OAM is: **In recognition of service to the sport of Rugby League.** In reviewing his career, it is clear why this recognition was so well-deserved. Don Furner devoted his life to Rugby League as a player, coach and administrator. He enjoyed a distinguished career as a player for a range of clubs across NSW and Queensland. Furner represented Queensland nine times in the mid-1950s and toured with the 1956/57 Kangaroos under captain/coach Ken Kearney. When he was forced to quit playing through injury, Furner turned to coaching with great success, most notably guiding the Queanbeyan Blues to ten premierships in thirteen years. In 1972, he coached Eastern Suburbs to the grand final in its 14–19 loss to Manly. Furner then added gravitas to Canberra's bid in their quest to join the NSWRFL competition and in 1982 the Canberra Raiders entered with Furner as head coach. Wayne Bennett joined Furner as co-coach of the Raiders for the 1987 season and they guided their team to its first grand final before suffering defeat at the hands of Manly, 18–8. However, even greater success for the Raiders was soon to follow. The winning Furner had helped to establish at the club enabled them to win the NSWRL (the renamed NSWRFL) premiership in 1989, 1990 and 1994 under coach Tim Sheens. Furner represented Australia again, this time as coach of the Kangaroos (1986–1988). He coached the 1986 Kangaroos – the "Unbeatables" – to win all 20 matches on the tour of Great Britain and France.

Richard Would Always Speak His Mind… No Matter What
Example 1) Officials and administrators

It is probably fair to say that Richard had, at times, a guarded, even oppositional relationship with those who controlled or officiated the game. The clashes he had with Water Polo officials over his amateur status were mentioned earlier in the book, and even though he had great respect for Ken Kearney, others such as Harry Bath, Ian Walsh and Don Furner were not always 'on the same page' as Richard. Richard didn't suffer fools gladly. Because he was always prone to speak his mind, it could sometimes lead to some rather awkward moments, such as the time that he was given the honour of presenting the Shore School Rugby 1st and 2nd XV jerseys to the players in 2011, only three months before his death. I was standing next to the coaches as Richard, in no doubt at all, told all and sundry in the room that coaches were unnecessary and superfluous, and that the players were good enough to train and think for themselves. It was all I could do not to dig a hole and bury myself there and then.

Example 2) My proposal… almost

Richard's propensity to speak his mind, much like Jim Carrey in the film "Liar Liar", didn't stop with officials and coaches. In 2002, after dating Sophie for three years, I decided that marriage was in order at last. Wanting to ask Richard's permission for his daughter's hand in marriage first, I was road-blocked initially because, as a schoolteacher, I had still eight weeks left in the term and weekend sport meant I could not get to Millthorpe to ask him. Eventually, we got there but it took a further two days for me to seize on an opportunity to speak to Richard alone, as Sophie was always there with us. One day, after several hours out fencing and drenching, Sophie announced, as we were slumped in the chairs in the lounge room sipping Richard's home brew, that she would collect the eggs from the chicken yard. This was my chance! I asked Richard the question and to my relief, he replied yes. Obviously, wanting to keep this news from Sophie, my thoughts turned next to when best to propose so I would surprise her.

Mission accomplished? Hold your horses. No sooner had Sophie returned with two egg-laden buckets did Richard stand up, raise a dark-brewed middy aloft and proudly tell her that I would be asking her to marry me some time very soon. Every lunch or dinner date after that was awkward to say the least, especially when the bill was paid and the car trip home was as icy as you can get. Richard didn't make it easy. But I did pop the question eventually, and we were married in 2004.

Brendan Morris, Author

Some thoughts looking back…

Richard on Don Furner (Easts' First Grade coach, 1972): "I don't mind, I'll talk about him. Oh well, I didn't like him. I can't think of words to describe him. I don't think he had the scope to understand the game as much as what he thought he had. No, I didn't like him as a person straight away. That was the reason why I retired. I think I could have had a couple of years. I was 32 then. I was turning 32 at the end of September, at the end of the season. I think I was fit enough, probably healthy enough to have another year or two; but I wasn't going to change clubs again. I didn't believe in players changing clubs. Well, even if you don't finish up on top, you can finish up running around in second grade and knowing full well that if you weren't a better player than Laurie Freier and you weren't a better player than Greg Bandiera or Jimmy Morgan, something's wrong."

Ron Lynch on he and Richard leaving Parramatta: "Parramatta made a big blue there – my contract finished and so had Dick's and although I went to them to see what was going on, they said 'Look, you can go back to the bush and we'll put no transfer on you, but if you go to another Sydney club we'll put a transfer fee on you that no club will pay because they're only going to get you for one or two years.' And I said, 'Well if that's the game, I'll give it away', and Dick was in the same position. So, during the summer months, that Dennis Tutty case came up, so that made me a free agent. So, Penrith rang me and I said, 'Seeing as Parramatta did that to me, yeah, I'll sign the contract.' So, I had two seasons there. And Dick did the same thing, he went to Easts. Well, at that stage, Parramatta wanted one of us and they didn't know which one, but they lost the two of us and they finished up last (in 1972)."

Bob O'Reilly: "Dick went to Easts and they just happened to pick him to play against us that day at the Sports Ground and well, he cut us to ribbons. I said, 'Why should I be surprised?' and Ronny Lynch was running around up here with Penrith doing everything he wanted to do and I said, 'I must have been on a different planet.' These blokes are at the top of their form. I just said to them after the season was over, 'Why was that decision made?' Anyway, Walsh left at the end of that year because the joint was in turmoil. That was the start of it and I wasn't happy."

John Quayle on Don Furner's thinking regarding Richard's role at Easts: "I worked closely with Don, and he said we knew that if Arthur or Richard got

1972 – THE ROOSTERS

injured, he always had that backup for a premiership club. And Don was very open and honest with all of us in all of that situation. He said, you're a back-up player. You've got to understand that you're never going to replace a Ronnie Coote in that situation. But if anything happens, you're going to be part of that squad. In those days, it was just … it wasn't the replacements that are there today. It was replacing an injured player with someone that needed to go the next step. So, he was always honest with everyone in that situation. And it used to offend a lot of people. And I suppose even in Richard's case, to be told that at a different club, was probably the first time he'd been told it."

John Quayle's summation of Richard's approach to Rugby League, other sports and aspects of his life outside of sport: "Oh, just leadership. Richard had a way about him with an intelligence… he had an educated view on everything rather than 'just let's take the ball up and belt them'. When you got a response from someone like Richard, I remember distinctly it was certainly an intelligent conversation. When you sat down or when you were having a beer with him, a conversation with him was different."

John Quayle on the ball players of yesteryear: "I get disappointed today when sometimes you hear them comparing forwards of the past. We have eliminated a lot of that wonderful play. If you go back to the English – go back to a Malcolm Reilly with Manly, you go back to a Cliffy Watson, their sole job was to offload a ball or set up and that was a wonderful time for people like me because your game was built off getting a ball from a Beetson or a Thornett that could make a break. And if you look back at the Cootes and all that sort of stuff, that so many times that those great runs were off a ball-playing prop. And the Beetsons and the Thornetts of the era, the Rasmussens and the O'Neills of that particular era, their sole focus was their eyes and their arms, because their arms in many cases would go above the tackle to be able to offload."

John Quayle on the thrill of playing with Richard: "It's different today from back then because there wasn't the media prominence, there wasn't the television prominence. But when you're a young guy from the country saying 'I'm playing with an Olympian or a rugby international' – it was a pretty big thing for a young country boy like me to get that opportunity. And even though we played in reserve grade a hell of a lot, it didn't matter to me. I wouldn't have cared what grade it was. I was playing with Richard Thornett, an Olympian."

Michael Cronin

Mick Cronin was chosen in 2014 as the ultimate Parramatta representative – the inaugural "Champion of Parramatta" – technically the greatest Parramatta player of all time. Michael William Cronin OAM was a stalwart for the Parramatta Eels club. He played in 22 Tests and 11 World Cup matches between 1973 and 1982. He retired as the NSWRL premiership's and the Australian Kangaroos' all-time highest point-scorer and has since been named among the nation's finest footballers of the 20th century.

In an interview for this book, Mick remembers Dick Thornett "as a unique player in that a man of his size could kick and was also a remarkable ball player under pressure, which was something quite unusual in those days." These observations were made as a young boy growing up watching Richard as a player in the mid-'60s. "I remember speaking to my great mate, Bob O'Reilly, who said that he regards Dick Thornett as the greatest player he ever played with or against. The two comments I remember Bob making (were) related to Richard's intelligence as a football player on the field and his ability to be able to read the play, as well as his toughness, never taking a backwards step." Mick also remembers Bob saying to him that he saw Dick as a role model, a mentor for him starting out as a Rugby League player at that top level in First Grade at Parramatta.

When the 1972 Easts side was discussed and the fact that Richard played most of the year in second grade, interestingly, Mick Cronin made a comment about his legendary coach, Jack Gibson, who would say that best practice was to pick the best 13 and find a spot for them somewhere.

When asked about whether the Parramatta club in his day placed great importance on players who had come before and the legacy that they left, Mick certainly remembered them. "I classify myself as a bit of a Rugby League 'nerd'... I knew the history of those players who'd come 15 and 20 years before me and I was aware of the legacy they left before I came to the club, and also having remembered watching them." He mentioned players like Billy Rayner, Brian

Hambly, Ron Lynch, Richard and Ken Thornett, and he certainly remembered the important part they played in the club's history.

To have someone like Cronin, a man and player of such great gravitas, one of the greats who 'bled blue and gold', say that he knew he walked in the shadows of those other greats who'd come before him, said much.

John Rhodes

Australian international winger, John Rhodes, admitted benefitting from the skills and offloading of both Dick and Artie Beetson, especially Beetson. "Artie didn't have the speed that Dick had but what I did notice with Artie was that he'd throw the ball on the ground at times, you know, he'd turn around and throw the ball on the ground and hopefully somebody would pick it up; whereas Dick would always throw to a player. I think he (Beetson) just knew his players would be there to pick up the ball, you know?" This aspect of Beetson's game tightened up under his coach at Eastern Suburbs, Jack Gibson. Nonetheless, when pressed for three words to sum up Richard Thornett, Rhodes didn't hesitate: "All-time great player."

Denis Fitzgerald

Denis Fitzgerald AM played in the 1970s (with Richard) for Parramatta, as well as for New South Wales and Australia, and he was a former Chief Executive Officer of the Parramatta Eels and the Parramatta Leagues Club. His views on Parramatta, coming from an interview for this book in 2023, are fascinating and founded in the very core of Parramatta's values and establishments. Few, if any, are better placed to comment on this great club and its history. Below is an extract from that interview:

"Well, it (Parramatta) was totally different. It was like a small country town. The first five years of my life I was at Castlereagh on a dairy farm there, but we moved to Dundas, now called Oatlands, which is only two miles from the centre of Parramatta. And so, I went to Saint Patrick's Primary School from kindergarten and then went to Parramatta, the Marist Brothers, and that was right next door to the church, Saint Patrick's Cathedral. And I got married there. So, I'm truly a Parramatta boy."

"I didn't see him or remember him (Richard) as a talker. And so, he wasn't going to waste his words. I got a bit closer to Dick because he was running the pub and putting up with all sorts of people at the pub, and I was just the new boy driving a delivery van. So, I'd pull up there in Miller Street and Dick would be there and we'd have a chat about football. Not for too long. We used to go to the pub, the Royal Oak Hotel, where I think all players from 1947 at Parramatta went to."

Like Mick Cronin, Denis remembers the legacy of men like Richard. "Oh, for sure. Oh, very much. He was not a father figure, but he was a senior figure who had done so much. But with Dick, the fact that he played for Australia and went to the Olympic Games….we thought only Julius Caesar went to Rome… but he did too. It was terrific to play with one of my heroes. And he was, I thought, such a big guy. And he *was* big compared to most other players going around."

On Richard and Lynch leaving Parramatta, Denis recalls, "Without knowing all the intimate details of what happened there with Lynch and Thornett, I was most disappointed that both of them left after our good year in '71… that was basically Ian Walsh who said, 'Well, these blokes have seen better days.' Lynch went to Penrith and Dick went to the Roosters and both of them had good years there at their respective clubs that they went to."

"I'll just finish the point about Ian Walsh; he didn't mix with the players much at all and he wasn't like that at all, especially when he's bagging them in the Tuesday papers. So that's where things gradually got worse. Sure, we weren't playing well, but when you're getting bagged by supposedly the bloke looking after you or (who) is in charge of developing teamwork and players getting on well, with relationships, that became a problem."

Peter Fenton

Peter Fenton OAM is described on the *Penguin Books* website as *"a punter, poet, raconteur, aging coach and writer who is a regular speaker at sporting and corporate functions."* He was awarded the Australian Sports Medal in 2000 for service to rugby. We asked him the following questions:

Could you give us a commentary on dynamic players who converted from union to league? How would you compare the success of when Ray Price converted to league to what you remember of Dick Thornett converting, because they both made an impact straight away?

With such invaluable experience in his field, Fenton's response was fascinating:

"The two best converts from union to league, because they were dynamic forwards, were Ray Price, certainly, and Dick Thornett, for the same reason. He was dynamic when he ran and he could also tackle and he could kick."

"Price of course was a back rower; he was the purest gold of flanker; and he was a sensational player. So, it's a bit hard to talk about whether the system was right or whether they were the right sort of players, because he (Price) was a freak. But very few of the tight forwards actually ever turned to Rugby League. Kevin Ryan was a 'rah rah' (Rugby Union player) who went to league and he was a success. And Ken Kearney, who came out of the '47/'48 Wallabies, he was a success too."

"I was a League kid and my Dad and I went to see the first league Test in Australia after the War, and that was at the Sydney Cricket Ground in 1946. I was ten and I remember it being so exciting; huge crowds, so noisy and blokes having 'blues' on the hill and all that sort of stuff. I thought, '*This is exciting stuff.*' And the 'Poms' started poaching the union players and the league players."

"Pat Devery was a five-eighth and Arthur Clues was a big, big success. He was a union player who had turned to league when in actual fact he played Parramatta union minor grades; Eric Tweedale used to tell me about this, the old mate of mine who just died at 102 (5 May 1921 – 16 October 2023)."

From the authors: It is important to note here that Arthur Clues introduced Ken Thornett to Leeds and hosted the 1963 Kangaroos when they toured.

"There are blokes who talk on YouTube, old English blokes about Arthur Clues being the best player in Rugby League that they ever saw. I watched all the backs go from Rugby Union, which was pretty bloody disappointing from my point of view – every year they took a few. Jimmy Lisle was a great player. Arthur Summons was a great player. (Michael) Cleary was a very good player. (Phil) Smith and (John) Brass went from Randwick rugby and Phil Smith broke down early; he was a good player too. But Brass was a wonderful player, as was Mick O'Connor. Well, Mick O'Connor's old man didn't speak to him for some years (for converting to Rugby

League). That's dead true. It just tore a hole in the family."

"(Russell) Fairfax was a wonderful player – but we kept filling up the gaps in the backs, but we didn't have the same ability to breed big, tough forwards like the All Blacks and the Boks who dominated the rugby game. So, when Thornett came in '61, '62 I think, he played 10 or 11 Test matches… he would have been there, I reckon, for 10 or 12 (or) maybe longer years, (as) one of the backbones of that Wallaby pack. So, Thornett was missed dramatically without the rugby people realising. League was smart to pick him up because he was a terrific player. He was a tough, hard, big man as well, who was, as Colin Meads said, as good as them (the All Blacks). He was a big, big loss, for sure, to Australia. Big loss. Well, at least until the early '90s. We never, ever got to the point where people didn't want to play the Australian forwards. They were only scared of the Australian backs."

CHAPTER TWENTY-FIVE
Post-Career, 1970s

Be yourself. Everyone else is taken.
Oscar Wilde

After Richard walked away from playing Rugby League at the end of 1972, he continued his interest in the hotel game. It was an interest that, initially at least, generated a highly successful business with several hotels across Sydney, although not usually at the same time. Richard recalls, "My first (pub) was *The North Star* at North Sydney, that's what it was called then; it's now *The Rag and Famish*. I went there in 1968 with Maureen. We had the first two children by then and Sophie was born while we were there. We had ten years there – I sold it in '77 and we went to *The Dolphin Hotel* at Surry Hills in early '77. While we were there, we bought *The Doncaster* in Kensington, so we had the two pubs at the same time. That was with Maureen… then when we sort of went our own ways and I stayed on at *The Dolphin* for a while (he sold it in 1989) and ended up finishing up at *The Phoenix* in Woollahra in 2000."

Richard and Maureen had some work to do getting *The North Star* ready for business. They worked extremely hard at internal refurbishing. After a particularly late night doing so, they decided to bunk down on the floor of the front bar rather than drive home. What they didn't count on was the traffic down Miller Street, North Sydney, the next morning during peak hour, and waking to the passengers of a double-decker bus, stopped at the traffic lights, looking in the window at them lying on a makeshift bed.

Journalist Norman Tasker remembers well the hospitality he enjoyed with Richard; he had wonderful friends but it came at a cost. "I can remember drinking with him down at *The Dolphin Hotel* with Norman May and David Morrow, two of his sort of regulars; (we) did a lot of damage there. And poor old Dick. I don't think it did him any good, really. But he was always the sort of guy that really liked people, enjoyed people's company. Yeah, he was a good man. He was a quiet sort of guy."

Fellow esteemed journalist, Adrian McGregor remembers those times as well: "I began writing a sports column for the Bulletin magazine called Sports World, and I had a pseudonym, Nicholas Fox because *The SMH* wouldn't let you write for any other organisation. So, I would go up to *The Dolphin Hotel* and say hello to Dick. I'd have a beer and I'd tell him what I was doing. He'd give me insights into Rugby League, people and all that sort of stuff, so I was able to write with some sort of authenticity in my column. But, after maybe my tenth visit, Dick said, 'You're here again, Macca. (You just) want to come up here to get inside information to write your column.' I said, 'Well, you're not wrong. Eventually, he got a little bit cranky. But, you know, I was flat out trying to make my living as a journalist."

Richard recalled, "When the children were young, Christmas was spent at *The Dolphin Hotel* with the cousins. The kids would live it up in a place normally reserved for adults, playing pool and pinball while the adult members of the family relaxed in another section of the hotel. It was a wonderful time for the extended family. We used to get the 2UE announcer Bob Rogers, if you remember him, and Des Hoysted… Tony Barber and, and the pianist, Geoff Harvey. We got quite a lot… Raper and those who would come over on Monday and celebrate their weekend of football, so we got a good mixture and we were running a pretty good food operation. It was a good business. We used to open at 10 and shut at 10… reasonable hours and we never had any real problems… there was no poker machines…. There were no complications and if you ran a good pub, they left you alone."

"Sometimes you regret that you never did a trade or a profession. It'd be a lot easier if you could go back to something. But I really enjoyed it; I had thirty years in the pub game and it was very kind to me. I met a lot of good people and I made a couple of bad decisions, I suppose. I played it a bit harder. I worked as a volunteer through the 2000 Olympic Games. Then I did some renovation-type work with a friend of mine for a couple of years and afterwards I bought a lawn-mowing run for 18 months. I moved to Millthorpe in 2002."

Richard leased the Millthorpe property where he kept many of John Thornett's sheep on agistment – John lived close by near Cowra. It would be his home until he passed away a decade later, although there is more, much more, to Richard's story in the interim.

In 1974, to the surprise of many, Richard wound back the clock 12 years by returning to the Rugby Union field, this time as coach of the Briars' Kentwell Cup team in the Sydney Rugby Union sub-district competition. Jim Webster, in *The SMH* on December 11, 1974, wrote that Richard had become involved with Briars after watching them in a social match. *"Although he has never done any, coaching appeals to Thornett. He once applied for the captain/coach job of Parramatta but failed to get it. As publican of the North Star Hotel at North Sydney, Thornett finds himself constantly in the public eye. With a sub-district club, he can avoid further exposure coaching might bring. Thornett has kept close ties with union since turning to league and this is a chance to become involved with it again. He lists amongst his best friends Michael O'Gorman, Mick Young, Ted Heinrich, Peter Johnson, Ken Catchpole and Roy Prosser, all union men."*

Unfortunately, Richard couldn't get the Briars up for a premiership in 1975, with St Patrick's taking out the title. Meanwhile, over at Moore Park, Richard's last Rugby League club, Eastern Suburbs, handed St George a 38–0 grand final thumping. Nine years later, Richard was back coaching, taking the reins at his beloved Randwick club with their third-grade side.

In *The Sun-Herald* on June 29, 1975, Jim Webster wrote an article on the great All Black, Colin Meads. While there was focus on the career-ending injury sustained by Ken Catchpole in the 1968 Sydney Test, prefaced by the quote – *"I'm no angel"* – Meads left time to reminisce on his clashes with Richard Thornett. After admitting that Richard was *"the hardest Aussie he's ever come up against,"* Meads was quoted as saying, *"He was something more than 16 stone and a wonderful mover around the field."*

On July 16, 1978, a gala day was held at Drummoyne Oval for former Australian Rugby Union captain Greg Davis who was seriously ill in New Zealand, raising $12,000 in the process. One of the highlights of the day was a touch football game between some of the greats of yesteryear. Names such as John Thornett, Peter Johnson, Tony Miller, Arthur McGill, Beres Ellwood, Stewart Boyce and Ken Catchpole lined up against Arthur Summons, Phil Hawthorne, Michael Cleary,

Reg Gasnier, Kevin Ryan, Jim Lisle and Richard himself. Four of the players that day had led Australia in Rugby Union Tests and three were former Rugby League Test captains. At the end of the day, Richard's team won convincingly, nine tries to three, although it was the cause that really mattered. Sadly, the mercurial Davis passed away from a brain tumour almost a year to the day later.

Exactly one week after the Drummoyne Oval gala day, Thornett matriarch Marjorie joined her sons, Ken and Richard, when TV's *This Is Your Life* compere, Roger Climpson surprised John Thornett for a memorable episode. Not only was it an emotional reunion with many of John's greatest friends and influences, but it was also a nod to the wonderful early days at Bronte, the nurturing provided by their mother and just how far the three boys had progressed in their lives and careers.

Five years later, Richard was still running around in 'Golden Oldies' tournaments with the likes of his brother, Ken, Hawthorne, Summons, Reg Smith, John Brass, Tony Miller and Brian James. Jim Webster's *SMH* headline on July 4, 1983, said it all – **Age Shall Not Weary Them… Well, Just a Bit**. The article may have been a little ironic as these aging warriors did all they could to prove that they could still stand on their own two feet (just).

Richard was still up to his old tricks in 1992 when Ian Heads reported in *The SMH* on August 20 on the 'Golden Oldies' day at Parramatta Stadium. Along with Stan Jurd, Ron Hilditch and Billy Rayner, Heads made comment on *"a 50-metre rolling maul inspired by ex-Rugby Union great Dick Thornett"*, probably the first move of its kind on the Rugby League headquarters of the west.

Close mate, Kevin Ellis wrote, *"In 1979 (I think) he entered a new life in developing The Dolphin Hotel in Crown Street – with his personality and wife's personality – they worked enormously to set up a memorable hotel in the city. It became the meeting place for all country and city people interested in all sports. I have seen so many country people (from south of the border to north of the border) relish friendships rarely seen in the big city – players, committeemen, administrators, spectators in all sports, the Royal Easter Show, horse racing, union, league, AFL and Test matches in all sports. Closely associated with Richard for many years was Norman May and his followers in (the) Olympics, cricket, union and league."* (Authors' note: Brian Hambly said, "Every time you go in, you would see Dick and Norman May sitting there… Oh, and [famous Australian cricketer] Neil Harvey.")

Ellis continued: *"Richard and all his friends helped me immensely whenever I was associated with various sports the country people attended in Sydney. Students competing in athletics one year were from far west of New South Wales – Broken Hill – they were all 'nationalities' (some were from the Flinders Ranges in South Australia, White Cliffs in NSW, etc.) They'd never been to any city, especially Sydney. Whilst unloading their equipment, many things were stolen. With Richard and Norman May's support, replacements for the stolen gear were provided, and the kids have never forgotten that act of kindness (they would all be in their 50s (now) or nearing that age)."*

"Richard assisted in the 2000 Olympic appeals which Norman May had organised to assist competitors with very little money – with their help, we held many functions in country towns – Gundagai, Tumut, Coffs Harbour, Dorrigo, Broken Hill, Glen Innes. They provided their help at no cost and they paid their own way to wherever they were held. I could write for days and never get to the end of such a well-known sportsman and gentleman and family man – he had tremendous wit but tended to be a quiet, unassuming man in all things he has done in sport and society. Richard is a legend in the names of (the) Olympics, union, league, hotelier, policeman and other unknown societies. He has blended us country people into the city society easily with his generosity and willingness to help all and sundry."

CHAPTER TWENTY-SIX
Post-Career, 1980s

A society grows great when old men plant trees in whose shade they know they shall never sit.
Greek proverb

In 1982, Richard's health continued to suffer. He was close to death and admitted to the Intensive Care Unit of St Vincent's Hospital in Sydney with a serious bout of pancreatitis on December 27. It was Richard's second admission for the same condition after he had been warned to slow down his lifestyle the first time, advice he failed to heed. He survived, but it could have gone either way. He was born a fighter, Richard Thornett, and after finding himself in combat with the enemy again, albeit a different one, there was fight in the 'old dog' yet.

Sadly, Richard and Maureen separated as 1985 started drawing to a close. Even though separated, and subsequently divorcing not long afterwards, Maureen continued to work at *The Dolphin* until the middle of 1986, before leaving to work as consultant for Nutrimetics and a representative for Seppelt, distributors of the popular *West Coast Cooler* beverage. It was said, tongue-in-cheek, that "If your Mum wasn't drinking *West Coast Cooler* in the mid-'90s, you lived in a dysfunctional family." Maureen bravely ventured out on her own in 1987 and bought the *Royal Oak Hotel* in Balmain, an establishment she still owns and for which she still works to this day, every day of the week. 1987 was also the year that Richard remarried, to Jan Andrew, as his youngest daughter, Sophie completed her HSC. There was certainly a bit going on, with more on the horizon…

Also in 1985, over 20 years after his last brush with conservative amateurism, Richard found himself in the news once again. The NSW and Sydney Rugby Union presidents expressed conflicting attitudes towards his reinstatement when he was coaching Randwick third grade in the Sydney Rugby Union competition. Jim Webster reported in *The SMH* on April 4, 1985, that *"The NSWRU President, Mr John Freedman, said the game had a problem with the laws relating to amateurism, which were drawn up in another generation with specific attention being given to other countries, namely Britain. The Sydney Judiciary Committee had recommended against the reinstatement only to have the NSW Rugby Union Executive, which has the last say on such matters, take the opposite view and allow him back. A Judiciary Committee member, Mr Frank Lawson, said he had followed guidelines in voting against the readmissions, but privately was pleased they had later been cleared by the more senior body."*

On April 26, 1988, highly respected journalist, Alan Clarkson retired after 33 years as a sportswriter for *The SMH*. The next day, he concluded a two-part series in the newspaper with a look back at some of the *"greats of the Greatest Game of All"*. The article concluded with him naming his all-time best team of players that he had seen. That team, starting at fullback, was: Clive Churchill, Michael O'Connor, Ken Irvine, Graeme Langlands, Reg Gasnier, Bob Fulton (Captain), Peter Sterling, Johnny Raper, Ron Coote, Dick Thornett, Duncan Hall, Ian Walsh, Arthur Beetson. Reserves: Steve Rogers, Rod Reddy. What a team, and what an honour it was to be chosen in a team selected by one of the doyens of the game, Alan Clarkson.

In 1989, after selling *The Dolphin Hotel* early in the year for around $4.5 million, Richard purchased the *San Pedro Motor Inn* in Redfern. He paid $900,000 for the 11-year lease of the 40-unit motel on the corner of Phillip and Marriott streets. It was a huge gamble on several fronts, not the least of which was the significant change in direction (and experience) that would have a huge impact on Richard's fortunes in the near future. One of Richard's weaknesses was his (often blind) trust in others – some might call it naivety, and his generosity to a fault. It proved to be his undoing more than once.

The next decade was going to present Richard with the greatest challenge of his life.

CHAPTER TWENTY-SEVEN
Post-Career, 1990s

You know, when you get old in life, things get taken from you. I mean that's...part of life. But, you only learn that when you start losing stuff. You find out life's this game of inches. So is football. Because in either game, life or football, the margin for error is so small -- I mean one-half a step too late, or too early, and you don't quite make it. One-half second too slow, too fast, you don't quite catch it. The inches we need are everywhere around us. They're in every break of the game, every minute, every second.

Al Pacino as coach, Tony D'Amato (*Any Given Sunday*)

Richard sold his Federation-style Mosman house in November 1991.

By 1993 and in the space of four years, Richard had gone from running one of the most successful pubs in the country, on the back of an illustrious sporting career, to driving taxis to make ends meet. His second marriage had also failed as Richard stared an imposing future dead in the eyes. In *The SMH* on February 21, 1993, journalist Peter Kogoy told the story:

"*Former Rome Olympian and dual rugby international Dick Thornett is battling to stave off bankruptcy after a $1,000,000 motel business at Redfern turned sour. Thornett, 52, once the owner of a large hotel-motel group, has been reduced to driving a taxi. 'All I know is the pub game. But given my current position, it's going to be hard to get back into it,' he said yesterday.*"

"*From a strapping 105 kg rampaging second rower for Randwick and Australia at Rugby Union, then later with Parramatta, Eastern Suburbs and Australia at Rugby League, his weight is down to under 90 kg as a result of his financial troubles and his battles with sugar diabetes. Friends have rallied around one of Australia's* *sporting greats and offered Thornett accommodation in Surry Hills after his second marriage to former Olympic swimmer, Jan Andrew, failed. For Thornett, his financial troubles began after investing $900,000 in taking out an 11-year lease in 1990 on the San Pedro Motel at Redfern. Thornett's financial woes took a turn for the worse after spending what he estimates was a further $700,000 of his own money in the 1990-91 financial year in refurbishing the motel. But business quickly dried up. 'When I took over, I was charging guests $100 a night to stay but by the time I was kicked out it was down to $60 – not to mention the drop-off in the nightly occupancy rate," he said. He has lost the motel business, and it has since been sold at auction, but this has still left Thornett with an 8-year lease arrangement."*

"This change of events has led to him losing:
- *A backpackers' hostel at Magnetic Island off the Queensland coast.*
- *A 930 ha property at Carroll, near Gunnedah in northern NSW.*
- *A fifth share in a Tamworth hotel."*

"'It all went wrong for me when the original motel owner went broke owing the Commonwealth Bank heaps,' said Thornett. It got to a stage where I was selling the progeny from the 200 breeders I was running on the farm near Gunnedah just to make ends meet at the motel. I got about $40,000 from the sale of my share of the pub at Tamworth. I had a couple of racehorses, but they've gone, too. The cars have as well, but I have no equity in them. They were on lease.'"

In an interview with Ian Warden for the National Library of Australia, Richard remembers, "*I carried on at The Dolphin until 1989 so that was quite a length. Then I remarried, to Jan, who I'd met in Rome. She was an Olympic swimmer who won two silver medals – she swam as Jan Andrew. We got married in 1987. After selling The Dolphin, I bought a property at Gunnedah and I bought the San Pedro in Redfern, and financially, things didn't go well. I drove a cab for a while and then in the mid-1990s I managed a hotel for Mike Willesee at Kincumber near the Central Coast. I came back to The Phoenix Hotel after that.*"

In between leaving *The Phoenix Hotel* and heading bush to Millthorpe in 2002, Richard did some house renovations with a friend before working for a lawn-mowing business for a year. He said to Ian Warden, "*(My) two brothers are living in the bush so I thought I'd get out of Sydney and come and live here. (It's) nice, peaceful; after 30 years in the hotel industry, I think it was a good move... I quite enjoyed getting out of it all. Your friends are your worst enemies."*

Paradoxically, both sadly and happily, Millthorpe is where Richard spent his last decade of life, a far cry from the baying crowds at Ellis Park or the Sydney Cricket Ground. He desperately missed his family and close friends in the city and would speak of the isolation and loneliness he felt at times. Conversely though, the country was always a place that gave Richard a sense of surety and contentment, and it was here, with his ever-loyal kelpie, Milo, that Richard found peace once more.

Norman May (who met Richard in 1961 during the Fiji tour of Australia) liked to drink at Richard's pub; so did Richard. "I drank in one pub. I wouldn't go to different pubs at all because I'd get ear-thrashed. But the reason I had more to do with him afterwards, because working on television in those days, the *ABC* had the rights to everything, all the major sport, and I couldn't go to say a leagues club or a place like that, or to even a pub where I wasn't known, because people would walk over and say, 'I'm drinking with you', people would walk between us and ask me questions, you see, and it got to be so impossible. So, I decided I was going to go to one hotel where I was known, and that would be my (one) place where I'd go for a drink, ever. Dick's at the *North Star* in North Sydney which was very close to – well not far away from – the *ABC* studios at Gore Hill, and we used to go there on Saturday nights, always Saturday night, with all the crew from the *Sports Review Program* on *ABC* and that's where we'd drink on Saturday nights. We stayed there with Dick for a couple of years and then he bought *The Dolphin Hotel* in Surry Hills, so we transferred from the *North Star* to *The Dolphin* and we stayed there, it must have been for oh, ten or fifteen years. When he sold *The Dolphin* he was managing *The Phoenix Hotel* in Woollahra. So, we went there with him there, so that's when he --- of course he retired from all drinking; he had to give up drinking, he was drinking twenty middies a day, you can't do that, you know, and he ended up in Millthorpe where he is now." (The interview was recorded in 2008).

"And Dick and I, you see on Saturday nights we sometimes used to bet on the dogs and things like that – never too well 'cause I'm a 'mug' punter, and away we went. And this went on for, well it must have been years. Well, '83 for a start, well I was still drinking with him when I was 70, so that was '98, so there's 15 years there. And that association went on for a long, long time, right. 'Cause I remember when I left for Montreal in 1976 for the Olympic Games, Dick gave me a party at the *North Star*, so that's '76 till about 2000 and – so yeah, it's about 30 years, isn't it, the association was there, just under 30. And there it was, all the way through. And we were great mates all the way through. He of course was at my 80th birthday party."

LA Olympics 1984

"Yeah, and when we went to Los Angeles in '84," May continued. "Dick came along there and Jan was there and they went to the Water Polo a lot, and they had a heap of --- we had a heap of tickets for the thing 'cause I'd done all this fundraising for the Olympic team and they gave me a heap of Games' tickets and we had tickets everywhere to the Games and away we went. We used to do a fair bit of scalping outside the thing itself, tickets.

Comparisons to the Ella Brothers

"The Thornett brothers were better in the sense that all of the Thornett brothers were international-class players, where all the Ella brothers were not (all at that elite level)," May said. "The Thornett brothers had the all-round strength that the Ella brothers don't have, although they didn't have the brilliance that the Ella brothers had. But I'd rate the Thornett brothers ahead of the Ella brothers in that sense because all of the Thornett brothers were elite international footballers."

CHAPTER TWENTY-EIGHT
Family

When it is dark enough, you can see the stars
  Ralph Waldo Emerson

Maureen Thornett (nee Kay)

Maureen first met Richard when she was 16 and Richard was about to finish his education at Randwick Boys' High School. She remembers:

Meeting Richard – "We both grew up in Bronte; he lived in Tomlin Street and I lived on the corner of St Thomas and Gardine Street. We were both still at school and I guess in walking up the street to do the afternoon messages I noticed this handsome young man, and so I readily found lots of excuses to do the afternoon chores. Eventually he asked me to go out to a Water Polo function – I was about 16 and he was just leaving school and he had to get my father's permission. At that stage, I wasn't really aware of his sporting career, I was just more interested in the physical aspect – he was a very attractive young man. He was obviously busy with his sport which distracted him from continuing the relationship."

"Then, it was most probably a couple of years after that when I had actually left school, that he did take me to my year dance and I guess we started to go out again at that stage. Our first date on that occasion was when he was playing for NSW (Rugby League) against the French. It was an eye-opener having come from a fairly sheltered background. I remember he told me to sit with the partners of a couple of international players in the team; I didn't know them and I was left there with a couple of women who seemingly had a much more exposed life than I had at that stage. I guess I was a bit dismayed at the comments, the language, but then I realised that my life had to expand and there were lots of other people in the world other than the little area I had grown up in."

FAMILY

The Good and the Bad – "I loved him and I enjoyed, I guess, being part of it – the sporting experience – because you were with Dick Thornett and we had some wonderful times together. But I didn't actually share a lot of his achievements because in those days the men celebrated and we had a young family and I think the difference was that it was very difficult to take babies to Parramatta Oval to watch a game. You knew that you were going to be there all the afternoon and that after the game he would obviously want to have drinks with the guys. It was cultural. I mean, they would train and go and have a few drinks and probably get home a midnight or 1 a.m. You did feel quite excluded from those sorts of achievements, however we by then had a business with our first hotel (*The North Star*), so I became quite involved with that. I remember, I walked into the public bar of my own hotel, *The North Star,* and was told very quickly to walk out, that women were not allowed in there; the barmaids were the only females allowed in."

Why I Loved Him – "We got engaged when I was 20, so we were young, but he was a very caring and a gentle, humble person, very loyal to his friends and family. I guess what attracted me to Richard most of all was his sense of humour. I mean, he could always make me laugh and bring me down to earth in that sense because he was able to mix with everyone. In fact, probably because of the experiences that I had with him in the league world, it gave me a far greater appreciation of life than if I stayed in my little box."

What Happened – "I think we both grew apart. We worked together and I think I guess I built up some resentment because of the cultural differences. Richard, being the male and in the era he grew up in – the wife did not work. We went through some really tough times; it was very stressful, and I was working very long hours and bringing up the children and because Richard was the sportsman and people came to see him, I felt that I was just the wife and I was doing all the work and he was there having a drink. Deep down we both loved each other but we both went in different directions and subsequently have spoken about it. I mean alcohol was a big part of it. Everyone came in to see him and have a drink, I mean even the reps. Johnny Raper had a cleaning contract with the *Dolphin Hotel* but sometimes he wouldn't turn up because he had had a big night with Richard at the hotel the night before."

Richard's Illness – "He got very ill and he was on life support for two weeks in the early '80s. The medical team said, 'Your husband looks OK, but I just want to warn you that in 24 hours he is going to be in intensive care and he is going to be fighting for his life.' I just thought, *'Look I can't do this.'* I've got the business and we had just renovated and had three children and he was in hospital for a long time. But look, I am not perfect, that's life. I think from our point of view, we have got three wonderful daughters and grandchildren, so we have been able to get over our differences, which we did fairly quickly."

Loss of Their Son - "Oh, it was difficult, that is all part I guess of the stress of our relationship. We did have a lot of stress at the time I lost our son; Richard had been in hospital just before that with blood clots and so he was in North Shore (Hospital), so we had the baby and he died about 2 weeks after that."

Authors' note: Maureen and Richard remained close friends until his passing. They often confided in one another and sought advice as well as comfort. They would often ring each other just to chat (Richard was never one for texts and emails). Richard's wake was held on October 18, 2011, at Maureen's Royal Oak Hotel in Balmain.

Jan Thornett (nee Andrew)

Richard's second wife first met him in 1960, although they did not marry for another 27 years. Jan recalls her memories of Richard:

Meeting Richard – "I first met Richard when we were training for the Rome Olympics in 1960 and we used to go into Tattersalls because they were the only ones with the heated pool in Sydney in those days. I think that my attraction was that he was very humble and just a very, very nice man, an extremely nice man. Tattersalls had quite a small pool but we used to go and do some weights and some exercises and then have a swim, and the Water Polo boys were included in the swimming team. That's probably where I first met Richard but I didn't really take much notice of him, to be quite honest."

"I first noticed Richard at the 1960 Olympics and I probably noticed him there when we were doing a little bit of training. When we came back to Sydney, I think he phoned my home after the Olympics but I wasn't home. I must have been training or doing something else, and Mum said, 'Oh, Jan's very busy with something,' and I think he was too scared to call back."

"So look, the years went on, I married and had two children, two girls, and of course he married Maureen and had three lovely girls. Then, Richard moved from *The North Star* to *The Dolphin* and I used to go in there occasionally. It used to be the busiest pub in town."

From John Singleton to Richard Thornett: "I mean he (John Singleton) wasn't really a boyfriend. He was just a friend that I used to date occasionally and we'd go into the pub because Norman (May) and Richard would be there and John knew Richard as well. We used to have a sort of a bit of a merry old time with a few drinks and a few laughs. John and I got on very well but I was just not interested in a relationship with him, my marriage was over, two girls to bring up, work, knuckle down; I wasn't interested. Richard maybe got wind that John was off the scene and we went out a few times and then it went from there."

Great Friends But Can't Live Together: "I can't say enough about Richard. People were quite sad when we split up, but they realised that we were going in different directions. We are such great friends – we sort of can't live together but we're much happier that way. We had a very brief time together; I think we were married for four or five years."

In an interview for this book, Richard was asked to reflect on how he rated himself as a father during those years in sports. Here is what he had to say:

"I was always there but I probably didn't have a lot of good hours with them (his daughters). I was probably in the hotel industry for most of their early years, up until they were fourteen or fifteen and it hasn't affected them at all. We lived above the premises. I'd always be there but I'd probably be in the bar most of the time and you might have dinner with them the odd night but I don't think they have been affected by it. I think they're all good kids and none of them got into drugs or got into any trouble and they've all been well-educated; they're good kids. We used to have holidays but, after school or when you'd get home from work – most fathers would have two or three hours. I probably never did that. Living in a pub… Maureen was with them a lot of the time. We had a housemaid, and she was only too willing to give a hand and stay back and stay a night to help. She was really good with the kids."

"And we had two good grandmothers who used to help out a lot. The pub game was different then, it was ten to ten. You could shut up at ten o'clock at night and still have time to go out and have dinner or do something, so it was a different industry. You know, we gave them opportunities in everything when they were growing up, like tennis camps, horse-riding camps, swimming, violin, the guitar and the piano."

Sisters Liesl, Amanda and Sophie were interviewed about their father for this book:

Q: What three words describe your father?

Amanda: "Soft, strong, humble."

Liesl: "Family-man, loving, dry (sense of humour)."

Sophie: "Caring, generous, loving."

Q: Who was your father?

Sophie: "I miss him. He was an amazing man. Funnily enough, I guess when we were younger, they (Richard and wife, Maureen) weren't around much because they worked so hard. They were workers. They wanted to give us everything that they could, to give us a life that we had; the schools we went to. And, I remember times, oh, my God, he didn't suffer fools. He was beautiful. He did as a dad would do and they were always working. We had nannies, we had people looking after us and when they were free, they (Mum and Dad) would spend time with us."

Liesl: "He was a very loving father and grandfather. He was just a very special man, to a lot of people. Family was a big part of his life, always, his family always came first. When I was younger, he didn't have a lot of time to spend with us because he worked very long hours. He and Mum both worked tirelessly to give us the best life. After we had left school, and they didn't have to support us financially as much anymore, he therefore became more involved in our lives."

Amanda: "He was caring, loving, hardworking, generous. He looked out for us. He was supportive in everything; in everything that we did. He gave us so many opportunities, I believe that we were his life. I think his work took a lot out of him both in terms of his time and perhaps his own relationship with our Mum. Our friends loved him. He was nicknamed 'Moby' Dick by my friends."

Sophie: "In those early days, it wasn't just about supporting us. They were trying to create a business. They were trying to make themselves. The first business they had, here in North Sydney, *The Rag and Famish* (*Hotel*), which was *The North Star* back then, was owned by the breweries who had control over it. They (Mum and Dad) wanted to do some changes and they couldn't because the breweries wouldn't allow it, and that's when they stepped away from that. The breweries started selling hotels off and then they bought the freehold of *The Dolphin (Hotel)* and they thought this is an opportunity that we can actually be ourselves and do our own thing. It was a pub on the corner (in Surry Hills), but they bought a burnt-out florist shop next door and joined it to the hotel and then created this massive business. And it *had* to work, because they had invested so much money. They were also the first creators of pub food in Sydney, which a lot of people that you talk to now, don't know."

Q: Did the pub business affect your dad's health?

Sophie: "Well, it was the social impact of it for him, obviously being the sportsman that he was, and when he was at *The Dolphin*, it was renowned for people to go to before and after rugby games at the Sydney Cricket and Sports Grounds. The council blocked off the side street to accommodate the crowds, and it was huge. People just wanted to be part of him – in his life – back in those days."

Amanda: "He didn't want to let anybody down. He was there for everybody."

Q: We have a story in one of the transcripts where (famous cricketer) Neil Harvey, who was representing a spirits company, would come in and it might be ten in the morning and that was the end of the day for your father. That would have had an effect on him if he was regularly spending his time drinking?

Sophie: "Yeah, big time. That's where Mum and Dad went their separate ways."

Liesl: "Working together and living together is hard. It's hard on any relationship (to do both). It is tiresome on any marriage."

Amanda: "The stresses of the business… they just grew apart."

Authors' note: Richard himself recalled the times when Neil Harvey arrived as he was carving the meat. "I was married to Maureen at the time and she'd be in the kitchen and I'd go into the kitchen because I used to cut up all our own meat; I'd buy the whole rumps and the scotch fillets. Maureen would look down the corridor and say, 'No more meat done today…'"

Q: Can you think of an anecdote of a time that you spent with your dad that was special, that still lives with you now?

Amanda: "I remember when we were really young and he used to make us swim at Bronte Beach. He used to make us go out in the surf and swim past the break. So, he made us go out, he's with us, made us feel safe. We were just gripping onto him for dear life. I was like, 'Oh, wow, I can do that!' But I'm still scared of the surf."

Liesl: "We'd all get dumped by the waves and he'd go into hysterics. He treated us as the sons he never had and throw us into the surf."

Amanda: "I remember him working with me when I had my café (*Zink*) at North Bondi. It was New Year's Day and I wasn't going to open but he said, 'You have to open this shop on New Year's Day. Everyone's closed. You have to, you'll make a lot of money.' I said, 'But I don't have any staff,' and he said, 'I'm going to help you.' So, he washed the dishes for me in the shop. He seriously worked all day. It was so busy and at the end of the day, my Dad drove us to the bottle shop. He topped his ute up with ice, got a whole lot of beers, put them in the back of his 'ute' and brought it back to the café. We all sat there drinking beers out of the 'ute'. It was the best thing ever. I would not have worked if it wasn't for my Dad that day."

Liesl: "Every time *The Sound of Music* was on (TV), my Dad used to ring me and he'd say, 'I've got tears in my eyes. I'm watching *The Sound of Music* and it's reminding me of you.' And then I'd start crying. He named me after Liesl in the film. I think the movie must have come out just before I was born. (Note: Liesl was the eldest of the Von Trapp children). And he loved it, which is probably unusual for a rugby person to like a musical like that."

Sophie: "I used to love packing my car for our girls for a weekend in Millthorpe. I'd get there and he'd have a roast on the table. I loved those weekends that we would have with him, where he had no other distractions in life and he just looked like it was his pleasure to just be a dad, a grandfather and look after us. And then we would leave on the Sunday and Dad would cry and wave goodbye. I had so many memories. I just loved the days when we used to go out, even going back to our early childhood, to Watson's Bay for these long lunches when we were all so young... and then we would hop back on the boat at night and come home. So many amazing things."

Amanda: "He had a big heart."

Liesl: "The gentle giant; and he was a soft, loving and devoted family man."

Sophie: "*The Coachman*! In Redfern! It was an institution and Dad used to take Amanda and I there for our birthdays (that were a couple of days apart). You would get the Greek guys that would come through and sell single roses. So, these guys knew Dad because he had *The Dolphin*. He also had *The Doncaster* (*Hotel*) for a while, so they'd come into a restaurant and they'd see him sitting there and yell, 'Hi Dick!' And he'd be sitting with his daughters, and he would buy all of us roses. And so, when Mum and Dad weren't together, that was his special thing. The other thing that he used to do was when he used to come by and pick us up on a Sunday. And we used to go to the Italian restaurant in Kellett Street in King's Cross with Dad. He always tried to take us out on a Sunday night. Every week."

Q: When did you realise that your father was perhaps a little different to most fathers?

Amanda: "I didn't really know that my Dad was famous until I started dating boys. So, it was, 'Okay, football?' Like, what was that? Because we were so young; I was probably two when Dad stopped playing, so it (football talk) wasn't around when we were growing up. We started dating and they knew the name and they'd go, 'Oh, my gosh, is your dad Dick Thornett, or one of the Thornett brothers?' I'd say, 'Yeah, why?' They were all so scared to meet him. I remember one night we had a few boys back when we were living in Point Piper and it was late and we were sitting down all huddled up watching TV. Dad walked in and said (to one of them) that he had a cricket bat. I'm not sure whether Dad did have a cricket bat but..."

Liesl: "I still get it to this day, usually comments made by my friends' parents."

Amanda: "Because we went to a girls' school, no one knew, and we didn't exactly talk about it in the family, if our parents were well-known. We just knew them as Mum and Dad. It wasn't talked about when we were young."

Sophie: "I remember the days where I first valued it, which was when Dad went back and played 'Golden Oldies' at Queens Park, where Tilly plays now. We would get cardboard and slide down the hill there at the top end. It made me think that maybe he was a good sportsman. Like, a really good sportsman."

Amanda: "You know, we all look back thinking we could have done things differently. Not just us, but anybody who's lost anybody. He just liked his own company."

Never Devalue Excellence by Rewarding Mediocrity

It is true that going out with a daughter of Richard Thornett can be a little daunting, a tad intimidating. He had high expectations. And he was Richard Thornett, for goodness' sake. Any father with daughters will naturally be fierce in their defence and protection of them. I should know; I have twin girls myself.

An example of how a champion views things: *One September afternoon in 2005, I was coaching the Shore School's 2nd XV rugby side that was playing the rugby juggernaut and my alma mater, St Joseph's College. We had stayed in touch with them for the majority of the match, even threatening to take the game at one stage, but Joeys sealed it with a late try. Nevertheless, I was proud of the effort. I bounded up the Northbridge grandstand stairs afterwards to speak to Sophie and her father, Richard, who was attending his first game of rugby that had me as coach. I was thrilled to have a man of such gravitas attending to watch a rugby team I was coaching. We had put in a worthy performance and I was eager to hear his opinion. I chuckle when I recall that, once again, I underestimated Richard's no-nonsense expectations. His analysis at the back of the stand tore apart our scrum, our breakdown, our game plan and our backline width and alignment. I was a little deflated you might say, but that's why champions achieve greatness; they only accept excellence and perfection, and I learnt a good lesson that afternoon.*

Brendan Morris, Author

CHAPTER TWENTY-NINE
Sunset

God, grant me the serenity
To accept the things I cannot change;
Courage to change the things I can;
And wisdom to know the difference.
   Reinhold Niebuhr (Serenity Prayer)

Richard Thornett: "Over the period of my sporting career I look back and see it as a very enjoyable period of my life. I met lots of nice people and I met lots of crooks and lots of thieves as well. Even though there were hard times, there were also good times and even though there were winning times, there were losing times too. Nonetheless, I personally enjoyed every minute of it. I've made a lot of good friends along the way. Many of my closest friends are those I played football with at Randwick way back when I was 17. I have no regrets in what I've done through my life. If I had to go through the same again, I would do exactly the same."

As mentioned previously, Richard settled in Millthorpe in 2002 at the end of an illustrious, if tumultuous, career and life. His love of the earth, nature and animals sustained and nourished him. In many ways, it revived him. Richard's great friend, Norman May, concurred. "Dick loves animals. Really, really loves animals. He spends most of his time outside. With Milo, the dog. And he loves the sheep and he's out there, always tending the farm. He loves it. And he's an egg man now. And tomatoes. He's got little cherry tomatoes. He was a great animal man, you know."

Like the countryside Richard loved so much, his journey was akin to the topography upon which his house now sat and the land it overlooked. He had scaled mountains and enjoyed the views from the summit; he had lived in valleys that challenged his resoluteness; and now, he had settled on the plains – in comfort – restful and serene.

The bond between Richard and his dog Milo was as strong as any he had with the special humans in his life.

During an interview with author Stephan Wellink, Richard said "Oh yeah. I… If I didn't have my dog, I'd… at least I can talk to her. She's waiting for me in the car now." As Richard spoke this sentence, both he and Stephan turned to look out of the restaurant window to his 'ute' which was parked on the street a short distance away. It was no surprise that Milo, sitting in the tray, turned to look at Richard at the same time.

A Man, His Dog and the Earth Beneath Their Feet

Milo: *Milo lived to 17 years of age, outliving her best friend by seven years. I have this belief that she lived for such an extraordinary length of time in the hope that one day Richard, who had disappeared so suddenly from her life, would one day return. Milo split her time between the homes and families of Amanda and Sophie, and I will never forget where she easily spent the most time when she stayed with us. It was in our courtyard, looking unwaveringly up the driveway, waiting to see the tail-lights of Richard's 'ute' backing down the drive. She sat at his feet whenever Richard sat and followed him everywhere whenever he was on the move. When Milo collapsed in that same courtyard, no doubt still waiting, one afternoon in 2018, we all cried, not just because we had lost our little, loyal friend, but because the last physical connection we had with Richard was gone.*

Millthorpe: *Our memories of Millthorpe and the times we spent there are precious. Richard could be himself and he was happy. Fire pits under the stars, Milo and my own dog, Nelson, walking in the snow and sleeping in front of the fire together, betting on the 7 dog and sipping Tooheys Old at the Railway Hotel with Nobby, beers at Forest Reefs, Spring Hill and lunches at the Union Bank and Tonic. I remember, too, chickens, tomatoes, figs, apples, roast dinners, golf at Duntryleague (in Orange, NSW) and drenching,* *marking and rounding up sheep on the quad bike with Milo and my daughters, Tilly and Ava.*

Brendan Morris, Author

Richard Norman Thornett passed away peacefully in his sleep from heart complications on the morning of October 12, 2011, at the age of 71. He was farewelled at All Saints' Anglican Church in Ocean St, Woollahra by a packed congregation. Many people who are mentioned in or contributed material for this book were there to say goodbye. It was a remarkable life well-lived, so very much enjoyed. He brought so much love and joy to all who knew him and who were entertained by him, from swimming pools and rugby fields to pubs and everything in between.

The third verse of the service's first hymn, *Amazing Grace*, said much:

Through many dangers, toils and snares,
I have already come.
'Tis grace hath brought me safe thus far,
And grace will lead me home.

Richard's favourite song, Roger Miller's *King of the Road*, accompanied him as he was carried from the church. Brendan Morris recalls, "We sang it often together – at his house in Millthorpe, at our place in Forestville and in our lounge room in North Sydney." Although Richard loved the song primarily because of the melody, two lines from it apply poignantly to him:

I'm a man of means by no means
King of the road

Money meant little to him – his extreme generosity reflected that. His wealth came from the love he shared with others, most particularly his family and close friends. That was his currency.

I wouldn't change my life for a million quid. I've had a great life. You know, you have your ups and downs whatever you do. I couldn't be happier to see the way

they've – my daughters – all turned out. I don't have to worry. *(Richard Thornett, 1940–2011).*

I will never forget the feeling of safety as my father carried me to bed in his arms after long days out with family and friends. I'd wish that he'd never put me down.

And I will never forget sitting with my father on his farm in Millthorpe; Dad's home brew in hand, fire roaring and Milo, his faithful dog at his feet. I looked at my father and realised he was as happy as he has ever been.
Sophie Morris, October 18, 2011

Career Statistics

Water Polo
Bronte Water Polo Club (1954–1961)
New South Wales (1958 - 1961)
Olympian: Rome 1960

Rugby Union
Randwick: 49 games (1957–1962)
Premiership winner (1959)
NSW: 4 games (1961)
Wallaby #465: 11 Tests: (1961, 1962)
Non-Test Caps: 11
Wallaby Tours: South Africa (1961); New Zealand 1962

Rugby League
Parramatta Eel #218: 1963–1971 (160 games)
Eastern Suburbs Rooster #627: 1972 (9 games)
City Seconds: 2 games (1963, 1966)
City Firsts: 4 games (1964, 1965, 1967, 1968)
Sydney: 2 games (1963, 1964)
NSW: 13 games (1963 – 1969)
Kangaroo #383: 11 Tests plus 3 World Cup games (1963, 1964, 1968)
Non-Test Caps: 13 (1963/64)
Kangaroo Tour: 1963/64

Honours

NSW Hall of Champions (1979)

Sport Australia Hall of Fame (1999) – Multiple Sports (Water Polo, Rugby Union, Rugby League)

The Greatest NSW Rugby Union Team of All-Time (1999) – *The Sydney Morning Herald* (Greg Growden)

The Australian Sports Medal (2000)

SCG Walk of Honour Plaque – Thornett Brothers (2001)

The 10 Greatest Wallabies (2001) – #10 – *The Sun-Herald* (Greg Growden)

Sport Australia Hall of Fame (2002) – Team Sport Australia Award: 1963 Kangaroos

Parramatta Eels Hall of Fame (2002)

Parramatta Eels Legends Team (2002)

The Top 10 Dual Internationals (2002) – *The Daily Telegraph* (Grantlee Kieza)

Greatest 100 Wallabies – #62 (2003) – *The Daily Telegraph* (Peter Jenkins)

Top 10 Waratah Hardmen – #8 (2003) – *The Daily Telegraph* (Peter Jenkins)

Kangaroo Team of the 1960s (2006)

The Police Team of the Century (2008)

Randwick Hall of Fame (2010)

NSW Waratahs Hall of Fame (2024)

Acknowledgements

Our thanks go to everyone who contributed anecdotes, observations and personal archives, including valuable photographs and press clippings. We also appreciated the helpfulness of archivists at the ARU who allowed open access to their collection of films, books and the volumes of press clippings from the 1950s and 60s.

We want to give special thanks to the magnificent men we interviewed who played alongside or against Richard from 1960 to 1972. Their wholehearted commitment to this project helped us tell a special story about a very special man.

Thank you, Steve Ricketts for your support and guidance which was, and is, invaluable. Peter 'Fab' Fenton contributed to this project on a number of levels and his ode to Richard Thornett perfectly captured the man and his monumental achievements. The renowned sports journalist and author Norman Tasker provided encouragement which was highly valued. We are forever grateful to these men.

This book exists because Bonita Mersiades of Fair Play Publishing said 'yes.' Thank you, Bonita, and team for making our dream a reality.

To Dawn Fraser, John Eales and Michael Cronin, your words mean a great deal to us and most certainly would have to Richard. Thank you.

We are also grateful for the support provided by the late John and the late Ken Thornett who shared their memories of the early days at Bronte through to the major sporting arenas they graced alongside their youngest brother. You will always have our admiration and respect.

To Richard's immediate family, particularly Liesl, Amanda and Sophie, thank you for your undying support throughout the ups and downs of this project.

We hope the story that unfolds between the covers of this book makes you even prouder – if that's possible – of your father.

Maureen Thornett speaks openly of her relationship with Richard and her insights allow the reader to understand something about the pressures of living in the spotlight of fame. For this and her generosity, we extend our sincere thanks.

Thank you also to the generosity and kindness of those who offered a place to get away to write that allowed both time and beautiful settings to inspire this great tale to be written and shared. To Di Thornett (your Boomerang Beach retreat, NSW), Will Armstrong and John and Liz Power (your Matarangi Beach batch, New Zealand), your contributions may not be obvious in words but they definitely exist in mind and heart. Golf and surfing helped, a lot.

Finally, to Richard. It was a privilege to tell your story. Thanks for the memories.

Brendan Morris and Stephan Wellink

Personal Thanks

None of this would have been possible without the undying support of my wife, Sophie. You allowed me to set sail up the North Coast and to the land of my heritage, New Zealand so that I could try to fulfil that promise I made and do justice to a truly great man. Ever since the seeds of this journey were first sown by Stephan, you have been by my side encouraging, supporting (and critiquing, at times) this beautiful journey that I took in writing about your father, Richard. You are, in so many ways, your father's daughter, and I know how deeply proud he would be of you.

Tilly and Ava, you are my world and my inspiration. I looked up often from the page while I was writing, many miles away, and I saw you there alongside me. I hope I can be half the father to you that Richard was to his daughters.

Brendan Morris

For my wife, Jennifer, who has been by my side throughout this roller coaster of a life, whose patience, calmness, kindness and love have given me the strength, resilience and purpose to follow my dreams. There are not enough words to express my feelings for you.

And for our children, Katrina, Simon, Laura, Suzanna and Ava – you inspire me through your words and deeds. I love you unconditionally.

And for our grandchildren Ebony, William, Amelia and Mackenzie – you are precious gifts, and it is a joy to see the world through your eyes.

Stephan Wellink

Bibliography

Books

Rome 1960 by David Maraniss, Simon & Schuster July 2009
The History of Bronte Water Polo Club
Sheilas, Wogs and Poofters: An Incomplete Biography of Johnny Warren and Soccer in Australia by Johnny Warren, Random House Australia 2002
The Top 100 Wallabies by Peter Jenkins, Random House 2004
Wallaby Gold: The History of Australian Test Rugby by Peter Jenkins, Random House 1999
The Wallabies: A Definitive History of Australian Test Rugby by Maxwell L. Howell, Lingyu Xie, Bensley Wilkes, GAP Publishing 2000
A Rugby Memoir by Peter Johnson, P. Johnson (self-published) 2000
Giants in Green and Gold Springboks vs Wallabies 1921 – 1993 by Ian Diehm, Boolarong Press 1994
Inside Rugby League by Ian Walsh & Keith Willey, Horwitz 1968
Playing with Legends, The Peter Dimond Story by Peter Dimond with Paul Dillon, Rugby League Publications 2008
The Johnny Raper Rugby League Book by Johnny Raper, KG Murray Publishing Company 196-?
Tackling Rugby by Ken Thornett with Tom Easton, Lansdowne Press 1966
The Kangaroos by Ian Heads, Ironbark Press 1994
Captaining the Kangaroos by Alan Whiticker, New Holland 2004
Parramatta: The Quest for Glory by Neil Cadigan, Lester-Townsend Publishing 1986

BIBLIOGRAPHY

100 Years of Rugby League by Brad Collis & Alan Whiticker,
    New Holland Publishers 2007
The Story of Australian Rugby League by Gary Lester,
    Lester-Townsend Publishing 1998
*A Centenary of Rugby League 1908 – 2008 : the definitive story of the game
    in Australia* by Ian Heads & David Middleton, Pan Macmillan 2008
Never Before, Never Again by Larry Writer, Pan Macmillan 1995
St George: Eleven Golden Years of the Dragons 1956–1966
    by Ian Collis & Alan Whiticker, New Holland Publishers 2015
For the Love of the Game : Ten Legends of Queensland Rugby League
    by Murray Barnett, Boolarong Press 2015
Auckland, 100 Years of Rugby League 1909–2009
    by John Coffey and Bernie Wood
Life is Worth Swimming by Murray Rose, Arbon Publishing 2013

Newspapers and Magazines

The Sydney Morning Herald
The Sun
The Daily Mirror
The Daily Telegraph
The Rugby League News
Rugby League Week
Tricolour, The Paddington Central Junior Technical School magazine, 1955
NSW Combined High Schools Sports Association archivist:
    School Sport Unit, Student Support and Specialist Programs,
    NSW Govt Education – courtesy of Grant Parker
Pegasus, The Randwick Boys' High School magazine, 1956 & 1957
Rugby News, August 10, 1957 (p8) – courtesy of Emma,
    NSW Rugby Union and Waratahs
The Code's Family Affair by Alan Hulls, Sports Magazine, June 1959
Sport Magazine (April 1963 edition)

Internet Resources

The Sydney Morning Herald Archives 1955 – 1995 https://archives.smh.com.au/

Trove https://trove.nla.gov.au/

Rugby League Project https://www.rugbyleagueproject.org/

Wikipedia https://en.wikipedia.org/wiki/Main_Page

Newspapers by Ancestry https://www.newspapers.com/

NRL Hall of Fame https://www.nrl.com/hall-of-fame/players/

Classic Wallabies https://classicwallabies.com.au/

Steve Ricketts: A site covering all things Rugby League https://stevericketts.com.au/

NRL News - *Kangaroos Legend: Noel Kelly* https://www.youtube.com/watch?v=reerIAaM42M

Noel Kelly – League Legends (FOX Sports) https://www.youtube.com/watch?v=WP9hO6wg5iQ

The Creative Writer: John Gleeson – Rugby League Legend Series https://thecreativewriter.com.au/john-gleeson-rugby-league-legend-series/

Randwick Rugby: https://randwickrugby.com.au/about/randwick-hall-of-fame

National Library of Australia: Richard Thornett – interview with Ian Warden (9/8/2008) https://catalogue.nla.gov.au/catalog/4464180

Oral History and Folklore collection of the National Library of Australia: Interview with Neil Bennetts (12/12/1979) https://catalogue.nla.gov.au/catalog/1158362

Water Polo Australia Archive 0405-156538 provided by Dr Tracy Rockwell

Interview with Noel Kelly, The Rugby League Digest 2018 https://www.youtube.com/watch?v=KwckzLG37-k

BIBLIOGRAPHY

Interviewed by the authors

Richard Thornett
John Thornett MBE
Ken Thornett
Maureen Thornett
Liesl Thornett
Amanda Oayda
Sophie Morris
Jan Thornett
Di Thornett
Tom Hoad AM
Mick Withers
Ken Catchpole OAM
Peter Johnson
Rob Heming
Beres Ellwood
Peter Fenton OAM
Warren Hurt
Sir Nicholas Shehadie AC OBE
Sir Wilson Whineray KNZM OBE
Sir Colin Meads KNZM MBE
Dick See
Ron Lynch
Brian Hambly

Keith Barnes AM
Peter Wynn
Arthur Summons
Michael Cleary AM
Kevin Ryan
Frank Stanton
John Cleary
Kevin Junee
Bob O'Reilly
Peter Peters
Denis Fitzgerald AM
Lionel Williamson
John Rhodes
Mick Veivers AM
Norman May AM
Norman Tasker
Adrian McGregor
Barry Rushworth
Michael Cronin OAM
Ivor Lingard
Fred Pickup
John Quayle

Endnotes

CHAPTER ONE
A Time of Change

Meanjin , Summer vol. 9 no. 4 (1950)
(Ref: https://www.austlit.edu.au/austlit/page/C85165)

CHAPTER TWO
Sunrise

Rhodes also represented Australia in the 1975 World Cup, playing seven games (Ref: https://www.rugbyleagueproject.org/players/johnny-rhodes/summary.html

CHAPTER TWELVE
The Kangaroos

Dr H.M. Moran, the captain of the first Wallabies, admitted to being 'unreasonably bitter' about the spirit of rugby in his autobiography, Viewless Winds: Being the Recollections and Digressions of an Australian Surgeon. "The objects of his bitterness were his former team mates who had formed the 'Wallabies' team against the 'Kangaroos' in 1909. 'In a sour moment', Moran wrote, 'I thought of

ENDNOTES

Judas Iscariot as the primate of all professionals in sport. They, too, must often have looked in anguish at the pieces of silver in their hand'". (Ref: Nielsen, E. (2008). 'Oh error, ill-conceived': The Amateur Sports Federation of New South Wales, rugby league and amateur athletics. In Centenary Reflections: 100 Years of Rugby League in Australia. Australian Society of Sports History).

For decades after McKivat and his teammates were suspended, the Australian Rugby Union administration imposed a life ban on players who 'defected' to Rugby League.

The 4th Kangaroos won the first Test 31–8 and lost the second 3–9. The third Test at Swinton ended 0–0 in controversial circumstances. A few minutes from fulltime, Australia's halfback Joe "Chimpy" Busch raced down the sideline to score what appeared to be a fair try, which would have given the Kangaroos the match and the Ashes. Referee Robinson was about to award the try when a touch judge ran onto the field claiming Busch had touched the corner post while diving over. Robinson reportedly told the Australians, "Fair try, Australia, but I am over-ruled." (Ref: NRL Hall of Fame https://www.nrl.com/hall-of-fame/players/joe-chimpy-busch/).
A fourth Test was needed to decide the winner of the Ashes series, which Great Britain won 3–0.

Barry Rushworth played for Parramatta between 1964 and 1971.
(Ref: https://www.rugbyleagueproject.org/players/barry-rushworth/summary.html)

Reg and Ron Kray built a criminal empire that ruled the East End of London in the 1950s and 1960s.
(Ref: Reg and Ron Kray (with Fred Dinenge), Our Story (2015). Published by Pan Macmillan).

Jack Lynch and Arthur Sparks, (Ref: Managerial Report, Australian Rugby League Touring Team 1963/64).

CHAPTER THIRTEEN
England

Several of Ken's teammates and family interviewed for this book, said Ken was very "professional" in the way he handled his finances and some further defined Ken's "professional" money management style as "frugality".

"Beatlemania" had captured the world by the time the Kangaroos returned home in early 1964 (Ref: Glenn A Baker, The Beatles Downunder – The 1964 Australia & New Zealand Tour (1982), published by Wild and Woolley Sydney.

Authors' personal communication with Murray Barnett, author of For the Love of the Game (2015). Published by Boolarong Press, and The Creative Writer: John Gleeson – Rugby League Legend Series, (https://thecreativewriter.com.au/john-gleeson-rugby-league-legend-series/ (courtesy of Murray Barnett).

CHAPTER FOURTEEN
The Ashes

Authors' personal communication with Murray Barnett, author of For the Love of the Game, (2015). Published by Boolarong Press and The Creative Writer: John Gleeson – Rugby League Legend Series, https://thecreativewriter.com.au/john-gleeson-rugby-league-legend-series/ (courtesy of Murray Barnett).

CHAPTER FIFTEEN
France

Kevin "Kandos" Ryan returned to Australia on December 3, 1963.

Ian Heads, The Kangaroos (1994). Published by Ironbark Press.

When his playing career ended, Frank Stanton enjoyed success as a coach with Manly-Warringah (premierships in 1976 and 1978), Balmain and North Sydney.

He coached the Kangaroos in 1978 and again in 1982 when his team "The Invincibles" were undefeated on tour.

CHAPTER EIGHTEEN
1966 – The Ashes In Australia

Interestingly, Watson was sent off for kneeing Peter Dimond in the 46th minute of the third Test of the 1963 Ashes series.

CHAPTER NINETEEN
1967 – A Difficult Season

Larry Writer, Never Before Never Again (1995). Published by Macmillan.

CHAPTER TWENTY
1968 – The World Cup In Australia/NZ

Keith Page was listed as the referee in The Rugby League News, Vol. 49, No. 10 (April 6,7, 1968).

"The Other Nationalities was a representative Rugby League team, which usually consisted of non-English players. They competed in the first ever Rugby League international in 1904 against England, fielding players from Wales and Scotland. The team was later represented by players from Australia, Fiji, New Zealand, Ireland and South Africa". Australians Harry Bath, Brian Bevan, Arthur Clues, Trevor Allan, Pat Devery, Lionel Cooper and Rex Mossop represented Other Nationalities. The team ceased to exist after 1975.
(Ref: Wikipedia, https://en.wikipedia.org/wiki/Other_Nationalities_rugby_league_team)

Harry Bath coached Balmain 1961–1966, Newtown 1969–1972 and St George 1977–1981, winning premierships in 1977 and 1979.

Peter Peters (Personal communication): "In those days there were transfer fees and mine was £800 and my father bought it, which was the most sensible thing that I could do because it allowed me to not have any ties for any long period at a club if I didn't want to."

Balgowlah is a beachside suburb north of Sydney.

CHAPTER TWENTY-ONE
1969 – Injury Plagued

Williamson is on the wing for the Newtown Jets' Team of the Century (1908–2008).
(Ref: https://www.newtownjets.com/about-newtown-rlfc/team-of-the-century/).

In his interview for this book, Kevin Ryan said he respected Richard as an opponent and teammate.

Kevin "Kandos" Ryan was the Queensland Amateur Heavyweight Boxing Champion 1958–1959.

Williamson (Heritage number: 826) played for Bradford Northern(1965–67).
(Ref: https://bullsfoundation.org/heritage-numbers-1-998/)

CHAPTER TWENTY-TWO
1970 – Annus Horribilis

While writing this book, the authors received news that former Wests Magpies, NSW and Australian representative John "Snoozer" Elford had passed away on February 4 aged 76.

ENDNOTES

CHAPTER TWENTY - THREE
1971 – Farewell Eels

Dennis Tutty was not alone in his courageous stand against inequity in Rugby League. Western Suburbs' John Elford did likewise and when "Snoozer" passed away in early 2024, journalist and author Steve Ricketts wrote, "Elford was also passionate about players' rights and fought a legal battle unsuccessfully against the NSWRFL's transfer system in the NSW Supreme Court, leading him to sit out the 1969 season in protest. Elford eventually resolved his differences with the Magpies and remained a one-club man for the rest of his career". (Ref: https://stevericketts.com.au/2024/02/06/vale-john-snoozer-elford/)

CHAPTER TWENTY - FOUR
1972 – The Roosters

John Quayle played Rugby League as a lock or second-row forward. He represented Eastern Suburbs (1968–72), Parramatta (1973–76), NSW (1973) and Australia (1975).
(Ref: https://www.rugbyleagueproject.org/players/john-quayle/summary.html)
From 1983 – 1997, Quayle was the General Manager of the NSW Rugby League (NSWRL) and then Chief Executive of the Australian Rugby League (ARL) (Personal communication).

CHAPTER TWENTY-EIGHT
Family

Tilly and Ava are the twin daughters of Sophie and Brendan Morris.

Career Statistics

Captain/Coach (Ref: The Rugby League News, Vol. 47, No. 16 June 4, 5, 1966).

MORE REALLY GOOD FOOTBALL BOOKS FROM FAIR PLAY PUBLISHING

 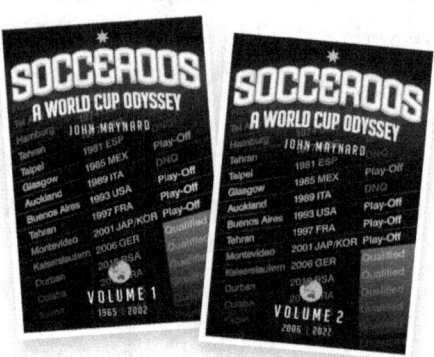 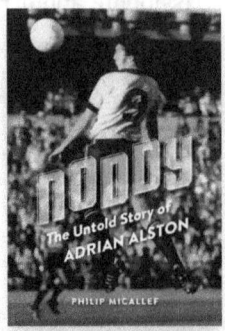

Turning The Tide   Socceroos – A World Cup Odyssey,   Noddy, The Untold Story
                                1965 to 2022 Volumes 1 and 2   of Adrian Alston

"Get Your Tits Out   Hell For Leather   Radicalised by FIFA   Football Fans
for the Lads"   In Their Own Write…

Available from fairplaypublishing.com.au/shop
and all good bookstores